MW00788807

Political Pedagogies

Series Editors

Jamie Frueh, Bridgewater College, Bridgewater, VA, USA
David J. Hornsby, The Norman Paterson School of International Affairs, Carleton University, Ottawa, Canada

Political Pedagogies is a collection of scholarly texts on methods of teaching and learning politics. The series seeks to be the premier assemblage of book-length contributions that explores all aspects of political pedagogy, from philosophical considerations about the role and purpose of pedagogy to practical guides and strategies for teaching political science and international relations. The proliferation of journals, conferences, workshops and institutional centers devoted to teaching attest to the accelerating interest in the pedagogy of Political Science and International Relations. The challenges of teaching in the twenty-first century span sub-disciplines and connect scholars from a wide variety of institutions in a common mission critical to the health of modern democracies. Indeed, teaching may be the only focus that scholars in these disciplines truly share, and the series seeks to elevate the importance of teaching in disciplinary and social advancement. *Political Pedagogies* strives to create an inclusive and expansive space where scholars can explore what it means to teach and foster learning and provides a much-needed platform for longer, deeper, creative and more engaged scholarship that melds the teaching and research responsibilities of Political Science and International Relations faculty.

Nathan Andrews · Nene Ernest Khalema
Editors

Decolonizing African Studies Pedagogies

Knowledge Production, Epistemic Imperialism and Black Agency

Editors
Nathan Andrews
McMaster University
Hamilton, ON, Canada

Nene Ernest Khalema
School of Built Environment
and Development Studies
University of Kwazulu-Natal, Howard
College
Durban, South Africa

ISSN 2662-7809 ISSN 2662-7817 (electronic)
Political Pedagogies
ISBN 978-3-031-37441-8 ISBN 978-3-031-37442-5 (eBook)
https://doi.org/10.1007/978-3-031-37442-5

Cover illustration: Jonny White/Alamy Stock Photo

This Palgrave Macmillan imprint is published by the registered company Springer Nature Switzerland AG
The registered company address is: Gewerbestrasse 11, 6330 Cham, Switzerland

Resurgent and Insurgent Decolonization of the Twenty-first Century—A Foreword

Nathan Andrews and Nene Ernest Khalema's book *Decolonizing African Studies Pedagogies: Knowledge Production, Epistemic Imperialism and Black Agency* is timely and is curated within a context of a resurgent and insurgent decolonization that is perceptible in the public sphere. This resurgent and insurgent decolonization is engulfing all imaginable areas of human life. This reality has raised fears of decolonization becoming a metaphor, a slogan, a buzzword and a catch-all concept with no precise meaning (Moosavi, 2020; Tuck & Yang, 2012). To the extreme end is Olufemi Taiwo (2022) who has openly declared his opposition to the concept of decolonization, arguing that it has served its purpose and now losing its way. To allay these fears, concerns and opposition, a number of clarifications have to be done.

The first clarification is that this decolonization is different from the previous one that was entangled with the global politics of shifting from empires to modern nation-states. The local native elites who assumed the name of nationalists were actively involved as were emerging superpowers—the United States and the Soviet Union. The local native elites sought to get rid of direct administrative colonialism and takeover the reigns of political power. The more radical local native nationalists sought to not only to attain self-determination but also to contribute to the re-making of the world after the empire (see Getachew, 2019). The emerging superpowers sought to re-organize the modern/colonial system after 1945 into modern nation-states for purposes of their own hegemonic interests. Basically, the modern/colonial world system was rebooting itself and modern power was being reconfigured. This reality is well-captured by Catherine Lu (2023: 143):

> Consequently, the political productivity of changes in the foundational organising principles of successive international orders—from empire to statehood, from civilization to self-determination, from sovereignty to human rights, from colonial law to rule of law, and from exclusion to inclusion—has yielded new disciplinary practices against historically marginalised and oppressed groups, while maintaining their structural disadvantages, and doing little to check domination, exploitation, and uses of force and coercion by dominant groups privileged through the structural power of imperialism, colonialism, global capital and white supremacy.

Inevitably, in the words of Christian Reus-Smit and Ayse Zarakol (2023: 1), "The post-1945 international order" fell into crisis—"it is condemned for its economic inequalities, social hierarchies, institutional unfairness, intergenerational inequities, historical injustices and accentuating all these, its normative and epistemic biases: the privileging of western—often 'white'—values and knowledge systems." It is these realities which make the resurgence and insurgence of decolonization in the twenty-first century also known as decoloniality necessary.

The second issue which needs clarification is that the resurgent and insurgent decolonization of the twenty-first century is no longer a state-driven and regulated project linked to elite politics of seeking to capture state power. It is emerging from political society and is very clear that sovereignty of the state is not sovereignty of the people (Mignolo, 2023: 2). Therefore, what is at the center of the resurgent and insurgent decolonization of the twenty-first century is a direct response to a question posed by Ugandan feminist scholar Sylvia Tamale (2020: 9): "Who will connect the ideological dots of racism, colonization, capitalism, sexism and heterosexism in ways that our children understand?" Decolonization of the twenty-first century connects the dots. It connects existential, material, justice and epistemic challenges, which inevitably makes it to express itself in multivocal ways because it "pieces together the planetary grammar of civil and epistemic disobediences and rebellions that connect peoples and their struggles worldwide" (Mignolo, 2013: 5; Ndlovu-Gatsheni, 2023). The multivocality is inevitable in a context that is well described by Nathalie Etoke (2019) in terms of "melancholia Africana." This Africana melancholia encases a number of complex existential-cum-epistemic questions:

> In a world where thought itself closes itself in language that strives to erase the sensitivity of existence, how can we make sense of sub-Saharan or Afrodiasporic life experience rooted in suffering born of social, economic, cultural, and historical structures dominated by unequal power relations? [...]. My process breaks with the habits that would have me speak of myself and mine as if I speak of another, step out of my self for the sake of objectivity, regurgitate the Other's way of thinking in the Other's rhetoric that I have learnedly digested. In all frankness, I take the risk of injecting subjectivity into my words. (Etoke, 2019: xix)

It is clear from Etoke's articulation of issues that there is an entanglement of existential, justice, material and epistemic issues within the condition known as melancholia Africana. The final issue which needs clarification is what Walter D. Mignolo (2023: 4) depicted as "the explosive preponderance of the words 'decoloniality/decolonization' in the recent past." It is this preponderance which has ignited fears of decolonization becoming a metaphor on the one hand and on the other attempts to dismiss it as a slogan and a buzzword. The critics of decolonization seem to be failing dismally to make sense of what Mignolo (2023) correctly depicted as "a change of era, no longer the era of changes" with decolonization pointing "to the emerging decolonial sensorium which is demanding concepts and theories to capture the tragedies and hopes of the change of era."

What the critics also fail to understand is that it took a lot of effort, sacrifices and struggles to push decolonization into its present status of a planetary consciousness. Fighters such as Ngugi wa Thiong'o and Angela Davis were detained in the course of their fight for decolonization. The planetary decolonial consciousness is drawing strengths from the blood of George Floyd. The students of South Africa who spearhead the Rhodes Must Fall and Fees Must Fall movements did not only endure tear-gas and button-sticks, some were arrested. So, for critics to emerge from their air-conditioned offices and try to minimize decolonization as a slogan, a buzzword and a struggle that is unnecessary emanates from arrogance of ignorance as well as ahistorical intellectual consciousness of the world of the oppressed and exploited peoples of the world.

These clarifications are helpful in situating Andrews and Khalema's book with its three entry points of pedagogy (teaching), epistemology (knowledge) and ontology (Africanity/Black agency). Re-storying is a decolonial strategy of connecting the dots. In its ten chapters, the book delves into complex issues of resilient whiteness, the colonial library, Eurocentric hegemony, epistemicide, African/Black agency, knowledge society versus knowledge economy, justice, engaged scholarship, curriculum, epistemologies, pedagogies and the syllabus. This is a book about the politics of knowledge, the dynamics of power in the knowledge domain and the orders of knowledge and truth. It reminds us of how the resurgent and insurgent decolonization of the twenty-first century has resulted in the re-opening of the basic epistemological questions: Where does knowledge come from? Is there any link between knowledge and identity? Does knowledge have a geography? What is the space for experience and biography in knowledge? How do we distinguish between scientific-driven and ideological-driven knowledge? Is knowledge free of ideology? These are long-standing questions which provoked debates over objectivity and subjectivity and their return to haunt us in the twenty-first century indicates that we have not yet offered adequate responses.

I highly commend Andrews and Khalema together with the contributors for mustering courage to interrogate the complex questions of today. Criticality cuts across the book, caution is sounded on issues of nativism masquerading as decolonization and decolonial Afro-futures are mapped out.

April 2023

Sabelo J. Ndlovu-Gatsheni
Chair in Epistemologies
of the Global South
and Vice-Dean of Research
in the Africa Multiple Cluster
of Excellence
University of Bayreuth
Bayreuth, Germany

References

Etoke, N. (2019). *Melancholia Africana: The Indispensable Overcoming of the Black Condition*. Rowman & Littlefield International.

Getachew, A. (2019). *Worldmaking after Empire: The Rise and Fall of Self-Determination*. Princeton University Press.

Lu, C. (2023). Progress, Decolonization and Global Justice: A Tragic View. *International Affairs, 99*(1), 141–159.

Mignolo, W. D. (2023). It is a Change of Era, No Longer the Era of Changes. *Postcolonial Politics*. 29 January 2023. Retrieved from https://postcolonialpolitics.org/it-is-a-change-of-era-no-longer-the-era-of-changes/

Ndlovu-Gatsheni, S. J. (2023). *Beyond the Coloniality of Internationalism: Reworlding the World from the Global South*. CODESRIA Book Series.

Reus-Smit, C., & Zarakol, A. (2023). Polymorphic Justice and the Crisis of International Order. *International Affairs*, *99*(1), 1–22.

Taiwo, O. (2022). *Against Decolonization: Taking African Agency Seriously*. Hurst & Company.

Tamale, S. (2020). *Decolonization and Afro-Feminism*. Daraja Press.

Tuck, E., & Yang, K. W. (2012). Decolonization is Not a Metaphor. *Decolonization: Indigeneity, Education & Society, 1*(1), 1–40.

Acknowledgments

This edited collection was made possible by sustained collaborative efforts. We are forever grateful for the opportunity to serve as editors and are indebted to everyone who has contributed in small and big ways to make this a success. First, we acknowledge the financial support provided by the Carnegie African Diaspora Fellowship Program (CADFP) that covered the cost of a six-week visit to the University of KwaZulu-Natal (South Africa) in the summer of 2021 which served as the birthing ground for the book. It is really refreshing to see such research collaboration between African scholars resident on the continent and those residing abroad supported and enabled. It is worth mentioning that CADFP also provided funding for us to attend and present some key findings from this book (mainly Chapter 1) at the International Studies Association conference held in Al Akhawayn University (Ifrane, Morocco) in June 2023.

Secondly, we are thankful for the editors of the *Palgrave Political Pedagogies Book Series* for their interest in the volume and the encouragement to get it completed. Both of us have published pieces that resonate with the themes covered in this book but this was our first shot at leading such a book-length endeavor on the topic of "decolonizing pedagogies" and we believe the encouragement went a long way in keeping our eyes on the end goal. Also, we appreciate all the contributors for their patience and sustained interest in this project despite a rather long peer/editorial review process.

Furthermore, we are grateful for colleagues who provided foreword and endorsements. The positive responses were pleasantly surprising considering everyone's busy schedules and the fact that, for colleagues like Prof. Sabelo Ndlovu-Gatsheni (who wrote a beautiful foreword) and Prof. Leon Moosavi, we had no prior connection. It is great to feel supported by colleagues from far and near! We also appreciate the thoughtful feedback received from anonymous peer reviewers of the book. Finally, we acknowledge Eric Adamo (Ph.D. student at McMaster University) who worked in the capacity of research assistant to help with various editorial responsibilities, including proofreading and indexing. It has been a wonderful labor of love and we truly appreciate everyone!

Praise for *Decolonizing African Studies Pedagogies*

"*Decolonizing African Studies Pedagogies* is a path-breaking attempt by an intergeneration group of outstanding scholars to walk the talk of decolonizing knowledge production and dissemination. Centering Africa as a subject of study, this innovative edited book offers nuanced, realistic, thought-provoking, and rich menu of ideas for addressing epistemic racism and disrupting oppressive structures of knowledge creation and mobilization. A great book for those seeking a fairer and an equitable world."

—Thomas Kwasi Tieku, *King's University College at The University of Western Ontario, Canada*

"This volume is a powerful intervention in the discourse and concrete action-oriented affirmation of the rights, need and urgency to, not simply reclaim, but systematically apply African agency in the critical sphere of knowledge. The theme and collection constitute a timely and an impressive cutting-edge contribution to both the theorizing and praxis of epistemic agency. This book will be powerful scholarly and practical reference for students and scholars across academic disciplines as well as practitioners and policymakers in treating with priority the defining knowledge matter."

—N'Dri T. Assié-Lumumba, *Cornell University, USA*

"This book makes a vigorous contribution to the struggle for epistemic decolonisation from Eurocentrism. It is daring yet still accessible. Look no further if you want to witness how to deploy postcolonial and decolonial theory to examine complex social issues, particularly in African contexts. Just like that, the contributors masterfully attain the elusive balance between realistic cynicism and uplifting hope. Read this book and learn! It's a gift to us."

—Leon Moosavi, *Department of Sociology, Social Policy & Criminology, University of Liverpool, UK*

Contents

Notes on Contributors

Nathan Andrews is an associate professor in the Department of Political Science at McMaster University. One aspect of his research focuses on the global political economy/ecology of natural resource extraction and development. His peer-reviewed publications on this topic have appeared in journals such as *International Affairs, Resources Policy, World Development*, *Energy Research & Social Science*, *Africa Today*, *Business & Society Review*, and *Journal of International Relations & Development*, among others. His latest books include a monograph, *Gold Mining and the Discourses of Corporate Social Responsibility in Ghana* (Palgrave, 2019), a co-authored monograph, *Oil and Development in Ghana: Beyond the Resource Curse* (Routledge, 2021) and co-edited volumes, *Natural Resource-Based Development in Africa: Panacea or Pandora's Box?* (University of Toronto Press, 2022). The second aspect of his research revolves around the scholarship of teaching and learning, in particular critical international relations, epistemic hegemony, racism and whiteness in knowledge production and dissemination. Some recent articles on this theme include "What/Who Is Still Missing in International Relations (IR) Scholarship? Situating Africa as an Agent in IR Theorizing" (*Third World Quarterly* with Isaac Odoom) and "Trends of Epistemic Oppression and Academic Dependency in Africa's Development: The Need for a New Intellectual Path" (*Journal of Pan African Studies*).

Olajumoke Ayandele is a postdoctoral research fellow at New York University Center for the study of Africa and the African Diaspora (CSAAD) and a non-resident fellow at the Center for Global Affairs. She is also the Nigeria Senior Advisor at The Armed Conflict Location & Event Data Project (ACLED). She is passionate about understanding the dynamic relationship and intersection between African governance, human development and political stability, and has won numerous awards and grants to conduct her research, with visiting research fellowships at the National Defence College, Abuja and the Center for International Studies (CERI) at the Institut d'études politiques de Paris (Sciences Po). A brilliant African Security Scholar, she continues to collaborate with international and regional decision-makers as well as government institutions in promoting human security initiatives and programs that can create a peaceful and secure Africa. She holds a Ph.D. in Global Affairs from Rutgers—The State University of New Jersey, an M.P.A. in International Development Policy and Management and a B.A. in Economics, both from New York University.

Savo Heleta is a researcher and educator with more than ten years' experience in higher education, academic research, curriculum development, teaching, research supervision and internationalization in South Africa. His research focuses on decolonization of knowledge, higher education internationalization, international research collaboration; climate justice, and social justice advocacy and activism. Apart from his work in higher education, he has worked on post-war peacebuilding and youth leadership development projects in Bosnia and Herzegovina (1998–2002) and post-war capacity building and leadership development in South Sudan (2009–2013). Survivor of the Bosnian war, he is the author of *Not My Turn to Die: Memoirs of a Broken Childhood in Bosnia* (AMACOM Books, 2008). He works as a researcher and internationalization specialist at Durban University of Technology in South Africa.

Nene Ernest Khalema is the dean and head of school of Built Environment and Development Studies (SoBEDS) at the University of KwaZulu-Natal (UKZN) in South Africa. Before joining UKZN he was a professor in various Canadian universities since 2001 and served as Chief/Senior Research Specialist (CRS) of the Human Sciences Research Council (2011–2016) where his seminal work on participatory action mixed methodologies in the areas of migration and mobilities, critical pedagogies, social epidemiology, social demography, critical race and gender studies, and sustainable development received (inter)national recognition. He is an author and co-editor of eight books and has published over 40 articles in accredited academic journals; 25 refereed book chapters; 40 technical research reports/policy briefs; and has presented over 75 papers and 25 academic posters in local, national and international conferences.

Blessings Masuku is a registered HR Professional with the South African Board for People Practices. He is also a registered trainer, assessor and moderator with several Sector Education and Training Authority (SETAs) for various qualifications. He is also part of the Quality Council for Trades and Occupations (QCTO) panel team of subject matter expert to develop occupational qualifications and review historic qualifications to suit the industry's needs. He has vast experience as a mentor and coach dealing with youth within the Education, Training and Development (ETD) space. He is an emerging researcher and contributor Southern African Institute of Government Auditors (SAIGA). He is currently a part-time research assistant at the University of KwaZulu-Natal where he is pursuing his Ph.D. in Community Development at the School of Built and Environment and Development Studies. His research focus is in the area of educational access, poverty and informality, energy studies, urban studies, food insecurity, service delivery, social policy review and youth development.

Sally Matthews is an associate professor in the Department of Political and International Studies at Rhodes University, South Africa. She teaches comparative politics, African Studies and African Political Economy. Her current research mostly falls into three broad areas. Firstly, she has a long-standing interest in post-development theory and more generally in how to challenge and move beyond the idea of development in Africa. Secondly, she is interested in rethinking how to research and teach about Africa in a way that acknowledges and challenges the colonial origins of African Studies. This area of interest also relates to the idea that we should "decolonize" university curricula which has led her to work on various teaching-related projects which seek to shift how we teach about Africa. Finally, she also has an interest in the politics of NGO work and of partnerships between privileged actors (like NGOs and universities) and the communities they set out to assist.

Zainab Monisola Olaitan is a Ph.D. candidate and an assistant lecturer in the Department of Political Sciences, University of Pretoria. She is also a project officer in the Litigation and Implementation unit at the Centre for Human Rights, University of Pretoria. She is researching the impact of gender quotas on the substantive representation of women in Africa. Her doctoral research interrogates the assumption that women's increased participation in politics improves the life of women substantively. She obtained her first degree in Bachelor of Science (Hons) in Political Science with first class from the University of Lagos. She completed her second degree in Philosophy, Politics and Economics Honors at the University of Cape Town as a 2018 Mandela Rhodes Scholar. In 2019, she was selected for the Mastercard foundation scholarship to study for a Master's in Political Science at the University of Pretoria. Her master's dissertation was on women's participation in peacebuilding in West Africa, using Sierra Leone as a case study. In 2022, she was awarded the Margaret McNamara Education Grant for her impactful research work on women and children. She is an avid researcher with published articles in journals, she is interested in contributing to research on political thought, gender and representation, conflict and peace studies, and African politics.

Samuel Ojo Oloruntoba is an adjunct research professor at the Institute of African Studies, Carleton University, Ottawa, Ontario, Canada and honorary professor at the Thabo Mbeki African School of Public and International Affairs, University of South Africa, where he was previously an associate professor. He obtained Ph.D. in Political Science from the University of Lagos, Nigeria. He was previously a visiting scholar at the Program of African Studies, Northwestern University, Evanston and fellow of Brown International Advanced Research Institute, Brown University, Rhode Island, United States. He is the author, editor and co-editor of several books including *Regionalism and Integration in Africa: EU-ACP Economic Partnership Agreements and Euro-Nigeria Relations*, Palgrave Macmillan, New York, 2016 and co-editor with Toyin Falola of the *Palgrave Handbook of Africa and the Changing Global Order, 2022*, among others. His research interests are in Political Economy of Development in Africa, Regional Integration, Migration, Democracy and Development, Global Governance of Trade and Finance, Politics of Natural Resources Governance, Indigenous knowledge and politics of knowledge production and EU-African Relations. He has won several awards and grants from local and international research institutions. He is also a member of the African Knowledge Network, Office of Special

Adviser on Africa UN Under Secretary-General, United Nations, New York.

Temitope B. Oriola is professor of criminology and associate dean in the Faculty of Arts, University of Alberta. A recipient of the Governor General of Canada Academic Gold Medal (first presented by the Earl of Dufferin in 1873), He is the author of *Criminal resistance? The politics of kidnapping oil workers*, one of a handful of book-length sociological investigations of political kidnapping in the English language. His research focuses on police use of force and terrorism studies. A decorated researcher and teacher, he is president of the Canadian Sociological Association (CSA), former president of the Canadian Association of African Studies (CAAS) and 2022 recipient of the Arts Research Excellence Award, University of Alberta. He is a member, Board of Directors, Canadian Federation for the Humanities and Social Sciences. He is also a recipient of an Alexander von Humboldt Fellowship and has served as special adviser to the Government of Alberta on Police Act Review. On the recommendation of the Alberta Legislature in January 2023, he received the Queen Elizabeth II Platinum Jubilee Medal for "exceptional qualities and outstanding service to our province in the field of Advanced Education and Public Service."

Hosea Olayiwola Patrick is a transdisciplinary researcher and postdoctoral fellow at the Department of Geography, Geomatics and Environment, University of Toronto, Mississauga. He has a Ph.D. in Political Science with a specialization in environmental politics from the University of KwaZulu-Natal, South Africa. His research focuses centrally on the United Nations' sustainable development goals application and implications in the areas of climate change (SDG 13), human security-conflict, water and food (SDG 2 and 6), as well as social and environmental justice (SDG 16). He also works on public policy, decolonization, peace and conflict, and academic exclusion research areas. He has published book chapters in Palgrave Macmillan, Routledge and Springer nature among others. He has also published in journals such as *African Insight*, *African Renaissance* and *Journal of Transformation in Higher Education* among others. He was the editor of a special issue of the *Journal of Inclusive cities and Built environment* on (De)-Coloniality, Autonomy, Identity and Spatial Justice in Africa and editor for the Alternation special issue on Migration, Identity Construction and Integration in Africa.

Sakhile Phiri is a lecturer and program leader of the undergraduate degree program in Development Studies at Nelson Mandela University in Gqeberha, South Africa. His main areas of teaching and research are around African economic development, development policy, decolonization and research methodologies. He supervises students in the broad areas of poverty alleviation, entrepreneurship, unemployment and employability. His other research focus areas include higher education and the labor market. He is currently busy with a Ph.D. which focuses on graduate employability.

Maïka Sondarjee is an assistant professor at the School of International Development and Global Studies (University of Ottawa). She obtained her Ph.D. from the University of Toronto and has been a Banting postdoctoral fellow at the University of Montreal. In 2023, she co-edited a volume entitled *White Saviorism in International Development. Theories, Practices and Lived Experiences* (Daraja Press) with Themrise Khan (Pakistan) and Kanakulya Dickson (Uganda). In her academic practice, she aims to support activists and movements for social justice.

Phumelele Makathini Zakwe is currently acting director of professional services at the College of Humanities and the substantive School Operations Manager in the School of Built Environment & Development Studies at the University of KwaZulu-Natal (UKZN). She holds a Doctor of Business Administration from at UKZN Graduate School of Business, an M.B.A., a B.Com. and the B.Ed. (hon). Her doctoral thesis examined the role of leadership in the provision of quality higher education institutions in South Africa. She is a member of local, national and international associations within the higher education sector and has worked in both private and public institutions in South Africa including the Presidency within the Government of South Africa. She has contributed immensely as an educational strategist to transformation and reform within higher education settings from both the educational governance and operational perspectives.

Nelson Casimiro Zavale is associate professor at the Faculty of Education at the Eduardo Mondlane University (UEM), in Maputo, Mozambique, a senior research fellow at Käte Hamburger Kolleg: Cultures of Research, the international center for advanced studies at the RWTH Aachen University, Germany. He previously held other positions, notably:

Fulbright visiting scholar at the Centre for Studies in Higher Education (CSHE), University of California, Berkeley (2021–2022), Humboldt Research Fellow at the International Centre for Higher Education Research (INCHER) of the University of Kassel, in Germany (2018–2021), a Swiss government excellence postdoctoral fellow (2015–2016) at University of Basel in Switzerland. His research interests focus on sociology of education, higher education, science and innovation studies. He is particularly interested in questioning existing assumptions about the contribution of higher education, science, technology and innovation to socio-economic development in Africa (and Global South in general). He has several research outputs in international journals such as *Higher Education, Scientometrics, Science and Public Policy, International Journal of Educational Development, Quality in Higher Education*, as well as monographs and book chapters in international publishers such as *Routledge and Springer*.

Acronyms and Abbreviations

ABU	Ahmadu Bello University
AIKS	African Indigenous Knowledge Systems
AJOL	African Journals Online
ANC	African National Congress
ASA	African Studies Association
CODESRIA	Council for the Development of Social Science Research in Africa
DHET	Department of Higher Education and Training
EDI	Equity, Diversity and Inclusion
GDP	Growth Domestic Product
GER	Gross Enrollment Ratio
GII	Global Innovation Index
GKI	Global Knowledge Index
HBU	Historically Black University
HWU	Historically White University
ICT	Information and Communication Technologies
IK	Indigenous Knowledge
INSEAD	Institut Européen d'Administration des Affaires
IR	International Relations
JPPS	Journal Publishing Practices and Standards
KEI	Knowledge Economy Index
MBRF	Mohammed Bin Rashid Al Maktoum Knowledge Foundation
NCHE	National Commission on Higher Education
NSFAS	National Student Financial Aid Scheme
NWG	National Working Group
OAU	Organization of African Unity

R&D	Research and Development
RDI	Research, Development and Innovation
SAP	Structural Adjustment Program
SJR	SCImago Journal Rank
SNIP	Source Normalized Impact per Paper
SSA	Sub-Saharan Africa
STISA-2024	Science, Technology and Innovation Strategy for Africa, 2024
TVET	Technical and Vocational Education and Training
UCT	University of Cape Town
UK	United Kingdom
UNDP	United Nations Development Programme
UNESCO	United Nations Educational, Scientific and Cultural Organization
UNIDESA	United Nations Department of Economic and Social Affairs
US	United States
USAf	Universities South Africa
VUT	Vaal University of Technology

List of Figures

List of Tables

CHAPTER 1

Re-Storying African (Studies) Pedagogies: Decolonizing Knowledge and Centering Black Agency?

Nathan Andrews and Nene Ernest Khalema

Introduction

For many decades, Africa has been a central figure in scholarly discussions in various disciplines. We can map out different trends in the study of Africa, including the euphoria that came with the post-independent Africa in the 1960s, the neoliberal structural adjustment programs (SAPs) in the 1980s that resulted in austerity-oriented reforms in higher education, the Africa-as-the-hopeless-continent trend in the early 2000s spearheaded by

N. Andrews (✉)
Department of Political Science, McMaster University, Hamilton, ON, Canada
e-mail: nandrews@mcmaster.ca

N. E. Khalema
School of Built Environment and Development Studies, College of Humanities, University of KwaZulu-Natal, Durban, South Africa
e-mail: Khalema@ukzn.ac.za

N. Andrews and N. E. Khalema (eds.), *Decolonizing African Studies Pedagogies*, Political Pedagogies,
https://doi.org/10.1007/978-3-031-37442-5_1

the popular article by *The Economist* and the current Africa-rising narrative. All these trends, which intersect with various global crises, have contributed to the growing interest in studying and teaching about this rather complex continent (Mamdani, 1993; Rutazibwa, 2018; Wallerstein, 1983; Zeleza, 1997). It is also notable that the notion and practice of decolonization in Africa have meant different things during these multiple eras. One can further point to the emergence of African Studies centers, academic associations, and journals that have privileged the production and dissemination of knowledge about the continent (Allman, 2019; Branch, 2018; Grosz-Ngaté, 2020).

Decades ago, some theorists established the link between economic/political imperialism and epistemic issues (see Ake, 1982; Mazrui, 1992; Mbembe, 2001). This is important in recognizing that knowledge is both political and social power, and whoever maintains control over the dissemination of such knowledge determines the narratives that are shared about the subjects (or countries) of study (Ndlovu-Gatsheni, 2012). In other words, the hegemony of the west in the broader global political economy mirrors the hegemony over knowledge production. As Branch (2018) notes, for instance, the powerful institutional structures that underpin knowledge production point to how we can examine the role of the twenty-first-century African Studies centers in Europe and elsewhere as part of the decolonization agenda or not. In fact, recent research has pointed to how initiatives to transform elite institutions where white privilege resides continue to center these same institutions as the ultimate echelon of knowledge (Coetzee, 2022). This implies that not all actions that are supposedly associated with the decolonial turn are truly serving the purpose of decolonization (Moosavi, 2020, 2023).

While many universities in postcolonial Africa have proclaimed intentions around the decolonization of higher education on the continent, the reality points to several challenges in Africanizing the curricula, pedagogical structures, and epistemologies (Andrews & Okpanachi, 2012; Assié-Lumumba, 2016, 2017; Mbembe, 2016; Nyamnjoh, 2019; Zeleza & Olukoshi, 2004). This explains how complex the work of decolonization is—especially as it entails both resistance to and intentional undoing (i.e., dismantling and unlearning) of hegemonic discourses, practices, institutions, and structures (see Kessi et al., 2020). Yet, it is a project that must be undertaken as part of efforts to unpack the manufacturing of Africa in the curricula of African Studies and other cognate disciplines, its empirical uptake in research as a subject of study, and the subsequent reproduction of certain 'truths' about the continent.

A discussion of critical pedagogy is inherently political, and so is the notion of decolonization itself (Sondarjee & Andrews, 2023; Tuck & Yang, 2012). This volume assembles the critical perspectives of scholars engaged in African Studies and other cognate disciplines (e.g., International Studies, Sociology, and Development Studies) who are located in African academic institutions and those located in North America. This cross-geographical specification is instructive since things that are said and written about Africa have historically excluded people whose daily lives and work intersect with such characterizations of the continent. It is also important to recognize how one's positionality as an 'outsider' or 'insider' contributes to one's approach to teaching and researching Africa. The goal is that, by assembling these varying insider–outsider and home-diaspora perspectives, the volume can contribute to a re-imagination and possible decentering of the Eurocentric pedagogical and research practices that inform entrenched narratives about Africa and African agency.

It is no doubt that Africa's decolonial knowledge production project remains important, especially given the persistent epistemic injustice that has been foreshadowed by the continent's deep colonial heritage (Crawford et al., 2021; Fanon, 1961 [2004]; Mbembe, 2021; Mudimbe, 1988; Ndlovu-Gatsheni, 2018, 2020, 2021; wa Thiong'o, 1992). Scholars like Walter Mignolo believe the decolonial agenda is possible "within academia through courses, seminars, workshops, mentoring students and working with colleagues who have the same conviction" (2013: 137). By focusing specifically on the perspectives of scholars with similar decolonial convictions, this book contributes to the movement in ways that help us as a collective to both challenge persistent oppressive structures and imagine possible futures where Black agency is neither marginalized nor stereotyped. The rest of this introductory chapter interrogates aspects of the scholarly debates on decolonization and the decolonial project within the context of knowledge creation and dissemination to help situate the respective contributions to the volume.

What's at Stake in Re-Storying African (Studies) Pedagogies?

> The reason being that the colonized intellectual has thrown himself headlong into western culture. Like adopted children who only stop investigating their new family environment once their psyche has formed a minimum core of reassurance, the colonized intellectual will endeavour to make European culture his own. Not content with knowing Rabelais or Diderot, Shakespeare or Edgar Allen Poe, he will stretch his mind until he identified with them completely. (Fanon, 1961 [2004]: 156)

The above observations by Frantz Fanon strike a nerve because many of us who have contributed to this volume operate within a western or *westernized* system although we may not readily admit to being completely absorbed by the culture. The role and positionality of the colonized intellectual is crucial to understanding both the possibilities and challenges of re-storying. Fanon could not have been more direct in pointing out what would be involved in getting African intellectuals to begin operating outside the colonial frame—a system they have been adopted into. For the two of us who had education in places like Ghana, South Africa, and Canada, we are somehow implicated in the western culture critique despite our best efforts to resist. What becomes necessary, then, is a detangling of our pedagogies from the status quo in ways that allow us to go beyond the single story of Africa and Africans (Adichie, 2009). In fact, Mbembe (2001: 241) has shown that "the order of truth in which Africa is situated is not unequivocal … Its reality includes several propositions that are, in one place, opposed or congruent, and, in another, parallel and perpendicular." Instead of the pervasive nature of single stories that surround the study of Africa, Mbembe's complex understanding of the continent and its peoples should inform a re-storying that is not unidirectional.

In her 2018 presidential address at the 61st Annual Meeting of the African Studies Association (ASA), which is arguably the largest professional organization for scholars who research and teach about Africa, Professor Jean Allman did not hold back in calling out the Association's first presidential address by Professor Melville J. Herskovits in 1958 (Allman, 2019). The Herskovits address set the tone for African Studies in North America (if not the rest of the western world) by entrenching white privilege and reforming the field along a more positivist American format of scholarship and knowledge production, partly captured in the following remarks: "... because we are from a country that has no territorial commitments in Africa, we come easily by a certain physical and psychological distance from the problems we study ..." (qtd. in Allman, 2019: 8). African Studies in the west has historically been informed by white superiority, American-style scientific objectivity and neutrality—a series of institutional standards which seem to justify the exclusion of non-white scholars, and especially those whose perspectives do not measure up to the American metric of quality or rigor. Allman (2019) obviously presents us with a problematic history of the field, explaining how decisions made by Herskovits facilitated the development of an 'Africanist enterprise' that excluded Black scholars and privileged White scholars. Thanks to the expressions of resistance at the 1968 annual meeting in Los Angeles and afterward that led to the realization that the Association was not serving the needs of Black people, ASA leadership and membership today are obviously more diverse than the 1960s (Allman, 2019). Yet, this diversity has not resulted in the systemic overhaul needed to centralize the contributions and perspectives of African scholars.

The Rhodes Must Fall and Fees Must Fall Movements in South Africa underscore the continued contribution of Africa to decolonization scholarship and the decolonial project globally (Ndlovu-Gatsheni, 2021). What transpired in South Africa has resonance with other higher education campaigns in the UK like Rhodes Must Fall Oxford and Why Is My Curricula So White, which challenge the persistence of Eurocentrism within knowledge production and the blatant absence of diversity among the professoriate as well as on reading lists and general course content (Andrews, 2022; Coetzee, 2022; Nyamnjoh, 2022; Swartz et al., 2020). These campaigns contribute to placing Allman's ASA presidential address into a broader perspective, which underscores why her predecessor also chose to focus her 2019 presidential address on the themes of knowledge and power, epistemic decolonization, and African self-determination (Grosz-Ngaté, 2020). Despite the buzz that such discussions have received in recent years, however, the issue of epistemic imperialism prevails as noted above. This volume, therefore, seeks to further reveal its influence on African Studies and highlight the necessity of countering such a hegemonic system.

Brazilian educator, Paulo Freire's (1972), seminal book *Pedagogy of the Oppressed* is quite instructive in understanding what is at stake in a re-storying that has direct decolonial ramifications. Freire (1972) differentiates pedagogical design into 'bank deposit education' and 'problem posing education.' The former sees students as passive individuals entrusted with storing information deposits entrusted to them whereas the latter sees students as having the freedom to think, imagine and create. Similarly, bank deposit education pathologizes the oppressed as marginal to the healthy society, whereas problem posing education speaks of the oppressed as having the agency to reflect on their oppression and, by so doing, maintains the capacities necessary for transforming the system that facilitates such oppression.

These two perspectives on pedagogical design by Freire (1972) bring the African Studies issue into perspective especially within the context of constructing a field of study that goes beyond the western gaze—one that represents people as not being simply oppressed and poor but as people with an imaginable future. It is rather interesting how ideas shared about half a century ago still resonate with the current times and with earlier works such as *The Wretched of the Earth* in which Fanon (1961 [2004]) reveals crucial weapons for the Black revolution. Here, Fanon (1961 [2004]) shows how the colonial struggles for power were created and maintained by the use or threat of violence which disrupted Indigenous ways of knowing and doing and positioned the African continent as a 'lesser power' heavily dependent on the colonizer for its 'progress.' As argued, "it is the colonist who *fabricated* and *continues to fabricate* the colonized subjects. The colonist derives validity, i.e., his wealth, from the colonial system" (Fanon, 1961 [2004]: 2, emphasis in original). It is this fabrication of the wretched colonized subject, often manifesting in stereotypes about the 'dark' and 'hopeless' continent, that distorts the capacity of Africa and Africans to be involved in knowledge creation.

The understanding of fabricated subjects connects with Mbembe's (2001: 237) description of the colonial relationship: "It works to preserve, in each time and circumstance, the possibility of telling oneself stories, of saying one thing and doing the opposite—in short, of constantly blurring the distinction between truth and falsehood." Wa Thiong'o (1992) shows how decolonization needs to begin with a transformed mindset. He sees imperialism's main weapon to be one of a cultural bomb which has the effect "to annihilate a people's belief in their names, in their languages, in their environment, in their heritage of struggle … and ultimately in themselves. It makes them see their past as one wasteland of non-achievement and it makes them want to distance themselves from that wasteland" (wa Thiong'o, 1992: 3). Despite the complexity proposed by Mbembe (2001), wa Thiong'o shows that with such a mindset the oppressed cannot imagine the possibility of breaking away from actual enslavement or even the fabrication of non-existence. Regardless of the tumultuous movements that have historically informed the decolonial project, some scholars are a bit more optimistic about the opportunity the current momentum presents:

> In Africa the stakes are high, but this is a fecund moment of opportunity. As the Global North experiences increasing economic and political instability (conditions that have long defined life in the Global South), the formerly colonised have the potential to rise to prominence as decolonising locus of enunciation – one informed by its own concepts, methods, categories, assumptions, and theories. (Swartz et al., 2020: 182)

The above remarks capture an important assertion of African agency given that existing scholarship has persistently marginalized African voices even on issues that are intricately connected to the daily lives of Africans. In other words, what once characterized 'the evolving role of the African scholar in African Studies' in the 1980s (see Wallerstein, 1983) still has not materialized four decades later into a substantive expression of agency, neither within the context of those individuals running the field of study nor those whose perspectives are valued as legitimate knowledge. We build on the theoretic foundations of reclaiming agency from its denigration by Eurocentric epistemological traditions. Firstly, as the basis of a decolonial theory, its objective is to reconfigure the logical connection between the implications of rigorously contextual African voices and the imperative of a commitment to an emancipatory discourse connected to the lived experiences of African peoples. Secondly, at the practical level, we provocatively explore the most pertinent approach to an agency-affirming decolonial discourse that centers what Jean-Paul Sartre (1948) describes in *Black Orpheus* as 'Africanity,' expressed in African ways of being, knowing, and doing borne of struggle (see also Sartre & MacCombie, 1964).

An agency-affirming decolonial discourse approach thus begins with transparency about one's own insider–outsider position and draws on the idea of resisting the immanent cultural hegemony cemented in colonial thinking by asking socio-ontological questions about agency and positionality. Sartre's (1948) praxis of agency allows for a legitimate application of the postulations to the current struggle for an authentic postcolonial African scholarship. Our formulation, therefore, seeks to step beyond the geopolitical critique of the western power matrix as a predominant theme and directs focus onto the dilemmas besetting contemporary African Studies on the continent and elsewhere.

What's in a Word? Coloniality and Epistemicide

Epistemic hegemony or imperialism is the outcome of entrenched epistemic racism that defines which knowledge contributions to a particular subject matter are deemed relevant, and it manifests in different fields of study that intersect with African Studies such as International Relations, Sociology, and Development Studies (Khalema, 2022; Ndlovu-Gatsheni, 2018; Odoom & Andrews, 2017; Rutazibwa, 2018; Shilliam, 2010, 2020; Tieku, 2021). This provincialization of knowledge and its sites of (re)production potentially explains why some of the 'key' scholars of African Studies (i.e., notable 'Africanists') have historically tended to be majority white men and a few women (see Allman, 2019). But this is not surprising given the enormous funding opportunities that exist in western universities for studies on Africa—research that often does not result in the co-creation of knowledge with scholars and organizations based in Africa (see Asiamah et al., 2021; Assié-Lumumba, 2017; Khalema, 2018; Mohammed, 2021).

An understanding of coloniality especially within the context of knowledge production and pedagogy may be characterized by what Andrews and Odoom (2021) discuss as the orthodoxies surrounding the propagation of monocultures, which are captured by Santos (2004) as the five logics that underscore the (re)production of non-existence. In no particular order, the logic of linearity sees the world in linear terms where core countries or superpowers come before the others (i.e., small powers) by measure of their supposed superiority in economic, political, military, or other sense.

Second, the logic of the universal and the global sees the world as more compressed than different. Therefore, anything that does not seem to capture this universalized understanding of the world is disregarded into non-existence. Third, the logic of capitalist productivity and efficiency is reinforced by neoliberalism and the practices associated with it. This logic privileges hyper-productivity and the grind culture (e.g., publish-or-perish mentality) without stopping to question the unequal nature of processes that inform knowledge production and dissemination. Fourth, there is also the logic of knowledge itself which tends to be focused on the disputed binary between science and tradition where the west has the former and the rest of the world have the latter. Finally, the logic of categorization that breaks down a much diverse world into units such as 'first and third,' 'developed and underdeveloped,' 'high income and low income' among other (often derogatory) descriptors that for instance make people associate 'third world' with dirty and inferior.

With the goal of underscoring the (re)production of non-existence or the 'zone of non-being' (Fanon, 1961 [2004]), these five logics or monocultures combined uphold a certain hegemonic rationality that sees the 'other' as "the residual, the inferior, the local and the non-productive" (Santos, 2004: 239). Coloniality, therefore, represents the continuities of colonialism and subjugation expressed in political, social, and economic forms operating at different scales. As argued by Quijano (2007: 171), race is fundamental to the coloniality of power because it served as the key criteria for the classification of the colonized and colonizers which, "under European colonialism were mutated in a relationship of biologically and structurally superior and inferior." This classification revealed a hierarchical structure for knowledge production, which are already well summarized in the five monocultures above. To overcome this coloniality, scholars like Ndlovu-Gatsheni (2018) have insisted on the need for a de-Europeanization which enables the emergence of decolonial consciousness. According to him, the process of de-Europeanizing also implies 'deprovincializing Africa'—"an intellectual and academic process of centering Africa as a legitimate historical unit of analysis and epistemic site from which to interpret the world while at the same time globalizing knowledge from Africa" (Ndlovu-Gatsheni, 2018: 4).

Santos (2014: 92) characterizes epistemicide as follows: "the murder of language ... unequal exchanges among cultures have always implied the death of the knowledge of the subordinated culture, hence the death of the social groups that possessed it." Santos (2014: 189) goes on to further argue that "social injustice is based on cognitive injustice," which manifests both as the unequal distribution of scientific knowledge and the potential of such knowledge to truly transform the 'real world' of social groups outside of the west. As noted by Ndlovu-Gatsheni (2015: 15), "genealogically speaking, coloniality is founded on theft of history. Theft of history for Africa translated into theft of its future." Epistemic freedom is, therefore, "that essential prerequisite for political, cultural, economic and other freedoms" (Ndlovu-Gatsheni, 2018: 4).

Despite the coloniality of power that underpins epistemicide as captured by Santos (2014), Kumalo (2020) argues that claims of epistemicide and linguicide within the context of South Africa in particular are misplaced. Focusing on the Black Archive, Kumalo (2020: 20) highlights how "language allows us access into knowledge that existed historically and remained irrespective of colonial imposition." The point is that what is thought to have been killed is only a result of the deliberate forgetfulness that hides the existence of Black/Indigenous epistemic traditions. Certainly, African academics must learn from their history and lived experiences (see Tieku, 2021). The postcolonial situation is something more complex and further concerns what Africans themselves have done or not done about their colonial past. This means that power and knowledge are inextricably intertwined; hence, control of the domain of knowledge creation/recreation and cultivation of knowledge should be overseen by political institutions which are considered as key sites of knowledge production. Political institutions occupy a significant and powerful position in society to guide and administer the creation of knowledge vital to human emancipation and development. Yet the effects of colonialism that undermine the knowledge of the 'Other' continue to be reflected in social structural settings of Africa's developmental agenda, notably in the institutions of higher learning (Mthembu, 2020). Due to the knowledge-power nexus, we can agree with Santos (2014: 207) that "there is no global social justice without global cognitive justice." In other words, the monoculture of scientific knowledge that informs western epistemology, colonial economies, and neoliberal rationality needs to give way to more pluriversal forms of knowledge and doing (see also Mbembe, 2021; Mignolo, 2007).

Decolonization and Decoloniality, or How Not to (Mis)use the D-word

The decolonization movement in higher education in Africa is clearly not new, as there has been a rich history of social activism that has sought to confront white supremacy and colonialism—for instance, the work of the Négritude movement spearheaded by African diaspora students such as Aimé Césaire, Leon Damas, Paulette Nardal, and Léopold Sédar Senghor (Pimblott, 2020; see also Falola, 2001; Mkandawire, 2005). This history recognizes the connection between institutional racism and its connection to the broader legacies of slavery and colonialism, which have had direct ramifications for the continent's positionality and epistemic contributions. One thing that unites the resurgent and insurgent decolonization struggles is the broader issue of rehumanizing people who have been dehumanized, which reveals the intertwined nature of the struggle for epistemic freedom with other struggles (see various contributions in Shilliam, 2010; also, Ndlovu-Gatsheni, 2021; Sondarjee & Andrews, 2023).

Garwe et al. (2021) note that despite being recognized as the cradle of humankind with a proven record of creativity and innovation as historically evidenced by its great empires and kingdoms, Africa remains positioned as an underdeveloped region contributing only about two percent to global knowledge production. Ndlovu-Gatsheni (2015) attributes this marginality to what he characterizes as the 'theft of history,' which leads to the questioning of Africa's contribution to human civilization. Motsaathebe (2020) also critiques the dismal failure of African governments to change historical injustices and the colonial structures, which has implications for how African politics can play a role in the rethinking that would serve as fundamental tool to decolonize the western pedagogy deeply embedded in African higher education (Heleta, 2018; Ndlovu-Gatsheni, 2020). As argued by Swartz et al. (2020: 175), "decolonising the canon therefore reminds us to consider everything we study from new perspectives. It draws attention to how often the only worldview made accessible to students is male, white, and European." Thus, epistemic decolonization is seen as a way out of the current Eurocentric pedagogy and the colonial continuities pervasive in Africa's higher education and the study of the continent (Alcoff, 2017; Assié-Lumumba, 2016; Mignolo & Walsh, 2018; Posholi, 2020; Santos, 2014).

Ndlovu-Gatsheni (2020: 37) posits that "decolonization/decoloniality is about connections and convergences... [it] does not authorize a simplistic conflation of human intellectual/academic productions and ideological ones." He further argues that this characteristic, for instance, points to how decoloniality and postcoloniality converge in terms of their critiques of modernity and yet diverge in terms of their intellectual genealogy that can be traced to thinkers like Aimé Césaire, Frantz Fanon, W. E. B. Du Bois, Kwame Nkrumah, and Ngugi wa Thiong'o among many others who originate from locations where people experience the negative ramifications of modernity. This intellectual genealogy (and its connection to the genealogy of centuries of colonialism) is crucial to understanding the context of decolonization in Africa. The following words by Fanon are instructive:

> Decolonization, therefore, implies the urgent need to thoroughly challenge the colonial situation. Its definition can, if we want to describe it accurately, be summed up in the well-known words: 'The last shall be the first.' Decolonization is verification of this. At a descriptive level, therefore, *any decolonization is a success.* (Fanon, 1961 [2004]: 2, our emphasis added)

Fanon's argument seems to suggest that any endeavor contributing to different causes that challenge the colonial situation, or the imperialism of today's world, is a good contribution. It is, however, important to note that the decolonization that Fanon refers to in the remarks above is more deeply politically rooted than the surface-level decolonization buzzword that has become prominent in recent times, especially within the context of higher education. Let us note take for granted that important movements like #RhodesMustFall continue to challenge the colonial situation (Coetzee, 2022; Ndlovu-Gatsheni, 2021). However, many people that use the D-word to capture all equity, diversity, and inclusion (EDI) efforts are not specifically addressing the systemic and structural nature of the problem at stake (Sondarjee & Andrews, 2023). This means that while we are all interested decolonization or at least love to use the word, it is useful to heed the wisdom expressed brilliantly in Tuck and Yang's (2012) popular article titled "*Decolonization is not a metaphor*." According to these scholars, the casual usage of terminologies such as 'decolonize our schools,' 'decolonize methods,' or 'decolonize student thinking' often provide little context about the immediacy of settler colonialism—thereby domesticating and metaphorizing decolonization by making it a substitutable term for all other things that need to be done to improve our societies and schools. The essence of their critique may be captured as follows: "When metaphor invades decolonization, it kills the very possibility of decolonization; it recenters whiteness, it resettles theory, it extends innocence to the settler, it entertains a settler future" (Tuck & Yang, 2012: 3).

Although we agree with Tuck and Yang (2012) about the overuse or misuse of decolonization, this book's focus on epistemic or pedagogical decolonization is one that seeks to disrupt or at least question whiteness and reimagine colonial imaginaries of the world as part of the process of revitalizing a pluriverse of perspectives and epistemic traditions emerging from places and people that are historically dehumanized and marginalized. Furthermore, although Tuck and Yang (2012) show that decolonization does not have a synonym, the decolonial turn in our academic disciplines and perhaps society in general has resulted in a plethora of D-words that sometimes get used synonymously without proper context. Ndlovu-Gatsheni (2021) provides a useful summary of these words that is worth rehashing here (see Table 1.1).

The D-words appear almost synonymous but a deeper reading of Table 1.1 should show that the decolonial movement even with respect to the question of epistemic (in)justice alone is vast and multi-dimensional, and "at the center of decolonisation are inextricably intertwined ethical, methodological, epistemological and political dimensions" (Ndlovu-Gatsheni, 2021: 883). In other words, and despite the current hype around decolonization, we cannot simply jump on the 'decolonial bandwagon' without understanding the foundations, goals, and even dangers of such endeavors (Moosavi, 2020). Despite this important caution, Ndlovu-Gatsheni reminds us in the Foreword to this volume that we should not allow critiques of decolonization to make us forget the effort, sacrifices, and struggles it took earlier pioneers "to push decolonization into its present status of a planetary consciousness," some of whom were detained in prison during their fight for decolonization (e.g., Ngugi wa Thiong'o and Angela Davis).

Within this context, epistemic decolonization, which is the main aspect of decolonization this book is primarily interested in, requires a shift in epistemology that accounts for and centers African history, culture, and context in our understanding of both the continent and the world at large. Dani Nabudere (2011), for instance, in his book *Afrikology, Philosophy and Wholeness: An Epistemology* posits that the idea of 'Afrikology' as an Africa-focused epistemology which is informed by the need for a redefinition of their world to advance both their self-understanding and an understanding of the world around them (see also Dastile, 2013; Ndlovu-Gatsheni, 2018). Kumalo (2020: 25) promotes the idea of the Black Archive as a way of attaining 'epistemic restitution' or epistemic justice by resurrecting it as part of the archives of the philosophy of history. He insists that decolonizing the curricula should start with decolonizing literature and the discipline of philosophy itself. He posits that "resurrecting the Black Archive concerns thinking about/through and theorising the

Table 1.1 The ten D-words of the decolonial turn

D-word	*Meaning*
1. Decanonization	Shifting or dethroning the boundaries that reinforce Eurocentric canons of knowledge (e.g., the 'classics') to allow the centering of African and other marginalized knowledges
2. Deimperialization	Reforming the modern power structures and hierarchies of the global political economy that undergird and enable the universalization of European knowledge
3. Depatriachization	Dismantling the androcentrism and heteronormativity in knowledge creation and opening up to feminist, queer, and womanist scholarship
4. Deracialization	Removing the color line and abyssal thinking in knowledge (i.e., de-essentializing race in epistemic justice)
5. Dedisciplining	Liberating knowledge from disciplinary empires, academic sub-cultures, and dominant epistemological churches
6. Deprovincialization	Positioning or re-asserting Africa as a quintessential site of knowledge production and removing it from marginality and peripherality
7. Debourgeoisement	Tackling white supremacy by liberating knowledge from dominant white male elite intellectuals and opening epistemic spaces for African intellectuals, peasants, workers, women
8. Decorporatization	Addressing the colonization of universities and the implementation of market-informed principles of commercialization and commodification of knowledge and education (i.e., not treating the university as a private corporation)
9. Democratization	Inventing new spaces to pluriverse epistemologies and ecologies of knowledges (i.e., diversifying knowledge systems)
10. Dehierarchization	Shifting or decentering hierarchies of thought and knowledge embedded in colonial rationality and western historiographies

Source Authors' adaptation based on Ndlovu-Gatsheni (2021: 884)

Fact of Blackness/Indigeneity, which continued even as Blackness/ Indigeneity was denied access to institutions of higher learning" (Kumalo, 2020: 31).

Other scholars have also pointed to the need to consider the African anticolonial archive as a vibrant body of work that provides a new way of thinking about the present (El-Malik & Kamola, 2017). Resurrecting the Black Archive can be seen as a useful way of tackling what Mudimbe

(1988) refers to as the 'colonial library,' including a body of dominant texts and associated discourses and epistemological orders that construct Africa as inferior. The persistence of this colonial library presents a challenge to the project of decolonizing the curricula and decentering the coloniality that places Africa in a position of servitude and otherness (see Matthews, 2018; Wai, 2015). El-Malik and Kamola (2017) describe the colonial library as the 'colonial archive' that has repeatedly been elevated as foundational to knowledge and history; it is, therefore, apt to imagine the 'anticolonial archive' as serving as a possible alternative—even as a representation of both the successes and failures of African anticolonial thought.

Quijano (2007: 170) shows that coloniality remains "the most general form of domination in the world today, once colonialism as an explicit political order was destroyed." Decoloniality as a direct response to coloniality, therefore, frees this dominant order from the universal rationality that imposes 'modern' paradigms of knowledge on people. It also involves new ways of intercultural communication as "part of the process of social liberation" from the coloniality of power (Quijano, 2007; see also Mignolo, 2007) as it "insists on Africa's ontological sovereignty and constructs its epistemological boundaries in broad pan-African geographic strokes" (Ochonu, 2020: 514). In the words of Ndlovu-Gatsheni (2020: 40), "decoloniality gestures toward the construction of the pluriverse as another possible world" which, for instance, can manifest by bringing suppressed or marginalized knowledge into the academy and as part of a general understanding of human life and existence.

Mbembe (2016) also notes that the decolonization process should result in a 'pluriversity' instead of a 'university,' which would represent a drastic break away from the neoliberal rationality and the monolingualism that informs the existing system. Pluriversity, therefore, captures an openness to diverse epistemic traditions. He asserts that decolonizing the university implies a reformation that results in "a less provincial and more open critical cosmopolitan pluriversalism—a task that involves the radical refounding of our ways of thinking and a transcendence of our disciplinary divisions" (Mbembe, 2016: 37). The issue remains whether such a reformation is possible, or such a university could be envisioned.

Nativist Decolonization as a Caution?

At this juncture, one may ask the following question: Can epistemic decolonization occur without romanticizing, essentializing, or even universalizing what may be considered as 'African,' 'Black,' or 'Indigenous'? Scholars argue that this ambiguity surrounding what sort of decolonization is possible or meaningful could result in 'nativist decolonization' or a certain form of nationalist exceptionalism that becomes a version of White supremacy or the very same colonial imaginary that epistemic decolonization is attempting to eradicate. Moosavi (2020: 347) considers nativist decolonization as "glorifying Southern scholarship or scholars just because they are from the Global South" or seeing intellectual decolonization as a way to promote the more populist political agenda of Third World Nationalism. Nativist decolonization can be dangerous because it leads to 'Southerncentrism' and a general distrust of Northern scholarship mainly because it hails from the North, which could result in useful scholarship being sidelined and less useful ones being valorized (Moosavi, 2020). The point here is that any sort of exaggerated romanticization of Southern scholarship or scholars could lead to a dangerous simplification of the much complex project of intellectual decolonization.

Since the destruction of knowledge (i.e., epistemicide) "involves the destruction of the social practices and the disqualification of the social agents that operate according to such knowledges" (Santos, 2014: 153), it remains unclear how epistemic decolonization can be attained without a deliberate overhaul of existing structures that flip things into the hands of social agents who have historically been ignored or only included as subjects of study, not actors in their own rights. In a paper ominously titled *Africanity as an Open Question*, Diagne (2010) draws attention to the fact that the discussion on the conceptualization of Africa, that is, the debate on *Africa* as an *invention,* a historical imaginary 'other' of European history, is not some recent postmodern deconstruction of the notion of Africanity. It is, in essence, a reclaiming of what was lost by those who were dispossessed.

Ndlovu-Gatsheni (2020: 6), for instance, characterizes 'deimperialization' as "the abandonment of Europe." But, like decolonization, he sees this as involving a "revolutionary transformation of the very immanent logics of Euromodernity, including colonialism, emancipation, and depatriachilization, and development" (Ndlovu-Gatsheni, 2020: 6). What this means is that abandoning Europe is not necessarily a romanticization of Africa but rather a deliberate act of revolutionizing the way people think about themselves vis-à-vis the rest of the world and how they deal with past atrocities/injustices as part of the process of imagining a future of possibilities. As argued by Kumalo (2020: 31) accessing the Black Archive, for instance, "empowers us to develop curricula that are locally responsive and globally relevant." Le Grange (2016: 6) also notes that decolonizing the curricula does not necessarily imply "destroying western knowledge but in decentring it or perhaps deterritorialising it." These insights suggest that a decolonial orientation should not result in what may be characterized as nativist decolonization, which could potentially further marginalize the histories and knowledge systems the process of epistemic decolonization is meant to resurrect. The following remarks by Prah (2017) is quoted in Swartz et al. (2020) nicely capture this sentiment:

> The decolonisation of knowledge and education does not and should not mean the facile rejection of western-derived epistemologies and their modes of construction. It means stripping western specificities from our modes of knowledge construction and the production of knowledge to suit and speak to our cultural/linguistic particularities. It means in short societal relevance. (qtd. in Swartz et al., 2020: 175)

The main contention with the argument raised above is that the redefinition of the world that is expressed in Nabudere's (2011) 'Afrikology' as an Africa-focused epistemology, for instance, might not be feasible if western-derived epistemologies are not entirely rejected. This leaves us with an interesting chicken-and-egg problem that defies easy diagnosis, which borders on some of the arguments raised by Moosavi (2020). Like Prah's (2017) is quoted in Swartz et al. (2020) argument above, the following remarks further highlight the caution with which nativist forms of decolonization should be treated: "Nativist education for decolonization must go beyond black against white, Europe against Africa or Britain against Zimbabwe but must interrogate all forms of hegemonic tendencies" (Hwami, 2016: 33). There will hardly be a decidedly clear verdict on this debate but a key implication we can point to is that the decolonial agenda should create spaces for multiple knowledges that co-exist to affirm the agency and epistemic justice of those who have historically been written off and/or colonized in different forms.

Moosavi's (2023) recent self-reflexive piece highlights how best efforts toward decolonizing a course, for instance, may inadvertently be sustaining exclusion while claiming to be inclusive, maintaining the status quo while claiming to be radical, or even reinscribing western-centrism while claiming to decolonize the western canons that underpin our disciplines. This evidence shows that pedagogical or academic decolonization is much harder than we often imagine. He, therefore, calls for 'decolonial reflexivity,' which should cause decolonial scholars "to introspectively locate the inadequacies, limitations, and contradictions within our own efforts at academic decolonisation, particularly in relation to the potential for us to inadvertently perpetuate coloniality rather than dismantle it" (Moosavi, 2023: 139). The need for this reflexivity also suggests to us that we must maintain some level of modesty or what Sondarjee and Andrews (2023) characterize as the 'epistemic humility' needed when associating our actions and practices with the wide variety of the D-words noted above, especially given the very political nature of what it would entail to say we are *truly* doing any of those things.

Overview of Chapters

The scholarly contributions in this volume are premised on the original goal of contributing to a re-imagination and possible decentering of the Eurocentric pedagogical and research practices that inform entrenched narratives about Africa and African agency. While some chapters take a broad approach and reflect on alternative pedagogies, Black agency, and the (im)possibilities of decolonial interventions, other chapters zoom in and illustrate the complexity animating an authentic decolonial intervention. Collectively, the chapters illuminate the particularity of African scholarship, the unique contextual challenges of interrogating the entrenched modes of curricula and pedagogies, research hegemony and practice that defines teaching about Africa, and possibilities of engaging with a non-essentialist decoloniality to redress and contest dominant modes of thinking and practice that have historically excluded African ways of doing and knowing, lived experiences, voices, attitudes, and positionalities. This volume, therefore, provides grounded conceptualizations about the academic project of producing African knowledge that is authentic and emancipatory to encapsulate the dynamic, ingenious ways in which African intellectuals on the continent and in the diaspora animate agency while navigating hostile and/or toxic neocolonial academic spaces.

The contribution by Zainab Olaitan and Samuel Ojo Oloruntoba (Chapter 2) tackles the issue of Africa's agency in the production of knowledge by arguing that the prevailing approach meant to establish Africa as a contributor of knowledge has been primarily reactionary rather than pragmatic. What this implies is that epistemic violence or epistemicide becomes sustained through the process of seeking validation and approval from the same system that denies the authenticity or validity of the knowledge produced from the continent. Also, a reactionary approach undermines the rich history of African Indigenous knowledge systems that have prevailed despite the role played by slavery, colonialism, neocolonialism in silencing such knowledge systems. The chapter begins by providing a historical understanding that contextualizes the silencing of African contributions to knowledge production, followed by an examination of the coloniality of knowledge itself. It then examines the resistance school—involving University of Ibadan School of History, Ahmadu Bello University School of History, Makerere University—that emerged on the continent to indigenize knowledge production. While key thinkers in these schools contributed to rejecting western ways of knowledge primarily through critique and resistance, these efforts have fallen short of going beyond the reactionary approach to effectively consolidate Indigenous African knowledge production and dissemination. The chapter, therefore, ends with some insights on how to overcome this existing challenge (i.e., embracing Indigenous knowledge systems) as a way to re-center Africa in knowledge production. This connects with existing calls to rejuvenate the Black anticolonial archive and Afrocentric epistemology (see Assié-Lumumba, 2016, 2017; El-Malik & Kamola, 2017; Kumalo, 2020; Nabudere, 2011; Tieku, 2021).

In Chapter 3, Ayandele and Oriola expand on the complexity of the global system of knowledge production by touching on the how, what, and why we must promote freedom of knowledge production on Africa. The chapter exposes the dilemma between academic freedom and the study of Africa within the dichotomy of the insider–outsider perspective vis-à-vis the impact of western pedagogies on research methodologies and the study of Africa. Drawing on sociocultural theories, the authors argue that scholarship about Africa must explicitly account for power dynamics that continue to reinforce the global North–South divide in the publishing regimes about Africa. In their analysis, Ayandele and Oriola address questions about voice, representation, agency with a particular emphasis on teaching, research, and knowledge production about the continent. The chapter poignantly advocates for reinvestment in local knowledge production that addresses African developmental challenges. To succeed in doing this, the authors point to the need for innovation and strategic actions geared toward nurturing academic collaborations, partnerships, and coalitions.

Answering the question, to what extent is the permanence of whiteness and epistemic exclusion or hegemony sustained in African Studies through institutionalized centers/programs of African Studies in North America and Europe, Andrews and Patrick's contribution (Chapter 4) engages with African Studies as a taught discipline and highlights the role of academic racism in pedagogy. The evidence presented in the chapter paints a stark picture of the dearth of Black agency in a field whose subject matter focuses on Black histories, experiences, and futures. The contribution specifically shows that the presence of whiteness across majority of the African Studies programs they examined as part of their pilot study—which manifests in who is teaching courses on Africa, who is included on course syllabi, who supervises students studying Africa, and who makes key decisions on African Studies curricula—is a function of powerful institutionalized hierarchies that have historically hindered the inclusion of others. This evidence resonates with points raised by Branch (2018), Allman (2019), Grosz-Ngaté (2020), and Sondarjee (Chapter 8 in this volume) among others (see also Odoom & Andrews, 2017). Andrews and Patrick note that representational diversity cannot be equated with decolonization but it is an important step in dismantling the prevailing whiteness and Eurocentric bias in African Studies pedagogy.

Sally Matthews' chapter (Chapter 5) centers the discussion on two fundamental questions of inquiry: (a) Is it possible to escape the colonial library and or Eurocentrism on knowledge production on Africa? How do we dismantle that? (b) Is replacing western scholars with African scholars a solution to decolonizing knowledge production on Africa? These questions underpin the danger of nativist decolonization, as discussed by Moosavi (2020) and also highlighted here in this chapter (Andrews & Khalema) and Chapter 7 (Zavale). Drawing on Mudimbe's (1994) concept of the colonial library, Matthews reflects on the way scholars of African Studies can encourage African students to engage with and reconfigure scholarly representations of Africa. In a very detailed manner, Mathews argues for the recognition of the tenacity of the colonial library as an opportunity to disrupt existing forms of knowledge production about Africa.

Drawing upon the song, *Monsters You Made*, by the popular Nigerian Afrobeat artist Burna Boy, Savo Heleta and Sakhile Phiri in Chapter 6 engage in a deep dive to unpack the coloniality and Eurocentric hegemony in African education and pedagogy. With a focus on the pitfalls and promises of epistemic decolonization, they highlight the intersectional legacies of colonialism, especially how colonial racism, white supremacy, and racial capitalist exploitation are intricately linked to the ongoing dehumanization of Africans through coloniality and neocolonialism (Ndlovu-Gatsheni, 2013). In particular, they examine how this reality (i.e., the making of 'monsters' through post-independence neglect, repression, and subjugation) has undermined the ability of African educational systems, institutions, and scholars to develop and valorize education and knowledge relevant for Africa and Africans. They do so by also pointing to the lack of willingness on the part of post-independence elites to break away from the colonial structure and systems to carve out a clear pathway for epistemic decolonization. This is also explained in Chapter 2 by Olaitan and Oloruntoba as yielding to the same structures we are attempting to dismantle or at least using established Eurocentric systems as the basis or metric to measure our own intellectual contributions. A central message from this chapter is that epistemic decolonization—involving decolonizing the mind and knowledge production—cannot occur in isolation of material decolonization and this undertaking requires the breaking down of political, geopolitical, and economic structures and systems that enable and preserve coloniality and neocolonialism.

Nelson Casimiro Zavale's contribution (Chapter 7) focuses on knowledge production but turns attention to conventional western-rooted approaches of measuring knowledge readiness and performance, including knowledge index, index of knowledge societies, global knowledge index, and global innovation index. Zavale argues that these metrics reveal persistent inequalities between developed and developing countries, a monolithic western-based view of science or knowledge, and geopolitical inequalities in the global system of knowledge production—all of which explain why sub-Saharan Africa is lagging in efforts to build a meaningful knowledge-based economy or society. Like Olaitan and Oloruntoba in Chapter 2, Zavale insists that pluralism of knowledge production as well as valorization of other (Indigenous) knowledges, through the lens of epistemic or cognitive justice (Santos, 2014), will contribute to the democratization and possible decolonization of African pedagogies. As we note in this chapter, Zavale also raises the caution of nativist decolonization (Moosavi, 2020), which involves an exaggerated romanticization of African scholarship to the point where it fails to be subjected to intellectual rigor. This implies not thinking of African knowledge systems as given but subjecting them to critical enquiry.

Presenting a rich exposé that challenges coloniality of knowledge and epistemic racism in the discipline of international relations (IR) as previous scholars have done (Andrews, 2022; Shilliam, 2010, 2020; Tieku, 2021), Maïka Sondarjee in Chapter 8 reflects on the role of the undergraduate course syllabi in perpetuating epistemic inequalities in the curriculum—a focus which is an in-depth extension of the pilot study of African Studies programs undertaken by Andrew and Patrick in Chapter 4. Sondarjee brilliantly explores the how and what educators minted in the postcolonial feminist paradigm ought to 'provincialize' western knowledge in IR, which is a field that is undoubtedly connected to Africa in terms of serving as a prominent subject matter. She argues that listening to student's critique of sanitized western curriculum and its masculine gaze of IR has mobilized her to be intentional about infusing critical pedagogies and epistemologies. For Sondarjee, decoloniality demands that we not only study how and what we teach in *our* institutions to expose *our* colonial legacies and biases but, also, we should always study relations of power and processes of marginalization.

In Chapter 9, Khalema, Masuku and Zakwe expand on Sondarjee's arguments as well as others in this volume by reflecting on the way post-apartheid institutions in South Africa have neglected the infusion of African-centered praxis in institutional governance and curriculum reform in favor of uncritical preservation of neocolonial practices and processes of engagement. The chapter interrogates the entrenched modes of colonial praxis in implementing 'transformation' in neoliberal South African universities. The authors maintain that transformation has morphed into a buzzword in South African universities often enacted as an emancipatory strategy to right the wrongs of the past, yet its implementation has tragically demonstrated a regressive move toward the institutional violence and victimization of the past. The chapter resolves on the intentional questioning of transformation beyond demographic pageantry particularly in relation to decoloniality and pedagogies of practices. The chapter concludes by advocating for an Ubuntu/Botho-focused approach to advance decolonial alternatives where historically marginalized knowledges, voices, and positions are illuminated in the teaching, learning, research, and governance spheres (see also Assié-Lumumba, 2017).

In Lieu of Conclusion: Black Agency, Africanity, and Decolonial Afro-Futures

The volume's concluding chapter, "*Agency, Africanity, and Some Propositions for Engaged Scholarship*" by Nene Ernest Khalema brings it all together and asserts an Afro-futuristic approach to teaching and learning about Africa on the continent and the Global North. This concluding chapter asserts that the challenges to effective decolonial action go well beyond intellectual intransigence. The prospects for a neo-imperialist subversion of the decolonial discourse itself remain possible. One does not need to theorize deeply to notice the anti-Black/African disguised as 'anti-woke' onslaught against Africa-centered history in America and elsewhere in the world.

Various chapter contributors to this volume have unpacked the notions of decoloniality, agency, and re-storying African Studies pedagogies from historical, material, and comparative perspectives to reflect upon the learning (and unlearning) of colonial practices and perspectives—further pointing to the need to critically interrogate pedagogies, curriculum, practices, governance, knowledge production, research methodologies, and epistemologies as equally relevant to undoing colonialism and its legacies. Within this context, decoloniality serves as a tool of Africa-centered analysis and it "seeks to retrieve Africa from the margins of global sociopolitical, economic and epistemic formations and inscribe it at the center of such configurations" (Ochonu, 2020: 514). Since the *coloniality of power* is closely tied to the *coloniality of knowledge* and the *coloniality of self/being* (see Fanon, 1961 [2004]; Grosfoguel, 2007; Mbembe, 2021; Mignolo, 2007; Ndlovu-Gatsheni, 2020; Quijano, 2007), a decolonial orientation forces us to reflect on how past and present forms of colonialism continue to shape what a social group knows about themselves, how they matter in this world, and how others see them—whether as mere subjects of dominant structures or as agents with some capacity to change something. Freire (1972: 61) posited that by consciously having dialogue about their lives and the conditions of their oppression, the oppressed should be able to "name their world," which also helps them to imagine the oppressive system not as one with no exit but rather as something that is only a temporary limitation to be overcome and transformed. In other words, by being able to speak and becoming accepted as speakers, the subaltern gains the agency to imagine a world of new possibilities.

The act of naming one's world also echoes strategies through which the 'cultural bomb' Mbembe (2001) refers to can be tackled as part of the process of decolonizing the mind. It is, therefore, fitting to reiterate that decolonization "is not as simple as removing some content from the curriculum and replacing it with new content—it is about considering multiple perspectives and making space to think carefully about what we value" (Swartz et al., 2020: 175). Although Andrews and Patrick (Chapter 4 in this volume) have emphasized the need to examine representation in course and program content (see also Chapter 8 by Sondarjee), it is crucial to admit that epistemic decolonization in its transformative sense goes beyond that. What this means is that although Mignolo (2013: 137) believes the decolonial agenda is possible "within academia through courses, seminars, …." Le Grange et al. (2020) point to how quick-fix solutions result in a 'decolonial-washing' instead of the revolutionary expectations of decolonization to dismantle structures of power and dominance inhabited in the colonial household. Moosavi (2023: 139) has also warned us to "avoid a self-righteous confidence in our status as enlightened decolonial scholars by being prepared to self-scrutinise our own decolonial efforts." This warning reverberates Sondarjee and Andrews' (2023) call for '*epistemic humility*' even as we encounter or embrace a 'decolonial turn.' Indeed, nothing can be taken as given and we must carefully examine all actions that supposedly derive from a decolonial conviction while keeping the fire burning under the feet of oppressive structures and systems.

According to Ndlovu-Gatsheni (2020: 6), decolonization needs to result in something new—i.e., "a new world, free from the paradigm of difference which enabled enslavement, colonial exploitation, and racist domination." It also needs to tackle the coloniality that reinforces racial hierarchies and dehumanizing structures of imperial cultural dominance (Quijano, 2007). Although the possibility of decolonization in higher education—especially its revolutionary political ambition that goes beyond just pedagogy—may be considered as quite far-fetched, if not counterproductive (Moosavi, 2020; Tuck & Yang, 2012), scholars have pointed to a decolonized (perhaps 'Africanist') curriculum as having the following characteristics: "Such a curriculum built on contextually produced theory will respond to empirical problems of population density, income poverty, unemployment, underemployment, precarious employment, forms of violence, and inequality from the perspective of theories of empire, practices of erasure, histories of dispossession, colonialism, enslavement, and appropriation" (Swartz et al., 2020: 181; see also Bhambra, 2014). This curriculum facilitates a re-storying that ensures that the stories are told from the perspectives of Southern people whose voices have been marginalized and their lived experiences shrouded in stereotypes of misery, poverty, and victimhood. It is also expected to encourage students to take ownership of knowledge creation instead of merely becoming recipients or users of received wisdom.

References

Adichie, C. N. (2009). *The danger of a single story*. https://sch.rcschools.net/ourpages/auto/2017/7/24/35784355/danger%20of%20a%20single%20story.pdf

Ake, C. (1982). *Social science as imperialism: The theory of political development*. University of Ibadan Press.

Alcoff, L. (2017). Philosophy and philosophical practice: Eurocentrism as an epistemology of ignorance. In I. J. Kidd, J. Medina, & G. Pohlhaus (Eds.), *Routledge handbook of epistemic injustice* (pp. 397–408). Routledge.

Allman, J. M. (2019). #HerskovitsMustFall? A meditation on whiteness, African Studies, and the Unfinished Business of 1968. *African Studies Review, 62*(3), 6–39.

Andrews, N. (2022). The persistent poverty of diversity in international relations and the emergence of a critical canon. *International Studies Perspectives, 23*(4), 425–449.

Andrews, N., & Odoom, I. (2021). Outside the orthodoxy? The crisis of IR and the challenge of teaching monocultures. In H. A. Smith & D. J. Hornsby (Eds.), *Teaching international relations in a time of disruption* (pp. 49–61). Palgrave Macmillan.

Andrews, N., & Okpanachi, E. (2012). Trends of epistemic oppression and academic dependency in Africa's development: The need for a new intellectual path. *Journal of Pan African Studies, 5*(8), 85–104.

Asiamah, G. B., Awal, M. S., & MacLean, L. M. (2021). Collaboration for designing, conceptualizing, and (possibly) decolonizing research in African politics. *PS: Political Science & Politics, 54*(3), 549–553.

Assié-Lumumba, N. D. T. (2016). Harnessing the empowerment nexus of afropolitanism and higher education: Purposeful fusion for Africa's social progress in the 21st century. *Journal of African Transformation, 1*(2), 51–76.
Assié-Lumumba, N. D. T. (2017). The Ubuntu paradigm and comparative and international education: Epistemological challenges and opportunities in our field. *Comparative Education Review, 61*(1), 1–21.
Bhambra, G. (2014). Postcolonial and decolonial dialogues. *Postcolonial Studies, 17*(2), 115–121.
Branch, A. (2018). Decolonizing the African studies center. *The Cambridge Journal of Anthropology, 36*(2), 73–91.
Coetzee, C. (2022). The myth of Oxford and Black counter-narratives. *African Studies Review, 65*(2), 288–307.
Crawford, G., Mai-Bornu, Z., & Landström, K. (2021). Decolonising knowledge production on Africa: Why it's still necessary and what can be done. *Journal of the British Academy, 9*(s1), 21–46.
Dastile, N. P. (2013). Beyond Euro-Western dominance: An African-centered decolonial paradigm. *Africanus, 43*(2), 93–104.
Diagne, S. B. (2010). Africanity as an open question. In S. B. Diagne, A. Mama, H. Melber, & F. B. Nyamnjoh (Eds.), *Identity and beyond: Rethinking Africanity* (pp. 20–24). Discussion Paper 12: Nordiska Afrikainstutet.
El-Malik, S. S., & Kamola, I. A. (Eds.). (2017). *Politics of African anticolonial archive*. Rowman & Littlefield.
Falola, T. (2001). *Nationalism and African intellectuals*. University of Rochester Press.
Fanon, F. (1961 [2004]). *The wretched of the earth* (R. Philcox, trans.). Grove Press.
Freire, P. (1972). *The pedagogy of the oppressed*. Penguin Press.
Garwe, E. C., Thondhlana, J., & Saidi, A. (2021). Evaluation of a quality assurance framework for promoting quality research, innovation and development in higher education institutions in Zimbabwe. *Journal of the British Academy, 9*(s1), 127–157.
Grosfoguel, R. (2007). The epistemic decolonial turn. *Cultural Studies, 21*(2–3), 211–223.
Grosz-Ngaté, M. (2020). Knowledge and power: Perspectives on the production and decolonization of African/ist knowledges. *African Studies Review, 63*(4), 689–718.
Heleta, S. (2018). Decolonizing knowledge in South Africa: Dismantling the 'pedagogy of big lies.' *A Journal of African Studies, 40*(2), 47–65.
Hwami, M. (2016). Frantz Fanon and the problematic of decolonization: Perspectives on Zimbabwe. *African Identities, 14*(1), 19–37.
Kessi, S., Marks, Z., & Ramugondo, E. (2020). Decolonizing African studies. *Critical African Studies, 12*(3), 271–282.

Khalema, N. E. (2018). Navigating race in higher education and beyond. In S. Swartz, A. Mahali, R. Moletsane, E. Arogundade, N. E. Khalema, C. Groenewald, & A. Cooper (Eds.), *Studying while black: Race, education and emancipation in South African universities* (pp. 50–67). HSRC Press.

Khalema, N. E. (2022). Transformational (re)encounters: Enacting a decolonial praxis at a UKZN School. *Journal of KZN Region of SAIA, 47*(2), 1–2.

Kumalo, S. H. (2020). Resurrecting the Black Archive through the decolonisation of philosophy in South Africa. *Third World Thematics: A TWQ Journal, 5*(1–2), 19–36.

Le Grange, L. (2016). Decolonising the university curriculum: Leading article. *South African Journal of Higher Education, 30*(2), 1–12.

Le Grange, L., Du Preez, P., Ramrathan, L., & Blignaut, S. (2020). Decolonising the university curriculum or decolonial-washing? A multiple case study. *Journal of Education (University of KwaZulu-Natal)*, (80), 25–48.

Mamdani, M. (1993). University crisis and reform: A reflection on the African experience. *Review of African Political Economy, 20*(58), 7–19.

Matthews, S. (2018). Confronting the colonial library: Teaching political studies amidst calls for a decolonised curriculum. *Politikon, 45*(1), 48–65.

Mazrui, A. A. (1992). Towards diagnosing and treating cultural dependency: The case of the African university. *International Journal of Educational Development*, *12*(2), 95–111.

Mbembe, A. (2001). *On the postcolony*. University of California Press.

Mbembe, A. (2016). Decolonising the university: New directions. *Arts and Humanities in Higher Education, 15*(1), 29–45.

Mbembe, A. (2021). *Out of the dark night: Essays on decolonization*. Columbia University Press.

Mthembu, N. (2020). Fundamentals of an African-Centred syllabus in higher education in the post-colonial era: The tehuti perspective. *International Journal*, *9*, 208–220.

Mignolo, W. D. (2007). Delinking: The rhetoric of modernity, the logic of coloniality and the grammar of de-coloniality. *Cultural Studies, 21*(2–3), 449–514.

Mignolo, W. D. (2013). Geopolitics of sensing and knowing: On (de)coloniality, border thinking, and epistemic disobedience. *Confero: Essays on Education, Philosophy and Politics*, *1*(1), 129–150.

Mignolo, W. D., & Walsh, C. E. (2018). *On decoloniality: Concepts, analytics, praxis*. Duke University Press.

Mkandawire, T. (2005). *African Intellectuals: Rethinking politics, language, gender and development*. Zed Books.

Mohammed, W. F. (2021). Decolonising African media studies. *Howard Journal of Communications, 32*(2), 123–138.

Moosavi, L. (2020). The decolonial bandwagon and the dangers of intellectual decolonisation. *International Review of Sociology, 30*(2), 332–354.

Moosavi, L. (2023). Turning the decolonial gaze towards ourselves: Decolonising the curriculum and 'decolonial reflexivity' in sociology and social theory. *Sociology, 57*(1), 137–156.

Motsaathebe, G. (2020). Towards the decolonisation of higher education in Africa: An 8-point plan. *African Journal of Rhetoric, 12*(1), 198–212.

Mudimbe, V. Y. (1988). *The invention of Africa: Gnosis, philosophy, and the order of knowledge*. Indiana University Press.

Mudimbe, V. Y. (1994). *The idea of Africa*. Indiana University Press.

Nabudere, D. W. (2011). *Afrikology, philosophy and wholeness: An epistemology*. African Books Collective.

Ndlovu-Gatsheni, S. J. (2012). Coloniality of power in development studies and the impact of global imperial designs on Africa. *The Australasian Review of African Studies, 33*(2), 48–73.

Ndlovu-Gatsheni, S. J. (2013). Why decoloniality in the 21st century? *The Thinker, 48*, 11–15.

Ndlovu-Gatsheni, S. J. (2015). Genealogies of coloniality and implications for Africa's development. *Africa Development, 40*(3), 13–40.

Ndlovu-Gatsheni, S. J. (2018). *Epistemic freedom in Africa: Deprovincialization and decolonization*. Routledge.

Ndlovu-Gatsheni, S. J. (2020). *Decolonization, development and knowledge in Africa: Turning over a new leaf*. Routledge.

Ndlovu-Gatsheni, S. J. (2021). The cognitive empire, politics of knowledge and African intellectual productions: Reflections on struggles for epistemic freedom and resurgence of decolonisation in the twenty-first century. *Third World Quarterly, 42*(5), 882–901.

Nyamnjoh, F. B. (2019). Decolonizing the University in Africa. In *Oxford research encyclopedia of politics*. Oxford University Press.

Nyamnjoh, A. N. (2022). Decolonisation, Africanisation, and epistemic citizenship in post-Rhodes must fall South African Universities (Doctoral dissertation, University of Cambridge).

Ochonu, M. E. (2020). South African Afrophobia in local and continental contexts. *The Journal of Modern African Studies, 58*(4), 499–519.

Odoom, I., & Andrews, N. (2017). What/Who is still missing in international relations scholarship? Situating Africa as an agent in IR theorising. *Third World Quarterly, 38*(1), 42–60.

Pimblott, K. (2020). Decolonising the University: The origins and meaning of a movement. *The Political Quarterly, 91*(1), 210–216.

Posholi, L. (2020). Epistemic Decolonization as Overcoming the Hermeneutical Injustice of Eurocentrism. *Philosophical Papers, 49*(2), 279–304.

Quijano, A. (2007). Coloniality and Modernity/Rationality. *Cultural Studies, 21*(2–3), 168–178.

Rutazibwa, O. U. (2018). On babies and bathwater: Decolonizing international development studies 1. In S. de Jong, R. Icaza, & O. U. Rutazibwa (Eds.), *Decolonization and feminisms in global teaching and learning* (pp. 158–180). Routledge.

Santos, B. D. S. (2004). The World Social Forum: Towards a Counter-Hegemonic Globalisation (Part 1). In J. Sen, A. Anand, A. Escobar, & P. Waterman (Eds.), *World Social Forum: Challenging Empires* (pp. 235–245). Viveka Foundation.

Santos, B. D. S. (2014). *Epistemologies of the South: Justice Against Epistemicide*. Routledge.

Sartre, J.-P. (1948). *Black Orpheus* (S. Allen, trans.). French and European Publications.

Sartre, J.-P., & MacCombie, J. (1964). Black Orpheus. *The Massachusetts Review, 6*(1), 13–52.

Shilliam, R. (Ed.). (2010). *International Relations and Non-Western Thought: Imperialism, Colonialism and Investigations of Global Modernity*. Routledge.

Shilliam, R. (2020). Race and Racism in International Relations: Retrieving a Scholarly Inheritance. *International Politics Reviews, 8*(2), 152–195.

Sondarjee, M., & Andrews, N. (2023). Decolonizing International Relations and Development Studies: What's in a Buzzword? *International Journal* (in print).

Swartz, S., Nyamnjoh, A., & Mahali, A. (2020). Decolonising the Social Sciences Curriculum in the University Classroom: A Pragmatic-Realism Approach. *Alternation Special Edition, 36*, 165–187.

Tieku, T. K. (2021). The Legon School of International Relations. *Review of International Studies, 47*(5), 656–671.

Tuck, E., & Yang, K. W. (2012). Decolonization Is Not a Metaphor. *Decolonization: Indigeneity, Education & Society, 1*(1), 1–40.

Wa Thiong'o, N. (1992). *Decolonising the Mind: The Politics of Language in African Literature*. East African Publishers.

Wai, Z. (2015). On the Predicament of Africanist Knowledge: Mudimbe, Gnosis and the Challenge of the Colonial Library. *International Journal of Francophone Studies, 18*(2–3), 263–290.

Wallerstein, I. (1983). The Evolving Role of the Africa Scholar in African Studies. *Canadian Journal of African Studies, 17*(1), 9–16.

Zeleza, P. T. (1997). *Manufacturing African Studies and Crises*. CODESRIA.

Zeleza, P. T., & Olukoshi, A. (Eds.). (2004). *African Universities in the Twenty-First Century: Knowledge and Society* (Vol. 2). CODESRIA.

CHAPTER 2

Beyond Reaction: (Re)-Imagining African Agency in the Decolonization of Knowledge

Zainab Monisola Olaitan and Samuel Ojo Oloruntoba

Introduction

Knowledge production is intensely political, and it usually reflects the wishes, interests, and values of dominant powers. The power dynamics in knowledge production can be explained by the African proverb which says until the lion tells his story, the hunter will always be the hero. Unfortunately, in many instances, the lion is the victim of hunting expedition, and as such, they are never able to tell their own stories. We ask ourselves why most of what is studied in universities in Africa are modeled based

Z. M. Olaitan
Department of Political Sciences, University of Pretoria, Pretoria, South Africa
e-mail: zainab.olaitan@tuks.co.za

S. O. Oloruntoba (✉)
Institute of African Studies, Carleton University, Ottawa, ON, Canada
e-mail: SamuelOjoOloruntoba@cunet.carleton.ca

Thabo Mbeki School of Public and International Affairs, University of South Africa, Pretoria, South Africa

N. Andrews and N. E. Khalema (eds.), *Decolonizing African Studies Pedagogies*, Political Pedagogies,
https://doi.org/10.1007/978-3-031-37442-5_2

on western ways of knowing. Without the necessary context, one might be tempted to argue that it is because Africa is devoid of its own Indigenous knowledge systems. But an extensive look into the subject begins to reveal centuries-long history of slavery, colonialism, neo-colonialism, all of which have contributed to the total silencing or what others might call epistemicide of African knowledges (Mignolo, 2011; Ndlovu-Gatsheni, 2018). This epistemicide is further maintained by coloniality through which colonialism finds expression without its physical structures.

The silencing of African knowledge systems led to an elevation of Eurocentric knowledge as the universal path to knowledge and development, a notion that is still being reproduced in the contemporary time through various means such as the establishment of various World Bank centers of excellence in African universities. How then has Africa navigated its way in this unequal relation of knowledge? From the 1960s to the contemporary times, African scholars have spent considerable energy and time debunking, negating, and carrying out epistemic disobedience against the tyranny of Eurocentrism. Efforts have been made by scholars in Africa and the diaspora to advance scholarship that rejects the superiority of western knowledge system over that of Africa by decrying the role of colonialism and imperialism in Africa's epistemicide (Ake, 1979; Arowosegbe, 2008; Oloruntoba, 2014; Olukoshi, 2006).

As part of the efforts of some post-colonial leaders to decolonize knowledge, they established several institutions which engaged in scholarship that tried to negate the false assumptions about knowledge from Africa. Among these were the University of Ibadan's School of History, Ahmadu Bello University School of History, Makerere university, and University of Dar es Salaam. In these universities were notable scholars such as Ade Ajayi, Kenneth Dike, Bala Usman, Walter Rodney, Claude Ake, and Dani Nabudere among others. Unfortunately, their scholarship transcended into adapting western models into the African contexts. Julius Nyerere's African socialism was modeled after Karl Marx's socialism, for instance. The constant need to remind the west that Africa matters in knowledge production is a major reason why most attempts at centering Africa have been reactionary rather than pragmatic. While such reactions have taken center stage, the position of Africa as a consumer of knowledge rather than producer has not changed, thus necessitating a new strategy.

There is a need for an alternative approach to be taken toward establishing Africa as an important contributor in knowledge production. The first step toward that is to re-imagine Africa's agency in the production of knowledge beyond reaction. The focus on reaction ignores the rich history of African Indigenous knowledge systems which are quite valuable to the discourse at hand. By critiquing the propensity of African scholars to react to western knowledge system, this chapter begins to delimit a new role for Africa in global knowledge production. This work is a critical analysis of the reactive position of Africa in global epistemology, and it argues for a new approach to decolonizing knowledge to re-center Africa. We argue that given the limited value in always reacting to theories and approaches from the west, it is important to start taking pragmatic steps toward Indigenous knowledge production by engaging with Africa's ritual archives and interacting with Africans to draw from their lived experiences as contributors to knowledge. The purpose is to chart a new course toward African studies and its pedagogies. In terms of structure, this chapter will start by providing context to the history of the silencing of knowledges in Africa drawing out how coloniality sustains this. It further discusses the contradictions of the post-colonial state and its contribution to perpetuating superiority of Eurocentrism. This is followed by an overview of some resistance to western knowledge system. The chapter concludes by suggesting how to re-imagine decolonization of knowledge toward creation rather than reaction.

History and Contexts of the Silencing of Knowledge(s) in Africa

The importance of knowledge is that it is "both foundational and fundamental to any attempt at imagining a future that is different from the present" (Ndlovu-Gatsheni, 2018: 95). Knowledge is dynamic, active, engaged and linked to social, political, cultural, or sustainable changes (Hall & Tandon, 2017). Thus, a people without their own ways of knowing are a people without both a history and a future of their own making. Ndlovu-Gatsheni points out that despite the significance of knowledge in determining people's destinies, the triumph of western-centered modernity perpetuated through colonialism negated the legitimacy of other knowledges and ways of knowing outside the western purview of seeing, imagining, and knowing the world. This is because the essence of colonial domination in knowledge production has always been the desire to control the minds and ways of knowing of the colonial subalterns to sustain and prolong the very project of colonization

(Ndlovu-Gatsheni, 2018: 96). It is important to acknowledge the long-lasting effect of colonialism on the life and psyche of Africans because of its continued domination of different aspects of the colonized existence in different forms decades after the end of colonial administration. This is made possible by the colonial structures, cultures, and epistemological systems in contemporary African existence which are still embedded within the modern, colonialist-capitalist world system (Grosfoguel, 2007). Ndlovu-Gatsheni (2018) further notes that Africa was re-imagined at the height of colonialism as a place of "darkness" devoid of any knowledge beyond superstitions. Racist philosophers and writers such as Hegel and Conrad among others demonstrated their ignorance of history by proclaiming that Africa was either not part of human civilization or occupies a heart of darkness. As a result, the epistemic problems of Africans are both recent and old. They are old in the sense that they were developed during the period of colonial encounter, and they are recent due to the coloniality of knowledge that ensures the continuation of colonial patterns of otherization and subordination of African forms of knowledges (Ndlovu-Gatsheni, 2018: 3).

Sifuna (2001) argues that it is known knowledge that colonization was an exploitation strategy, and that education during this time was planned with the colonialists' interests in mind. Colonial education was selective because it was created for the reproduction and accumulation of capital. All these actions were taken to ensure that the educated labor in Africa, which was mostly made up of low-level employees, would only serve to sustain and advance the status quo. The colonial curriculum placed no premium on areas that would benefit their African subjects. Rather, African students were trained to fulfill tasks appropriate to their presumed intellectual, and social inferiority. On this account, Fomunyam states that "Africans are unaware that they can pursue knowledge that is endogenous to their environments" (Fomunyam, 2020: 248). Unlike Asia where decolonization involved a systematic reengagement with Indigenous forms of knowledge, African countries have not yet made a substantial attempt to alter the ethos and principles of colonial education even though the colonialists have long since left. Moumouni (1968) explains that the philosophy and content of African education have not changed much, and post-colonial education in Africa remains a colonial heritage. Fomunyam argues that "African higher education is still modeled after western models and paradigms that are either irrelevant to or completely unrelated to life in Africa. These models have persisted in depersonalizing African knowledge and obliterating the African educational curriculum's epistemological framework" (Fomunyam, 2020: 249). He continues: "the educational and curriculum practices of the colonial masters were devoid of the cultural epistemologies of the African people, and this is equivalent to killing African knowledge, epistemicide" (Fomunyam, 2020: 249).

According to Bennett (2007), epistemicide is the systematic destruction of any Indigenous knowledge base in which the perpetrator has no concern for the victims' knowledge and has no interest in fusing or exchanging their own. Fataar and Subreenduth see epistemicide as a "metaphor for the epistemological marginalization, or evisceration, of African-centered intellectual traditions in formal education. It is caused by the constantly dominant western paradigm of knowledge generation, production, and consumption that unproblematically circulates within educational discourse and practice across the African continent as relevant, valuable, and best practice" (Fataar & Subreenduth, 2016: 107). They also highlight the ways in which epistemicide is a consequence of the persistently dominant western-framework of knowledge generation, production, and consumption that uncritically permeates African educational discourse and practice as meaningful, pertinent, and best practice (Fataar & Subreenduth, 2016: 107).

Rendering other knowledges invisible is essential to the success of western knowledge; this was the situation in South Africa during the colonial and apartheid eras (Cross, 1986). Thus, it is possible to view western epistemology as contributing to the epistemicide of African knowledge. A deep-rooted and normalized epistemological confinement caused by abyssal epistemology inhibits the creation of critical African knowledge forms from meaningfully circulating within the predominant knowledge system (Fataar & Subreenduth, 2016: 109). Africa is one of those epistemic sites that experienced not only colonial genocides but also theft of history (Goody, 2006). Epistemicide, which is the killing of Indigenous people's knowledges, and linguicides, the killing of Indigenous people's languages, occurred simultaneously in Africa (wa Thiong'o, 2009a, 2009b) and continue today in the way foreign languages remain official languages in virtually all African countries. A consequence of this epistemicide, as Ndlovu-Gatsheni (2018) argues, is that African scholars are always yearning for recognition and acceptance of their work in Europe and North America, of which publication in the so-called international, high-impact, and peer-reviewed journals serves as this affirmation and validation from the west. He explains that the international inflects Europe and North America, whereas the rest of the globe is rendered local. Since they are in Europe and North America, high-impact, peer-reviewed international journals, and reputable publishing houses and presses are also there. Universities with high rankings can be found across North America and Europe. Together, these facts attest to epistemic hegemony's reality. The concept of knowledge as opposed to "knowledges" is the hallmark of this epistemic hegemony (Ndlovu-Gatsheni, 2018: 8).

The above submission makes it imperative to refer to Blaut who asked the following unsettling question: "is it possible for people, whose ways of knowing, which is subject to colonial domination, to imagine another way of living, outside of that which is determined by the 'colonizer's model of the world?" (Blaut, 2012: 1). Such a question begins to open doors to the realization that the silencing of African knowledge is a systemic problem that is often further maintained by coloniality.

Coloniality of Knowledge

The discussion of the silencing of African knowledges would be incomplete without examining how coloniality sustains the unequal colonial legacy of global knowledge production. Coloniality is a broad concept that encompasses the principles and methods of western colonialism, particularly how knowledge is used as a tool of power. This term is particularly associated with the Latin American decolonial studies with names including Anibal Quijano, Walter Mignolo, Ramón Grosfoguel, and others. Coloniality is a structure of colonialism that is both prescriptive and performative (Ndlovu, 2018: 93). Based on coloniality being a prescriptive structure, it can be seen as a power structure that deprives the African subject of agency or sovereignty over his or her destiny, especially one that goes beyond being a target of colonial exploitation. As wa Thiong'o (2012) emphasizes, coloniality refers to a vertical global power structure wherein some people enjoy the privileges and benefits of living under modernity while others suffer the negative consequences of the "darker side" of the same modern world. This modernity is not just any modernity; it is a modernity that is primarily focused on the west. Maldonado-Torres states that "coloniality refers to a long-standing pattern of power that emerged because of colonialism but that defines culture, labor, intersubjectivity relations, and knowledge production well beyond the strict confines of colonial administrations to capture the longevity of coloniality beyond colonial structure" (Maldonado-Torres, 2007: 243). Thus, coloniality survives colonialism; it is all-encompassing since it incorporates historical foundations, theorization, and social action in its quest to pinpoint colonialism's ongoing effects on current social structures (Nwoma et al., 2021).

To expose the fundamental reasoning behind all modern/colonial imperialisms in the west, Quijano projected coloniality as a necessary component of modernity. His argument that modernity and colonialism are two sides of the same coin was thus advanced. To deceive the anti-systemic movements that are working to destroy it, coloniality, which is a structure made up of continuously shifting colonial hierarchies, has always performed the production of "dust of history" that passes for "actual history." Therefore, many today confuse the end of colonialism with the end of coloniality (Ndlovu-Gatsheni, 2018). Coloniality is preserved in literature, in the criteria for academic performance, cultural norms, common sense, peoples' perceptions of themselves, aspirations for oneself, and several other facets of contemporary life. When it comes to the creation of knowledge, coloniality takes the form of "colonization of imagination," (Quijano, 2007) "colonization of the mind," (wa Thiong'o, 1986), and colonization of knowledge and power (Ndlovu-Gatsheni, 2013). The fact that the types of colonization are invisible makes it possible for the colonized subjects to engage in activities that support and sustain the very structures of coloniality in which they are victims is even more problematic (Ndlovu-Gatsheni, 2018). In a sense, coloniality is something that we as modern subjects live with every day. The longevity of coloniality strengthens the hegemony that exists in knowledge production whereby the continued use of western-centered knowledge translates to the silencing of other knowledges. Africa is suffering from the consequences of coloniality by being tagged a consumer of knowledge stemming from the inability of African scholars to be recognized in knowledge production.

Another consequence of coloniality of knowledge or western hegemony on knowledge production is the concept of disciplinary boundaries. Imposition of strict disciplinary boundaries is one of the hallmarks of Eurocentric knowledge systems. The university system in Africa has followed this model to the detriment of an inclusive knowledge system which can ensure broadness, inter- and multi-disciplinarity, and overall development. Buck-Morss argues that disciplinary boundaries are often used to perpetuate the superiority of Eurocentric knowledge, she states that:

> When national histories are conceived as self-contained, or when separate aspects of history are treated in disciplinary isolation, counter evidence is pushed to margins as irrelevant. The greater the specialization of knowledge, the more advanced the level of research, the longer and more venerable the scholarly tradition, the easier it is to ignore discordant facts. It should be noted that specialization and isolation are also a danger of those new studies that were established to remedy the situation. Disciplinary boundaries allow counterevidence to belong to someone else's story. After all a scholar cannot be an expert in everything. But such arguments are a way of avoiding the awkward truth that if certain constellations of facts can enter scholarly consciousness deeply enough, they threaten not only the venerable narratives but also the entrenched academic disciplines that reproduce them. (Buck-Morss, 2000: 822)

The strict division among disciplines, especially those in the humanities, does not advance the specialization of knowledge as intended but rather fails to ensure trans-disciplinarity. This trans-disciplinarity is often found in Indigenous knowledge. Western knowledge system has devised means to separate knowledge into different disciplines as though political science and sociology do not deal with understanding the society using different lens. And as argued above by Buck-Morss (2000) this is a deliberate attempt to keep reproducing the hegemony of Eurocentrism as non-western knowledges are often interconnected and cannot be separated such that it allows for disciplinary boundaries. Stating the consequences of disciplinary boundaries, Geetz explains that "the way academic disciplines function in the modern world creates a Durkheiman solidarity among concerned scholars. Academic disciplines provide not only cultural frames to us but also social identity and locations in the institutions of knowledge. Academic disciplines not only help us classify the world but also classify ourselves, and both functions and objectives are due to the erection of rigid boundaries among them" (qtd. in Giri, 1997: 2). However, in recent times, these boundaries are beginning to fade away. What becomes of this re-organization of disciplinary interactions, Giri tells us, is that it "can be understood by looking into the way new disciplines and sub-disciplines are emerging which embody the limits of conventional disciplinary boundaries" (Giri, 1997: 2). This trans-disciplinarity can be found in the works of scholars such as Amartya

Sen. Giri explains in more detail that "when asked how he negotiates the boundaries between economic, sociology he asserts that his ability to negotiate a different disciplinary boundary comes from his fundamental belief that both economics and sociology deal with the complexities of social living" (Giri, 1997: 3).

The rigorous division of disciplines in the modern world is largely due to the logic of modernity, demonstrating that Eurocentrism is a significant influence in its development. Modern disciplines operate under the ideologically oriented premise that disciplinary boundaries represent the many essences of various facets of reality. But what we are increasingly coming to realize is that the boundaries between them are contrived ones and their specialization and monopoly over their disciplinary territory were part of a modern academic division of labor. Hence, Indigenous knowledges are struggling to thrive within these strict disciplinary boundaries created by Eurocentric system of knowledge.

Contradictions of Post-Colonial States and Entanglement with Eurocentrism

Oloruntoba (2014) argues that a contributing factor to the perpetuation of hegemony of western knowledge system is the workings of universities in Africa being dependent on state's directives. This argument is in synch with Mkandawire who points out that "in thinking about social sciences in Africa, the state looms so menacingly and enticingly large. No single social force has affected the social sciences as profoundly as the state" (Mkandawire, 1997: 3). This is because for most of the post-independence era, the establishment and funding of universities were in the exclusive preserve of the state.

The dependent nature of the social sciences and universities in general is directly related to the conditions under which they came into being in Nigeria and other African countries. This reveals that universities in Africa post-independence were not created with the intent to embody non-western teachings/knowledges. The haste in setting them up was to ensure economic development based on western notions of what the latter constitutes. Mkandawire (1997) notes that there were two reasons for the establishment of most universities. The first reason expressed the need to produce qualified manpower to drive the process of economic development. The second concerned the need to protect a certain ideological connectedness between political leaders and academics wherein national unity was a necessary vehicle in nation building enterprises, most of which were supported by twin ideologies of modernization and developmentalism (qtd. in Oloruntoba, 2014: 344). This endeavor contributed to their stunted growth as research-intensive institutions and fed into what they are meant to achieve. This is evident in how universities in Africa validate the superiority of Eurocentric ways of knowing and learning while relegating African knowledges. The role of the post-colonial state in facilitating the creation of universities did not consider the need to build African universities that serve the interests of Africans. But rather universities that are structured after western models of universities to mirror development in the west. The implication of this is the gradual silencing of African knowledge, the churning out of students that revere western knowledge as the basis of all knowledge thereby consolidating the myopic thinking that Africa is not a producer of knowledge. While the initial intention was to further economic development, Jinadu contends that political science as a discipline in Nigeria manifested a reproduction of the dominant perspective of western knowledge in terms of its pre-occupation with issues of modernization and development of political institutions (Jinadu, 1987). What this signifies is that there was an evident deviation between their initial aim and what they currently do. It is, therefore, not a stretch to argue that the state after independence is largely responsible for the silencing of African knowledges through its prioritization of Eurocentric way of knowing to advance economic development.

This inadvertent silencing has led to the failure of African scholars to empower the continent to create its own educational theoretical and methodological framework for knowledge production and sustainable development despite decades of self-rule. Chavunduka (1995) argued that since its inception in Africa and other non-western countries, the western concept of "knowledge" has lacked an understanding of the holistic character and method of non-western ways of knowing and knowledge production. According to Nkondo (2012), the western view of traditional African knowledge as merely a repetition of actions without any theory to explain them reflects the cultural and intellectual hubris of the west. A traditional healer who can treat a certain illness with a particular herb has knowledge and understanding of the plant species and their traits, however this practice of knowledge is not acknowledged as such, or at worse it is demonized and regarded as inferior to exogenous knowledges.

This perverse situation is compounded by the fact that links between African institutions themselves are largely neglected in favor of partnerships with the western countries. Currently, there are more academic and research connections between African and western institutions than between African institutions themselves, as most of these institutions compete to improve their rankings, which are frequently based on western ideals, by enlisting the help of foreign partners. Hountondji (2002a, 2002b) and Hountondji (1995) add that the fact that most academic and research activities are still conducted in colonial languages, particularly English, French, and Portuguese, undermines the growth of research and theory based on Indigenous conceptual framework and paradigms is another notable aspect of extraversion in Africa. Justification of the theoretical presumptions of western institutions and scholarship regarding the primitive nature of Africa are just two examples of how the intellectual and research activities in these institutions of higher learning continue to support the economic exploitation of natural resources (McCarthy, 2004; Moodie, 2003).

Sites of Epistemic Resistance in Africa

Attempts have been made by scholars in Africa to position the continent as an important contributor to knowledge production. From the 1960s to the mid-1980s, a few top universities in Africa engaged in epistemic resistance to the dominance of Eurocentrism, especially in history and social sciences. These universities embraced Indigenous paradigms to critique the epistemic hegemony of the west in a bid to establish Africa's presence in global episteme. Some of these efforts yielded results which led to the creation of schools such as the University of Ibadan School of History, Ahmadu Bello University School of History, and Makerere University's development of African Socialism. These schools were created at the dawn of political decolonization on the African continent where most independent states were beginning to re-imagine their agency within their new status as "free from their colonial masters." These institutions were at the forefront of this re-imagining by engaging knowledge production from the prism of rejecting western ways of knowledge mostly through critique and resistance, which has helped demystify the hegemony of western knowledge to an extent. For instance, Chris Ogbogbo records how the Ibadan School of History was created to respond to the devastating realities of the newly independent Nigeria by creating a history school that centered Africa rather than the predominant European history. He narrates:

> Kenneth Dike and some of his colleagues at Ibadan provided the tonic with which to quench the thirst of African students and nationalists who needed to study African history from the periscope of Africans. Dike began what has come to be regarded as a revolution with the introduction of African history courses to the Ibadan history curriculum. This was a major feat to pull off in the University of Ibadan of the 1950s, especially at a time when the existence of the discipline of African history was still contentious. The Ibadan scholars persisted, and, over time, the character of the curriculum metamorphosed from the dominant European history bias to mainly one of Africa. The Ibadan model became a major export to other universities within and outside Nigeria. The point of emphasis is that the academics at the Ibadan School of History succeeded, through their intellectual engagements, in becoming very relevant. (Ogbogbo, 2020: 84)

He explains that academics from the Ibadan School of History contributed to historical knowledge by focusing their research on African issues and using cutting-edge methods. A unique contribution of this School is foregrounding orality as a valid source of data. Whereas racist European philosophers like Hegel had argued that Africa was not part of history and that any history about Africa was the one written by Europeans, historians at Ibadan School like Ade Ajayi, Kenneth Dike, Obaro Ikime among others proved beyond reasonable doubt that oral history is a valid history because it represented the experiences, knowledge, and voices of the people. The best evidence of their efforts in this field may be found in the titles of their publications under the Ibadan History Series, the Journal of the Historical Society of Nigeria, and the Tarikh Series (ibid., 85). The renowned and well-known Ibadan School of History, Ahmadu Bello University (ABU), Zaria School of History, and Ife School engaged in critical historicizing of the Nigerian condition within the framework of the Africanist tradition of locating the unique condition of the people within the structural and functional factors that brought them into existence. These researchers devoted their time to the scholarly debate and examination of conventional ideas and paradigms of development, particularly those that originated in Europe and are frequently tinged by racism.

In Makerere and Dar es Salam, critical scholars like Claude Ade, Walter Rodney, Issah Shivji, Dani Nabudere engaged in crucial studies of Marxism using African socialism as an Indigenous alternative to the Eurocentric origin and relevance of the former (Arowosegbe, 2008). At the continental level, attempts were made to support these Indigenous sites of epistemic resistance. Molla and Cuthbert (2018: 252) affirm that the Organisation of African Unity at the time also attempted to center Africa within global knowledge production. They argue that the OAU can be commended with establishing the commitment to re-positioning Africa in global knowledge economy by bringing about African Renaissance and adopting African solutions to African challenges to achieve its goal of Pan-Africanism.

These schools of resistance (i.e., The ABU School of History, Makerere University, and Ibadan School of History) were instrumental in rejecting western models of learning and teaching in universities in Africa, a mission which they were dedicated to. This positioned them as notable agents for the critique of Eurocentrism present in the model of education.

Beyond this resistance and reaction, their role as producers of knowledge has been undermined by political and structural factors that have impeded such possibility. The heroic efforts in these sites of resistance did not last long. From the 1980s, many countries in Africa fell under the structural contradictions of the economies they inherited from the colonialists. Lacking in diversification through manufacturing and industrialization, commodity exports predominated. Fall in commodity prices led to serious macro-level economic problems that necessitated the intervention of the Bretton Woods institutions, the World Bank, and the International Monetary Fund. The reforms introduced by these institutions effectively turned the state against radical scholars and eventual defunding of the sites of epistemic resistance. In what Mamdani (2007) refers to as scholars in the marketplace in a book of the same title, the onslaught of market principles against the universities led to rationalization of departments, little or no money for research and less competitive salaries. These forced many academics to migrate outside the continent or join the non-for-profit organizations, which paid more competitive salaries.

Due to the Eurocentric foundations and ontology of the universities in Africa, as well as other structural problems, the education provided by these institutions has not contributed to solving the myriads of challenges confronting the continent. Scholars have attributed the failures of these universities to their locus of enunciation and ontological orientation. In this regard, a distinction has been made between universities in Africa and

African universities (Fredua-Kwarteng, 2019). The phrase "universities in Africa" refers to institutions whose academic curricula imitate with a high degree of exactitude the objectives, content, assessment techniques, and learning materials of western universities (Fredua-Kwarteng, 2019). In other words, the replication of western archives in African universities and continued otherization or subordination of African archives even in post-colonial state show evidence of coloniality of knowledge (Ndlovu-Gatsheni, 2013). African universities, on the other hand, will be universities that are not only physically located in Africa but are rooted in African archives and modes of knowing while not neglecting knowledges from elsewhere.

We look at the African socialism introduced by Makerere university, and we still see traits of adapting to western frameworks rather than embracing an African model for ensuring economic growth. Surely, there are several Indigenous models to advance economic development devoid of western influence, we can look at the Igbo apprenticeship model in Nigeria as a venture capital system, or the "Ajo" or stokvel as a way of ensuring shared prosperity. All these have been abandoned for Bretton Woods backed neoliberal policies that continue to stunt the development of African countries. Beyond resistance, reaction, and rejection of/to western and Eurocentric models of knowledge, there is the need to start consolidating efforts for Indigenous African knowledge production. The ideal scenario is to create African universities that focus on finding solutions to African issues and disseminate best practices to the entire world. Wright et al. (2007) point out that while challenging colonial stereotypes, prejudices, and mental devaluations of western knowledge, it is crucial to have confidence and make deliberate attempts to create and incorporate Indigenous African knowledge. This argument is at the core of our discourse that is: Africa should rise beyond resistance to western imposition of knowledge and create its own knowledge in ways that acknowledge and incorporate its history, cultures, and knowledges.

Reimagining Decolonization of Knowledge Beyond Reaction

The call for decolonizing knowledge in Africa often starts by looking at how universities in Africa can shed their western models of teaching and learning for more Indigenous ways so they can be African universities. However, the tendency for such calls to be reactive rather than pragmatic cannot be ignored in this chapter. Hence, this section provides a new lens within which we can begin to decolonize knowledge to re-center Africa in global knowledge system. Decolonization, according to Klose (2014), entails the mobilization of the peoplehood of Indigenous communities, their rejection of the imperial European control over their everyday lives, and their fight for autonomy and self-expression by utilizing their Indigenous power and wisdom. However, the path to decolonizing knowledge in Africa is impossible without ensuring both epistemic freedom and cognitive justice. Ndlovu-Gatsheni (2018) notes that academic freedom is different from epistemic freedom because the former primarily refers to the institutional autonomy of universities and the freedom to communicate a variety of viewpoints, including those that are critical of authorities and political figures. He asserts that "epistemic freedom on the other hand is much broader and deeper. It speaks to cognitive justice; it draws our attention to the content of what it is that we are free to express and, on whose terms" (Ndlovu-Gatsheni, 2018: 4).

Boaventura de Sousa Santos' (2007) definition of cognitive justice is predicated on acknowledging the various ways that people all around the world come to understand their existence. Cognitive justice "promotes the recognition of alternative knowledges by enabling dialogue between what is often regarded as incommensurable knowledges" (Fataar & Subreenduth, 2016: 108). Epistemic freedom aims to democratize knowledge by changing it from its existing single form to the plural known as knowledges.

Additionally, it is positioned against the disproportionate prominence of European ideas in knowledge, social theory, and education. Ndlovu-Gatsheni (2018: 4) explains that because it facilitates the creation of the essential critical decolonial consciousness, epistemic freedom is fundamental to the larger decolonization fight. Knowledge cannot be confined to philosophical and scientific forms alone in the pursuit of epistemic freedom. Recognition of various forms of knowledge and knowing is called for in decolonization. Hountondji elaborates that the task of epistemic freedom is "that of organizing in Africa an autonomous debate that will no longer be a far-flung appendix to European debates, but which will directly pit African philosophers against one another" (Hountondji, 2002a, 2002b: 104). All these actions reflect the essential processes of provincializing Europe and deprovincializing Africa (Ndlovu-Gatsheni, 2018). Suffice to say deprovincializing Africa addresses marginality and peripherality of Africa in the knowledge and education domain through recentering it. One form of knowledge that is marginalized, silenced in academia and education on the continent is Indigenous knowledge. Therefore, Hoppers (2009) suggests that Indigenous knowledges must be included in dialogues between knowledges without having to adhere to the frameworks and norms of western knowledge. Hountondji (2002a, 2002b) asserts that the changing of audience by African academics to consider his or her African public as his or her major goal is also required for the development of Indigenous knowledge systems. One of the ways to re-imagine knowledge production in Africa beyond reaction is the need to embrace African Indigenous Knowledge Systems (AIKS). This allows Africa to re-center itself as a producer and contributor of/to knowledge production rather than as mere consumers of knowledges from elsewhere. The embrace of AIKS would require decolonization of the state and the minds of the populace, in ways that ensure a belief in the originality and authenticity of African knowledges. A decolonized state will not only support the creation of or strengthening African universities but would accept the knowledges produced by African scholars as authentic. Such a decolonized state will also support the design of curricular that incorporate AIKS in teaching and learning as well as in research. Decolonized citizens, on the other hand, will accept to be taught about the history of their continent, as well as various non-western modes of learning such as orality, stories, artifacts, and so on, without feeling these are substandard.

Embracing Indigenous African Knowledge(s) in Recentering Africa

Oloruntoba (2020) suggests that academics in Nigeria, as in much of Africa, have been reactive, rather than responsive, to the global politics of knowledge production. Rather than wait and allow Africanists from the Global North to throw theories and ideas to intellectuals in Africa, the latter must now anticipate and pre-empt such and develop or build on existing, Indigenous epistemology of development on the continent. Emeagwali explains that "African Indigenous Knowledge Systems (AIKS) are a collection of different fields of study, as well as intersecting epistemologies and value systems, formed by societies that have their own paradigms and ways of existing in their ancestral lands" (Emeagwali, 2020: 37). The accumulated knowledges have emerged out of trial-and-error experimentation as well as tested empirical practices and paradigms related to ecological, geographical, economic, social, and other traditions of existence. Indigenous knowledges have substantial implications for the curriculum, development strategies, employment generation, sustained endogenous growth, and social movements. The fundamental tenet of AIKS is that they inform and link to all realms of life and the environment (Nel, 2008). Additionally, the concept of AIKS defines a cognitive framework for conceptualizing theories and perceptions of both nature and culture (Hoppers, 2005). As a result, there is a connection between Indigenous knowledge, the people who possess it, and the tools and technology used to apply it (Nel, 2008). AIKS incorporates ethical norms, standards of accountability, transmission, and a system of rules and practices, just like any discipline. By incorporating knowledges about different aspects of nature and the society, AIKS is interdisciplinary, multidisciplinary, and transdisciplinary in scope, methods, and application.

One may argue that AIKS's primary characteristics are represented in its comprehensive approach because it considers all facets of life, but fragmentary as no one person knows them all. Informed by conventions, practices, rituals, proverbs, and oral stories, it is also based in the community, unwritten but kept in the oral tradition and the collective memory, dynamic and fluid, and it is neither complete nor systematized (Dondolo, 2005: 115; Nel, 2008). In response to the question why then IK is often called a system, Nel (2008) argues that system refers to the holistic nature of the knowledge as it links up and relates to all aspects of life and the environment as it also refers to the plurality of both its properties and functions. Based on their surrounding reality, societies around the world have varying cultures, environments, experiences, and methods of resolving issues (Matike, 2008). As a result, knowledge is regional, incomplete, and fragmented (Kolawole, 2012), and its creation and application are potent drivers for socioeconomic advancement (Gurak, 2004). The struggle for humanity's survival has made knowledge production pervasive, with knowledge being created, communicated, and/or transferred anywhere there is life (Harari, 2014). Hence, AIKS should be turned to as we begin to explore new ways of recentering Africa as producer of knowledge.

Emeagwali (2020) explores the different pre-colonial ways of Indigenous system ranging from culture, business, metallurgy, soldering, etc. She traces Africa's knowledge systems to the period where the continent had and embraced its knowledge systems and practices. Such endeavors need to be amplified to recognize Africa in knowledge production rather than constantly being the object of knowledge or reacting to it. By amplifying this knowledge system, Africa can begin to be seen as an important contributor to global knowledge while creating new ways to engage with this knowledge. For instance, Emeagwali provides a view of pre-colonial political systems in Africa by noting that African political systems included democratic village republics without kings, queens, and dynasties; constitutional monarchies with dynasties, such as the Keita and Askiya dynasties of the Malian and Songhai empires; city-states with constitutional monarchies such as the Yoruba and Hausa city-states; and a wide variety of transitional political systems.

There is need to revamp the intellectual sites of resistance that we mentioned above and build capacity of new ones to move from resistance to reimagination of knowledge architecture in Africa. These universities should dedicate more funding to carrying out research on the pre-colonial knowledges to create more visibility for them, while entrenching them in school curriculum to start engaging the minds of African students on the existence of such knowledge. The teaching of these systems allows for them to balance out the Eurocentric ways of knowing that they have been used to.

A devastating implication of western knowledge system for higher education on the continent is that it is no longer acceptable to do research in Africa with local communities and people as if their opinions and life experiences are unimportant. This is because Eurocentric biases still heavily influence much of the existing research on African populations (Hountondji, 2002a, 2002b). Research should not be seen as an innocent academic exercise but rather as an activity that occurs in a specific set of ideological, political, and social frameworks given the extraversion of African knowledge systems. The mindset, attitudes, and behaviors of researchers and extension personnel of working with African local communities must be changed. They must abandon the presumption that the traditional must give way to the new. They must be receptive to learning from the locals who hold the information because they are outsiders. Locals or insiders must simultaneously value and respect their own local knowledge as the cornerstone of their community's survival and growth. This is because when people reject their own knowledge and wisdom, it gradually disappears and is open to abuse (Battiste, 2002).

There is need to consider interactions with Africans as Indigenous ways of knowing, just as the Ibadan school notes that orality is a valid source of data. Such approach needs to be embraced in our quest to uncover more Indigenous knowledge systems. Relying on western models of data that prioritize objectivity will often affect this endeavor as the latter is a means to consolidate the universality of western knowledge. In recentering Indigenous knowledge system, its ways of knowing must also be embraced to allow for holistic approach to understanding these knowledge systems. Rather than learning Indigenous system based on Eurocentric prejudices, there needs to be epistemic freedom wherein these systems are learnt within their own contexts separate from western ways of knowing. By rejecting the use of the dominant western worldview of knowing and knowledge creation as the exclusive method of knowing, African intellectuals should assist Africa in closing the gap produced by more than four hundred years of dominance and marginalization of African people's knowledge systems. This concern was well articulated by Ngugi wa Thiong'o in his seminal work, "Decolonizing the mind" (dre). African Indigenous knowledge should not only be seen as an alternative knowledge but as one domain of knowledge among others.

Concluding Reflections: Embracing African Indigenous Knowledge Systems in African Studies Pedagogies

This chapter delves into the reactionary position of most African scholars to rethink Africa's position in knowledge production. It argues that reacting or rejecting western way of knowing is not the same thing as producing knowledge, as the former still perpetuates the universality of Eurocentric ways of knowing. Although by reacting, there is an acknowledgment of the ills and effects of colonization and coloniality that silenced African knowledges which led to epistemicide, this is not enough. Spending too much time to react wastes precious time that could have been used to deepen the production of African Indigenous knowledges. While the critique of Global North's exclusion of non-western knowledge is not a futile endeavor, efforts at producing knowledge need to move beyond that to showcasing existing knowledges that are present in Africa.

A major recommendation of this chapter is that universities in Africa need to rethink their purpose toward actualizing their role as institution of learning, teaching, and research. The tokenistic teaching of western models of learning, consolidation of Eurocentrism which only produces qualified manpower for economic development rather than students that are grounded in African knowledge system, needs to be abandoned for a more holistic curriculum. A curriculum that highlights the importance of Indigenous knowledge to the progress and development of Africa needs to be introduced and recentered in the academia. This chapter also notes the role of the post-colonial state in perpetuating Eurocentrism through its initial intention of the creation of universities in Africa. The foundation was wrong from the beginning, creating universities to contribute to development should not be the only reason for such endeavor. Knowledge should be acquired due to its own value rather than as mere meal ticket.

The role of the universities as the theater of knowledge production needs to be better supported through research funds from governments and alumni donations. The continued reliance of these universities on foreign donors contributes to the stunting of their capability in furthering an African knowledge system devoid of western control. Hence, independence is needed from these western agents such as those use funding to set research agenda that reflects suboptimal interests. To advance African knowledge system, there is need to relax the rigorous disciplinary boundaries that currently exist to ensure trans-disciplinarity within Indigenous knowledge system. The task of centering Africa in knowledge production is not complete without embracing Indigenous ways of knowing which should start from understanding these knowledge systems.

References

Ake, C. (1979). *Social Science as Imperialism: The Theory of Political Development*. Ibadan University Press.

Arowosegbe, A. (2008). The Social Sciences and Knowledge Production in Africa: The Contribution of Claude Ake. *Africa Spectrum, 43*(3), 333–352.

Battiste, M. (2002). *Protecting Indigenous Knowledge and Heritage*. Purich Publisher.

Bennett, K. (2007). Epistemicide! The Tale of a Predatory Discourse. *The Translator, 13*(2), 151–169.

Blaut, M. J. (2012). *The Colonizer's Model of the World: Geographical Diffusionism and Eurocentric History*. Guilford Press.

Buck-Morss, S. (2000). Hegel and Haiti. *Critical Inquiry, 26*(4), 821–865.

Chavunduka, M. (1995). The Missing Links. Keynote Address to the Workshop on the Study and Promotion of Indigenous Knowledge Systems and Sustainable Natural Resources Management in Southern Africa. Midmar, KwaZulu-Nata, presented on 24 April.

Cross, M. (1986). A Historical Review of Education in South Africa: Towards an Assessment. *Comparative Education, 22*(3), 185–200.

Dondolo, L. (2005). Intangible Heritage: The Production of Indigenous Knowledge in Various Aspects of Social Life. *Indilinga: African Journal of Indigenous Knowledge Systems, 4*(6), 110–126.

Emeagwali, G. (2020). African Indigenous Knowledge Systems and the Legacy of Africa. In S. O. Oloruntoba, A. Afolayan, & O. Yacob-Haliso (Eds.), *Indigenous Knowledge Systems and Development in Africa*. Palgrave Macmillan.

Fataar, A., & Subreenduth, S. (2016). The Search for Ecologies of Knowledge in the Encounter with African Epistemicide in South African Education. *South African Journal of Higher Education, 29*(2), 106–121.

Fomunyam, K. G. (2020). Theorizing the Itinerant Curriculum as the Pathway to Relevance in African Higher Education in the Era of the Fourth Industrial Revolution. *International Journal of Education and Practice, 8*(2), 248–256.

Fredua-Kwarteng, E. (2019). African Universities—Imitation or Adaptation? *University World News*, 12 December 2019.

Giri, K. A. (1997). *Transcending Disciplinary Boundaries: Creative Experiments and the Critiques of Modernity*. Working Paper 150. Madras Institute of Development Studies.

Goody, J. (2006). *The Theft of History*. Cambridge University Press.

Grosfoguel, R. (2007). The Epistemic Decolonial Turn: Beyond Political-Economy Paradigms 1. *Cultural Studies, 21*(2–3), 211–233.

Gurak, H. (2004). *On Productivity Growth*. ICS.

Hall, B. L., & Tandon, R. (2017). Decolonization of Knowledge, Epistemicide, Participatory Research and Higher Education. *Research for All, 1*(1), 6–19.

Harari, Y. (2014). *Sapiens: A Brief History of Humankind*. McClelland & Stewart.

Hoppers, C. O. (2005). Culture, Indigenous Knowledge, and Development: The Role of the University. *Centre for Education Policy Development*. Occasional Paper No. 5.

Hoppers, O. (2009) From bandit colonialism to the modern triage society: Towards a moral and cognitive reconstruction of knowledge and citizenship. *International Journal of African Renaissance Studies* 4(2), 168–180.

Hountondji, P. J. (1995). *Second Bashorum MKA Abiola Distinguished Lecture Address*. Reported in Khosa, Meshack M., 1996.

Hountondji, P. J. (2002a). Knowledge Appropriation in a Post-colonial Context. In C. Odora Hoppers (Ed.), *Indigenous Knowledge and the Integration of Knowledge Systems: Towards a Philosophy of Articulation* (pp. 23–38). New Africa Books.

Hountondji, P. J. (2002b). *The Struggle for Meaning: Reflections on Philosophy, Culture, and Democracy in Africa*. Ohio University Research in International Studies Africa Series No. 78.

Jinadu, L. A. (1987). The Institutional Development of Political Science in Nigeria: Trends, Problems and Prospects. *International Political Science Review, 8*(1), 59–72.

Klose, F. (2014). *Decolonizationa and Revolution*. Leibniz-Institut für Europäische Geschichte.

Kolawole, O. D. (2012). Intersecting Western and Local Knowledge: Critical Issues for Development Research in Africa. *Journal of Knowledge Globalization, 5*(2), 1–23.

Maldonado-Torres, N. (2007). On the Coloniality of Being Contributions to the Development of a Concept. *Cultural Studies, 21*(2–3), 240–270.

Mamdani, M. (2007). *Scholars in the Marketplace: The Dilemmas of Neo-Liberal Reform at Makerere University: 1989–2005*. Human Science Research Council.

Matike, E. (2008). *Knowledge and Perceptions of Educators and Learners in the Incorporation of IKS into School Curriculum*. BA (Honours) Thesis, North-West University, South Africa.

McCarthy, S. (2004). Globalization and Education. In B. William (Ed.), *The Book of Virtues*. Simon and Schuster.

Mignolo, W. D. (2011). I am Where I Think: Remapping the Order of Knowing. In F. Lionnet & S.-M. Shih (Eds.), *The Creolization of Theory* (pp. 159–192). Duke University Press.

Mkandawire, T. (1997). The Social Science in Africa: Breaking Local Barriers and Negotiating International Presence. *African Studies Review, 40*(2), 15–36.

Molla, T., & Cuthbert, D. (2018). Re-imaging Africa as a Knowledge Economy. *Journal of Asian and African Studies, 53*(2), 250–267.

Moodie, T. (2003). Alternative Ways of Knowing—Doing Justice to Non-Western Intellectual Traditions in a Postmodern Era. *Journal of Education (kenton Special Edition), 31*, 7–24.

Moumouni, A. (1968). *Education in Africa*. Andre Deutsch.

Ndlovu, M. (2018). The Coloniality of Knowledge and the Challenge of Creating African Futures. *Ufahamu: A Journal of African Studies*, *40*(2), 95–112.

Ndlovu-Gatsheni, S. J. (2018). Seek Ye Epistemic Freedom First. In S. J. Ndlovu-Gatsheni (Ed.), *Epistemic Freedom in Africa: Deprovincialization and Decolonization*. Routledge.

Ndlovu-Gastheni, S. (2013). *Coloniality of Power in Postcolonial Africa*. Myths of Decolonization. Council for the Development of Social Research in Africa.

Nel, P. (2008). *Indigenous Knowledge Systems: Conceptualization and Methodology*. Unpublished Lecture (Presented October 21).

Nkondo, M. (2012). *Indigenous African Knowledge Systems in a Polyepistemic World: The Capabilities Approach and the Translatability of Knowledge Systems*. Paper presented at the Southern African Regional Colloquium on Indigenous African knowledge systems: Methodologies and Epistemologies

CHAPTER 3

Africa, Knowledge Production and Scholarly Prestige

Olajumoke Ayandele and Temitope B. Oriola

Introduction

Evaluating scientific quality is a notoriously difficult challenge. However, comparing journals in a subject category is one significant tool to measure scientific influence. This has led to variegated journal metrics. Journal metrics and impact now constitute a field of their own—bibliometrics or scientometrics—the measurement and analysis of scholarly literature.

The corresponding author would like to extend her sincere gratitude to the Center for the Study of Africa and the African Diaspora at New York University for their generous support, which made the completion of this book chapter possible.

O. Ayandele (✉)
Center for Global Affairs (CGA), New York University, New York, NY, USA
e-mail: jumo@nyu.edu

T. B. Oriola
Department of Criminology and Sociology, University of Alberta, Edmonton, Canada

N. Andrews and N. E. Khalema (eds.), *Decolonizing African Studies Pedagogies*, Political Pedagogies,
https://doi.org/10.1007/978-3-031-37442-5_3

Journal impact factor, Source Normalized Impact per Paper (SNIP), Cite Score, SCImago *Journal* Rank (*SJR*), acceptance rate or rejection rate, arc increasingly ubiquitous tools. The science of measuring the impact of scientific publications has taken a life of its own since Eugene Garfield established the Institute for Scientific Information in the mid-1950s, with impact factor being one of the most widely used journal metrics. Impact factor is a measured frequency that accounts for the average number of citations received by papers published in a journal usually within a two- or five-year period. For many who want a career in academia or research, publishing in peer-reviewed journals with high impact factors remains the conventional medium through which research findings are disseminated. That in turn routinely plays a role in hiring, tenure, promotion, merit incrementation and funding decisions.

Nonetheless, the importance of a journal's impact factor is a contentious matter. There are controversies surrounding its value in assessing high-quality work. Such issues range from downright manipulation of publication numbers to self-citation and disciplinary differences in the peer-review process. Despite the above challenges, recognition and progression in academic and research careers continue to hinge on publishing in journals with high impact factors. This is a cyclical process—such journals generally confer significant citation advantages (Nabyonga-Orem et al., 2020).

There have been increasing calls in the last decade to center and assert Africa as an agent of knowledge production by decolonializing current research methodologies and the impact of western pedagogies on the study of Africa (Agozino, 2004; Falola, 2022). Journal metrics are implicated in these issues. This chapter aims to explore the above problematic vis-à-vis the state of knowledge production and dissemination in Africa. What is the current state of knowledge production and dissemination in Africa? How is knowledge dissemination regarding Africa influenced by the scientometrics economy?

Using the SCImago Journal Rank (SJR) indicator to track the impact factor for about 25,000 selected journals in 27 major categories across the humanities, social sciences, hard sciences and medicine, we found that the total number of journals published in Africa is less than one percent.

---

e-mail: oriola@ualberta.ca

Additionally, less than 10% of journals from the continent occupied the top quartile of journals on the list. In contrast, the total number of journals published in North America and western Europe accounted for 75%, and out of this number, more than three quarters of journals from both regions occupied the top quartile of journals on the list.

This "invisibility" of research published in Africa may be attributed to reasons that include, finances, inequalities in geography, language barrier and the unwillingness of commercial indexing companies based in the Global North to include publications from the Global South (Andrews & Okpanachi, 2012; Bickton et al., 2019; Murray & Clobridge, 2014; Seglen, 1997). The ubiquity of knowledge from the Global North, however, does not mean that African-published research papers or journals are necessarily of low quality. There are a number of cases where an article from the Global South was ignored because it was published in an unknown and obscure journal. When the same work was published in high impact and well-read platforms from the Global North, however, said work gained a lot of credit (SCI Journal, 2022; Tarkang & Bain, 2019).

Furthermore, considering that important areas of research in Africa are not necessarily covered and published by the Global North, the availability of western scholarship coupled with the hegemonic nature of western theories, methods and research practices have resulted in scholars from Africa and the Global South being more versed in a world of thinking that perpetuates Eurocentrism without taking into consideration the diversity of perspectives that exist elsewhere (Andrews & Okpanachi, 2012; Mazrui, 1975; Nabudere, 1997). Indeed, as Andrews and Okpanachi (2012: 87) argue, the hegemony of western theorists have led many African institutions to adopt their writings in course syllabi, resulting in "knowledge dependence" that is not well suited for the development of the continent. This reinforces the Global North–South divide as research papers published in Africa remain underutilized, undervalued and under-cited in global and African scholarly arenas.

There are online services such as the African Journals Online (AJOL) that provide access to research published in Africa and increase worldwide dissemination of scholarship on the continent. Despite these platforms, there remains a need to indigenize knowledge production about Africa, by focusing on what we teach, learn and how we collect and analyze data. Endogenous factors, such as institutional attitudes toward critical reflection of course syllabi along with the localization of journals, the politics of language and scholarship, and the challenges of knowledge production in a fragile context, influence, and in some cases, are responsible for the "invisible" state of knowledge production and dissemination about Africa by African scholars.

Moreover, undergirding this notion of the invisibility of African research is what Andrews (2020: 271) terms, "epistemic imperialism," defined within this context as the tendency to privilege one's ways of knowing or theorizing over others based on the perception of one's own superiority. This trend of epistemic imperialism is also the major cause of the inability of many African countries and scholars in Africa to write and speak about their own situations without relying on already established western knowledge (Andrews & Okpanachi, 2012). Western orientations and ontologies may result in scholars failing to appreciate how things operate differently in other parts of the world. Indeed, the perpetuation of epistemic inequality often leads to what Andrews and Okpanachi (2012: 98) acknowledge as, the "I-am-the-knower-and-you-are-not" syndrome, a case where a researcher from "outside" thinks they know more than the people they are interviewing or investigating.

Nevertheless, efforts to decolonize current pedagogies and research methodologies will be dependent on conditions that are conducive to local knowledge production in addressing the continent's various developmental challenges. Consequently, this chapter accentuates the insider–outsider positionality of African academics on scholarship about Africa. We do this because a growing subset of African scholars based in the Global North, such as ourselves, face a unique challenge of being both insiders and outsiders concurrently. For these scholars who have left "home," usually situated in the Global South, to pursue graduate studies in the west, with an eye to returning to their country of origin to conduct research or start an academic career, they often find themselves questioning the ambiguities of their belonging, particularly, how they are positioned and what this means for their research experience (Oriola & Haggerty, 2012).

These are the same questions we have asked ourselves—and keep asking of ourselves and each other—in our reflections on the role of African intellectuals in repositioning Africa as an agent of knowledge production. For example, we are both of African origin—born and raised in Nigeria. And yet we are also "academic homecomers," having left "home" to pursue our graduate studies and academic careers. Although we regularly return to our country of origin and other African countries to conduct research, the geographic location of our higher education training in North America has meant that our coursework and syllabi have been heavily influenced by western ontologies and approaches. How does our positionality affect our ability to answer questions related to who disseminates information about Africa and the implications on teaching, research and knowledge production?

The remainder of the chapter is divided into two sections. The first section assesses the current state of knowledge production in Africa. In the second section, we present an alternative framework that incorporates African voices and perspectives in bridging the North–South divide in transforming knowledge production about Africa.

Assessing the Current State of Knowledge Production in Africa

The continuous call to assert Africa as an agent of knowledge production raises important and legitimate issues about who disseminates information about Africa and the ways in which current understanding of the continent reflect and reinforce asymmetrical power relations between scholars in the Global North and South (Adebanwi, 2016; Andrews & Okpanachi, 2012; Clapham, 2020; Crawford et al., 2021; Zeleza, 2002). Central to this process to center Africa's agency is also the tendency of the African intelligentsia to blame the Other, reflecting on the legacies of colonial power relations on the current state of knowledge production about the continent, its peoples and societies. Many of the scholarly articles on knowledge production about Africa have tended to blame the legacy of colonialism for the invisibility of Africa-based research and the predominance of non-African writers, who are necessarily speaking, "outsiders," on African issues. These scholars are correct to some degree. Much as scholarship in anthropology and sociology has acknowledged that researchers are "multiple insiders and outsiders" (Deutsch, 1981: 174). When it comes to the study of Africa, it has commonly been assumed that Africans studying the continent are too close to their communities to be objective despite their access and authentic understanding of the culture under study. In contrast, Northern scholars studying the continent are generally given the benefit of the doubt with their outsider status, or in some cases, "privileged near-insider" positionalities with regard to their "curiosity with the unfamiliar, the ability to ask taboo questions, and being seen as non-aligned with subgroups, thus often getting more information" (Merriam et al., 2001).

The debate surrounding Mara and Thompson's peer-reviewed article in *African Studies Review* as the "one stop shop for all things Africanist Autoethnography" exemplifies this tension (Mara & Thompson, 2022). It raises the question: Who are the "peers" in peer review? In an open letter to the Editorial Board of the journal, scholars of African heritage in the Global North expressed their discontent with the published paper, particularly, the hailing of the two western authors as the purveyors of a new form of autoethnography, even though there had been African scholars doing the exact auto-ethnographic work for several generations. For these African scholars, the article was a reflection of enduring colonialism in western academe and the double standard that privileges Northern scholars' reflexivity while undermining African scholars' research findings about the continent as lacking objectivity.

Nonetheless, reference to the legacies of colonial institutions to explain Northern dominance in the study of Africa may be too simplistic in illuminating the causes of the continent's current state of knowledge production. Most African states have been independent for at least 50 years. And although it is necessary to acknowledge that power inequalities silence some, while amplifying the voices of others (Crawford et al., 2021), it is also important to take a step back and, look inward at our own domestic social structures, and curriculum in renegotiating our agency and positionality when it comes to research and knowledge about Africa. We observe six trends in our assessment of the current state of knowledge production in Africa.

A Lack of Critical Reflection in Course Syllabus

To begin, a brief glance at course syllabi in African universities illuminates how course instructors generally rely on western theories in understanding African societies (Andrews & Okpanachi, 2012). In most cases, students are expected to reproduce these theories for their research projects, often with little or no critique of these perspectives. Although a few renowned African scholars receive minimal mention in course outlines, the dearth of non-western perspectives in the study of Africa may be attributed to African scholars not valuing scholarship from the continent. This is quite consequential for knowledge production. As Andrews (2020: 278) concludes, accounts of western scholars are usually deemed to be theoretically significant to the field while contributions by African scholars maintain the stereotypical categorization as "area" or "development" studies. This division of labor in the study of Africa where scholars in the west are responsible for theory production while African scholars produce data and local expertise for theory testing has unfortunately continued to augment the hegemony of western theorists. This reinforces the North–South divide and dependence of the continent on the west for knowledge.

Moreover, the current structure of Africa's education systems has also continued to have detrimental implications on knowledge production suited for the development of the continent. For example, comparison of the curriculum and education system of the USA and Nigeria indicates that the former has several courses that range from the liberal arts to natural sciences, with a focus on critical thinking, scientific innovation and entrepreneurship as major drivers of the economy (Andrews & Okpanachi, 2012). Nigeria's education system, however, emphasizes learning by memorization, without much thought to how subjects taught in the classroom translate into organic entrepreneurship and innovation that may inform development (Adjei, 2007). While we acknowledge that most current education systems in Africa emerged within the context of colonialism (Moore-Sieray, 1996), to improve the visibility of Africa-based research, there is a need for critical reflection on curriculum. More needs to be done to encourage the use of pedagogies that directly speak to African knowledge, history, ways of knowing and lived realities, rather than abstract formulations of the "ideal world" from elsewhere (Andrews & Okpanachi, 2012).

External Validation, Publishing and Knowledge Production

African scholars based on the continent who want a career in academia or research are compelled to publish in overseas journals with high impact factors in order to receive higher promotion points from their institutions. This "Impact Factor Fundamentalism" has continued to create a situation where the best articles about Africa by African scholars are published outside the continent (Murray & Clobridge, 2014). Of course, publishing continues in Africa, but quality research about Africa is dominated by entities outside the continent. This has implications for local journal publishing. In particular, when quality research done on the continent by Africans is sent overseas for publication, African-based journals are at a disadvantage in generating and disseminating high-quality work that can help in boosting their impact factor. Consequently, African universities' promotion policies that reward authors for publishing in western-based journals need to be reviewed. Such practices consign African local journals to the periphery, undervaluing their worth and potential (Gray & Wiens, 2014).

Furthermore, given that many African countries' annual budgets are over-reliant on donor support and loans from international financial institutions, the issue of academic dependency, as Andrews and Okpanachi (2012) demonstrate, remains real vis-a-vis the level philanthropy that surrounds higher education in Africa. While donor funding has no doubt supported knowledge production in Africa, in many cases, the knowledge that emerges from this endeavor trivializes African culture and knowledge. Beneficiaries of such grants often write for their foreign audience by adopting western ontologies to explain African societies and issues. This persistent solicitation of external validation from the west on scholarly worth (in the form of publications in certain ranked western presses and the ability to write successful international grant proposals) constitutes a constant blow to production of knowledge that is relevant to Africa. External donor funding also remains siloed and fragmented, lacking mechanisms for systematic collaboration with local stakeholders. Higher education in Africa will do well to systematically reduce and overtime eliminate reliance on western philanthropy in education (Andrews & Okpanachi, 2012).

The "Localization of Journals"

Another key setback to knowledge production in Africa is what we term the "localization of journals." Many African-based journals are personality-oriented journals—defined within this context as journals that are supported by a few individuals (Murray & Clobridge, 2014). There are cases where journals are established within a local university department for the sole purpose of publishing the research of faculty and other colleagues without much regard for the peer-review process. This hampers the development of Africa-based journals and their ability to offer ancillary services that are related to manuscript writing and author outreach campaigns in the form of conferences that can help to improve the international visibility of the journals' publications (Bickton et al., 2019).

Although organizations such as the Dakar-based Council for the Development of Social Science Research in Africa (CODESRIA) have made important strides over the past 50 years in serving as a Pan-African organization to promote African scholarship and facilitate the participation of African scholars in its publications, conferences and workshops, this initiative has not been effectively replicated on the continent (Andrews & Okpanachi, 2012).

The poor succession planning of African local journals further complicates the impact factor and usability of journals. For example, when an editorial staff member leaves a journal, there is often no one available or prepared to continue the staff member's duties (Bickton et al., 2019). The effect of this situation is the high-mortality rate of journals in Africa. Figure 3.1, for instance, illustrates the categorization of African local journals on the AJOL website using its Journal Publishing Practices and Standards (JPPS) framework in our assessment of the publishing practices of African journals.

Of the 583 journals currently hosted on the world's largest and preeminent platform of scholarly journals published in Africa, more than a

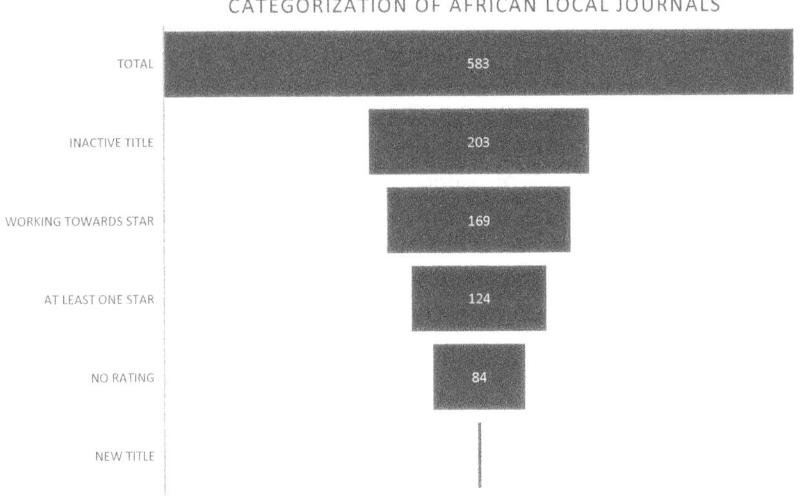

Fig. 3.1 Categorization of African Local Journals on AJOL (*Source* Categorization based on AJOL (2017) JPPS Framework and Criteria)

third of journals on the platform were categorized as inactive. For many academics and African researchers, this high-mortality rate of Africa-based journals is a major factor that has encouraged them to prefer publishing their works in international journals with longevity (Tarkang & Bain, 2019).

The Realities and Politics of Language

The way scholars write varies by region. Therefore, if more African scholars want to publish in foreign journals, this may mean reinventing themselves. Research papers from Africa are often rejected at a higher rate when submitted to foreign journals for publication. This affects capacity to generate and disseminate knowledge. Besides genuine gatekeeping issues, African researchers face language barriers and the challenge of "double consciousness" (Du Bois, 1903 [1999]). For example, English and French—two of the most common languages for foreign journal publication—are ubiquitous official languages in many African countries. However, there is variation in how English, for instance, is spoken and written in various societies. Besides, there is an enormous number of widely spoken indigenous languages and diverse speech patterns which African researchers may be more familiar with. These are useful in shaping scholars' research experience and the types of data they have access to and can collect (Labaree, 2002; Oriola & Haggerty, 2012). However, the imperative of publishing in English and/or French may make it difficult for African scholars who have legitimate knowledge claims to proceed as their local languages are not widely used in academic circles (Andrews & Okpanachi, 2012). These scholars are thus faced with the conundrum of how to position themselves and their research—should they measure their scholarly worth by their ability to reinvent themselves and publish in international peer-reviewed journals or the ability of their research findings to privilege indigenous ontologies in addressing local issues, which usually are of little interest to international audiences?

Knowledge Production in a Fragile Context

Furthermore, Africa's growing trend of civil and political instability and related problems have created a protracted period of stagnation in knowledge production and education advancement (Andrews & Okpanachi, 2012; Clapham, 2020). Assessments of the education sector, for instance, illuminate the migration of Africa's intellectual elites to the well-financed centers of international scholarship. While some gains have been made toward democratization and good governance on the continent in the last two decades, academic staff who show signs of dissent are usually dismissed and, in many cases, forced to flee into exile because of state censorship and harassment (Anyidoho, 1997). Scholars who choose to remain may leave positions in the formal university structure to establish research consultancies geared toward external funding (Clapham, 2020). The resulting research is, however, guided by the priorities of donors. This may have detrimental implications for publishing and knowledge production in Africa, as discussed above.

In addition, the declining ability of Africa to generate and disseminate knowledge is further compounded by the lack of strong political leadership to create enabling policies and environments that champion local knowledge production and the dissemination of data. There are major challenges when it comes to the reliability and validity of data as a result of political censorship. Many African countries, for instance, still operate under the auspices of dictatorial regimes. In many cases, government officials censor empirical data, intimidate and coerce knowledge producers that publish contrary or sensitive information that expose state leaders that abuse power, and in certain occasions, have deliberately published misleading statistics for political and personal gain.

The justification given is often based on the need to protect matters of national security. However, without strong African institutions and leaders dedicated to creating environments conducive to investments in research and development, African scholars are limited in their abilities to harness, utilize, disseminate and continually refine relevant indigenous knowledge that can prove useful for Africa's development. Strong political will in the form of support for scientific knowledge by African political leaders is, therefore, critical in addressing gaps in African knowledge production. Support is needed to encourage the freedom to produce as well as disseminate knowledge that is critical for Africa's economic advancement and much needed development.

The Research and Development Funding Gap

Another challenge, and perhaps the biggest challenge to knowledge production and dissemination on Africa, is the lack of funding for

Research and Development (R&D). Although in the last decade, countries, such as Kenya, Egypt and South Africa, have emerged as research hubs, many African governments still only marginally fund research and development. Most African Union member states, for example, have been unable to meet their commitments made in 2006 regarding spending at least 1% of their GDP on R&D initiatives (Midega et al., 2021). As of 2021, the continent's research and development funding accounted for 0.42% of GDP, which is low when compared to the global average of 1.7% (Midega et al., 2021). This non-prioritization of domestic programs for targeted research funding has continued to undermine Africa's ability to establish research centers that advance indigenous scholarship in addressing the continent's many challenges. Many of the knowledge production hubs in most African states were built during the colonial period, and unfortunately still bear the legacies of historical injustices of racial, gender and social discrimination and exclusion (Nyamnjoh, 2012, 2019). Transforming African knowledge production will thus require capital investments to bolster the capacity of African scientific research labs, libraries and universities in advancing the needs of the continent and African peoples.

An Alternative Framework

African or African-oriented scholarship need not be anti-west. What is important is that African scholarship is processed through platforms, journals, presses and institutions with Africa at their epicenter. In other words, knowledge produced by Africans about Africa should not continue to be assessed through the lens of entities that do not share the micro or macro-sociology of Africa. This approach emphasizes the nuances of local context and relevance.

Our proposed framework, below, presents the opportunity of reinventing African scholarship in our efforts to promote scholarship on the continent. Our framework is informed by the consortium model promoted by CODESRIA and the forward-looking recommendations of Moore-Sieray (1996), Olukoshi (2006), and Andrews and Okpanachi (2012) on Africa's intellectual path. It focuses on three pillars: (i) indigenizing African scholarship by making it more African and unmoored from western pedagogies, models and theories; (ii) creating an enabling environment in which the ideals and objectives of research are easily accessible and translated into practical solutions; and (iii) improved cooperation with and sponsorship from the private sector and the African diaspora.

With these three pillars in mind, we propose a consortium model across various regions in Africa that brings together the top universities to establish journals in each discipline/field. The idea is to have editorial boards drawn across the continent as well as diaspora. Such a synthetization of efforts will help to create greater links between Africa and the African diaspora. Current tendencies toward insularity have unfortunately continued to affect knowledge production about the continent. Encouraging such collaborations would, therefore, be useful in rethinking and reformulating guidelines on the philosophical orientation of what scholarship in Africa should be and would additionally create an enabling recruitment environment that can improve the ability of African scholars to generate and disseminate indigenous knowledge that are rooted in African realities.

The consortium model can also be implemented at both the national and subregional levels. However, given the high-mortality rates of Africa-based journals, it may be necessary for African journals to make efforts to create mergers to ensure longevity and improve the international visibility of publications. In addition, Africa-based journals should ideally be hosted under open-access repository platforms such as the AJOL. Submissions should undergo the highest level of rigor in the peer-review process. Local institutions within the consortium model may collaborate with the private sector to improve their technical capacity in running open-access journals and repositories. Professional training in Africa's booming technology ecosystem may address the technical aspects of supporting journals, moving print journals online, deploying online submission systems, indexing and other ICT-related skills that will be essential in bridging the North–South divide in publishing about Africa. Many Africa-based journals are not indexed, have low impact factors, and generally comprise editorial board membership from the country of origin of each journal. These characteristics and demands for fees unfortunately place such journals in the predatory-like category (Bickton et al., 2019; Tarkang & Bain, 2019). Therefore, partnerships with the private sector will be helpful to boost the confidence of researchers to publish in Africa-based journals. Such collaborations may generate advertisement revenue for the financial sustainability of open-access journals and repositories.

Apart from the regular peer-review process, senior researchers may also assist emerging scholars and graduate students to improve the quality of their papers through formal and informal mentoring opportunities. Kumwenda et al. (2017) identified a lack of mentorship of junior researchers by senior researchers as one of the challenges facing young African scientists in their research careers. Providing help and mentoring for first-time authors, by organizing seminars, soliciting manuscripts that target junior scholars, and communicating with junior authors about the publishing process could prove useful in ensuring a steady supply of quality articles in the long run. Other models of knowledge dissemination should also be encouraged. The current tendency to focus on peer-reviewed publications sometimes makes scholars to forget the vital role of being able to disseminate their published research to a wider audience (Bickton et al., 2019). Support for publishing formats other than a conventional research paper structure would be useful not only in promoting dialogue and cooperation with the media, private sector and even the government, but also in transforming knowledge production and narratives about Africa.

Nevertheless, this consortium model in order to be effective and replicated requires a sound administrative structure and sustainability plan that can convince the private sector and government about the value of academic research. Keeping in mind that there is no one size fit all and that these structures may be different in each country and subregion, the future of scholarly research about Africa will require intellectual engagement, material investment in R&D and a sense of urgency. Finally, concerted action is required from higher education administrators, African leaders and African intellectuals to promote research methods, theories and tools that acknowledge realities, positionalities and indigenous knowledge in advancing non-hegemonic viewpoints, approaches and voices that are clearly rooted in Africa. African governments in particular have a decisive role in strengthening national research programs and partnerships through collaborations and policies that promote regional integration of ideas, skills, knowledge production and empirical data dissemination within the African continent. To achieve this, the education system needs to be properly funded to reduce dependence on foreign grants, as well as other material and symbolic support.

References

Adebanwi, W. (2016). Rethinking Knowledge Production in Africa. *Africa, 86*(2), 350–353.

Adjei, P. B. (2007). Decolonizing Knowledge Production: The Pedagogic Relevance of Gandhian Satyagraha to Schooling and Education in Ghana. *Canadian Journal of Education/Revue Canadienne De L'éducation, 30*(4), 1046–1067.

Agozino, B. (2004). Imperialism, Crime and Criminology: Towards the Decolonization of Criminology. *Crime, Law and Social Change, 41*, 343–358.

Andrews, N. (2020). International relations (IR) Pedagogy, Dialogue and Diversity: Taking the IR Course Syllabus Seriously. *All Azimuth: A Journal of Foreign Policy and Peace*, 9(2), 267–282.

Andrews, N., & Okpanachi, E. (2012). Trends of Epistemic Oppression and Academic Dependency in Africa's Development: The Need for a New Intellectual Path. *Journal of Pan African Studies*, 5(8), 85–104.

Anyidoho, K. (1997). *The Word Behind Bars and the Paradox of Exile*. Northwestern University Press.

Bickton, F. M., Manda-Taylor, L., Hamoonga, R., & Mwenda, A. S. (2019). Challenges Facing sub-Saharan African Health Science Journals and Benefits of International Collaborations and Partnerships. *Science Editor, 42*(4), 116–119.

Clapham, C. (2020). Decolonising African Studies? *The Journal of Modern African Studies, 58*(1), 137–153.

Crawford, G., Mai-Bornu, Z., & Landström, K. (2021). Decolonizing Knowledge Production on Africa: Why It's Still Necessary and What Can Be Done. *Journal of the British Academy, 9*(s1), 21–46.

Du Bois, W. E. B. (1999). *The Souls of Black Folk* (H. L. Gates & T. H. Oliver, Eds.). W. W. Norton.

Deutsch, C. P. (1981). The Behavioral Scientist: Insider and Outsider. *Journal of Social Issues, 37*(2), 172–191.

Falola, T. (2022). *Decolonizing African Studies: Knowledge Production, Agency, and Voice*. University of Rochester Press.

Gray, E., & Wiens, K. (2014). *Open Access Dialogues: Report on the Global Electronic Debates*. https://www.ids.ac.uk/download.php?file=files/dmfile/OpenAccessDialoguesReport.pdf

Joannah, W. (2022). *What's a Good Impact Factor (Ranking in 27 Categories) 2022*. SCI Journal, 4 August 2022. https://www.scijournal.org/articles/good-impact-factor

Kumwenda, S., El Hadji, A. N., Orondo, P. W., William, P., Oyinlola, L., Bongo, G. N., & Chiwona, B. (2017). Challenges Facing Young African Scientists in Their Research Careers: A Qualitative Exploratory Study. *Malawi Medical Journal, 29*(1), 1–4.

Labaree, R. V. (2002). The Risk of 'Going Observationalist': Negotiating the Hidden Dilemmas of Being an Insider Participant Observer. *Qualitative Research, 2*(1), 97–122.

Mara, K., & Thompson, K. D. (2022). African Studies Keyword: Autoethnography. *African Studies Review, 65*(2), 372–398.

Mazrui, A. A. (1975). Academic Freedom in Africa: The Dual Tyranny. *African Affairs, 74*(297), 393–400.

Merriam, S. B., Johnson-Bailey, J., Lee, M. Y., Kee, Y., Ntseane, G., & Muhamad, M. (2001). Power and Positionality: Negotiating Insider/Outsider Status Within and Across Cultures. *International Journal of Lifelong Education, 20*(5), 405–416.

Midega, J., Kyobutungi, C., Okiro, E., Okumu, F., Aniebo, I., & Erondu, N. (2021). *African Countries Must Muscle Up Their Support and Fill Massive R&D Gap*. The Conversation. 24 January 2023. https://theconversation.com/african-countries-must-muscle-up-their-support-and-fill-massive-randd-gap-161024

Moore-Sieray, D. (1996). Towards a Decolonization of Scholarship in Africa and a Vision for the 1990s and Beyond. *Journal of Third World Studies, 13*(2), 25–50.

Murray, S., & Clobridge, A. (2014). *The Current State of Scholarly Journal Publishing in Africa*. African Journals Online (AJOL). https://www.ajol.info/public/Scholarly-Journal-Publishing-in-Africa-Report-Final-v04c.pdf

Nabudere, D. W. (1997). Beyond Modernization and Development, or Why the Poor Reject Development. *Geografiska Annaler: Series B, Human Geography, 79*(4), 203–215.

Nabyonga-Orem, J., Asamani, J. A., Nyirenda, T., & Abimbola, S. (2020). Article Processing Charges Are Stalling the Progress of African Researchers: A Call for Urgent Reforms. *BMJ Global Health, 5*(9), e003650.

Nyamnjoh, F. B. (2012). Potted Plants in Greenhouses: A Critical Reflection on the Resilience of Colonial Education in Africa. *Journal of Asian and African Studies, 47*(2), 129–154.

Nyamnjoh, F. B. (2019). *Decolonizing the University in Africa Oxford Research Encyclopedia of Politics*. Oxford University Press.

Olukoshi, A. (2006). African Scholars and African Studies. *Development in Practice, 16*(6), 533–544.

Oriola, T., & Haggerty, K. D. (2012). The Ambivalent Insider/Outsider Status of Academic 'Homecomers': Observations on Identity and Field Research in the Nigerian Delta. *Sociology, 46*(3), 540–548.

Seglen, P. O. (1997). Why the Impact Factor of Journals Should Not Be Used for Evaluating Research. *BMJ, 314*(7079), 497.

Tarkang, E. E., & Bain, L. E. (2019). The Bane of Publishing a Research Article in International Journals by African Researchers, the Peer-Review Process, and the Contentious Issue of Predatory Journals: A Commentary. *Pan African Medical Journal, 32*(119), 1–5.

Zeleza, P. T. (2002). The Politics of Historical and Social Science Research in Africa. *Journal of Southern African Studies, 28*(1), 9–23.

CHAPTER 4

#RepresentationMatters: Unpacking the Prevalence of Whiteness in the Teaching of African Studies Abroad

Nathan Andrews and Hosea Olayiwola Patrick

Introduction

The discourse on decoloniality and the power dynamics in knowledge creation and distribution have been an ongoing contention among African Studies scholars within and outside Africa for several decades. While there is literature that has extensively discussed the need for

N. Andrews (✉)
Department of Political Science at McMaster University, Hamilton, ON, Canada
e-mail: nandrews@mcmaster.ca

H. O. Patrick
African-Caribbean Faculty Association of McMaster University (ACFAM), McMaster University, Hamilton, ON, Canada
e-mail: patrich@mcmaster.ca

N. Andrews · H. O. Patrick
Hamilton, Canada

N. Andrews and N. E. Khalema (eds.), *Decolonizing African Studies Pedagogies*, Political Pedagogies,
https://doi.org/10.1007/978-3-031-37442-5_4

a decolonial construct in knowledge creation on Africans, few have addressed the issue of representation in terms of what Kessi et al. (2020) referred to as the scholarship in, of, by, with, and from Africa (*tagged as* African Studies) outside the shores of the African continent. As Arowosegbe (2016) argued, the African Studies field has been historically clouded by asymmetrical power relations regarding what knowledge is, the producers of knowledge, and the production and dissemination structure of such knowledge.

While the field of African Studies was birthed as a post-enlightenment drive to study non-western societies from a Eurocentric (Anglo-American) lens using an area studies approach (Allman, 2019; Arowosegbe, 2014; Hammett, 2010), the emergence of African scholars striving to tell their own story creates an authenticity struggle. It queries who is qualified as an 'expert' to tell the African story, to what extent is this story African, and how the African Studies discipline can be more African, among others (Arowosegbe, 2014, 2016; Falola, 2017). Though these questions are fundamental, Black scholars within the African Studies field have been historically disadvantaged as institutions in the Global North often privilege White scholarship over Black scholarship (Hammett, 2010).

Branch (2018) argued that the African Studies field in the U.K., for example, appears to be largely the preserve of White scholars. This assertion is true in the U.K. as it is elsewhere within the Global North, though there are some notable distinctions within the context of the U.S. for instance, which will be discussed subsequently. But the general premise is the fact that Eurocentric traditions have largely influenced knowledge production within the field, and a colonial notion of Africa as constituting darkness and primitiveness has contributed to the continent serving as an object for research rather than a place of knowledge creation (Allman, 2013; Branch, 2018; Kessi et al., 2020; Odoom & Andrews, 2017). As Arowosegbe (2014) opined, the alienation of Africans within the African Studies field is problematic in several ways. In view of this, the issue of epistemic exclusion vis-à-vis academic racism and the manifestation of practices and structures that underpin the dominance or superiority of whiteness (see Dotson, 2012, 2014; Dutt, 2020) beg for urgent research and policy attention. In this chapter, whiteness is understood to be the absence of any ancestral, ethnic, or geographical connection to Africa. While 'African' and 'Black' are used interchangeably, we specify the connection between the historical African root and the continent of Africa.

Considering the historical dynamics of knowledge production in general, the discourse of representation and misrepresentation, with the latter referring to various modes of distortion within the African Studies field, has influenced Kessi et al.'s (2020) argument on the need for redressing the inequalities prevalent within the African Studies field. While this is pertinent, it is crucial that close cognizance is given to addressing representation issues like who is telling the African story, the content of the message, and the source of information used in delivering the narrative. For instance, Mendonça et al.'s (2018) study on representation and journal governance argued that Africa-based editors constitute a minority in the editorial composition of top journals on African Studies. Also, all the 'top' most influential and widely cited African Studies journals are published in Global North countries, and the biggest African Studies conferences are all held outside of Africa. This evidence and its implications are quite alarming, which leaves one to wonder why the supposed Africans themselves constitute a minority in the production of knowledge or in 'gatekeeping' their own stories and perspectives.

This chapter primarily explores the issue of representation in the knowledge production and dissemination of African Studies in the diaspora by unpacking the role of whiteness in the teaching of African Studies outside the shores of the African continent. We focused on African Studies centers or programs abroad and sought to examine the color configuration of the field in terms of who is teaching African Studies, what it means for subject matter, knowledge (re)production, and the overall inclusion of African voices in Africa and the diaspora. The rest of the chapter proceeds with a discussion of the theoretical framing for our arguments. This is then followed by the methodology employed in the collection of data for the pilot study, a discussion of key findings, and concluding reflections.

Theoretical Underpinnings

This chapter's arguments align with scholarly discussions of epistemic exclusion and academic racism which have also been influenced by the notion of epistemic oppression and imperialism (see Ake, 1982; Alatas, 2003; Andrews, 2020, 2022; Andrews & Okpanachi, 2012; Mazrui, 1992; Ndlovu-Gatsheni, 2018; Noda, 2020). The central argument here is that colonialism and historical imperialism have perpetuated a system whereby the political and socioeconomic system is designed to benefit some people at the detriment of others, creating discriminatory and exclusionary outcomes. As Dotson (2014: 115) argued, epistemic oppression implies the "persistent epistemic exclusion that hinders one's contribution to knowledge production *due to* an unwarranted infringement on the epistemic agency of knowers". In this sense, the inability to effectively participate or utilize available shared resources in the production of knowledge can negatively impact an individual's or a group's agency leading to epistemic injustice.

Fricker's (2017) conceptualization of epistemic injustice, divided into testimonial and hermeneutical injustice, is relevant here. Dotson (2012, 2014) posits that testimonial injustice occurs in a situation whereby the credibility of a knower as a producer of knowledge is vilified as inconsequential based on certain prejudices such as race. Here, the credibility and authenticity of the message are disregarded or perceived as inferior due to the knower belonging to a social or racial class that is perceived as intellectually inferior. In contemporary and western traditions, the manifestation of practices and structures that underpin the dominance or superiority of whiteness is consciously and unconsciously seen as given. This perception of intellectual inferiority creates and continuously reinforces an ideology which coincides with White supremacy, which Liu et al. (2021: 106) refer to as "a historically emergent, socially constructed and institutionally embedded racial hierarchy that enshrines White physical, cultural, cultural, intellectual and moral superiority." Monarrez et al. (2022) argue that such a notion projects the perception that the White race's ideas, beliefs, actions, and thoughts are superior to those of people of color. This produces a continued and subtle bias and conviction in relation to the intellectual inferiority of Black people (Hawkins, 2021). This perception of inferiority vis-a-vis superiority leads to the kind of systems that (re)produce some level of White privilege and invariably lead to unequal opportunities and outcomes at the detriment of non-White people within academia (Arday & Mirza, 2018). This form of unfair discrimination in academia is referred to as academic racism (Dutt, 2020). The ignorance of epistemic agents in the maintenance of these injustices also leads to a contributory injustice which further creates epistemic harm to the agency of the knower (Dotson, 2012, 2014).

In essence, the historical configuration of western societies which is influenced by colonial and imperialist orientations perpetuated racial inequalities and discrimination that privilege one class over the other.

Historically, the system is configured in a manner whereby the slave owner is privileged over the slave, the White colonialist over the colonized, and White race over people of color (Bertocchi & Dimico, 2014; Summerhill, 2010). This disadvantage for people of color premised on the enduring historical, and societal structure produced some form of structural racism evident in implicit bias, open and subtle racism, and inequality in employment and education, among others (Acosta & Ackerman-Barger, 2017; Vanjani et al., 2022). This race-based discrimination and inequality is evident in contemporary western societies, including academia (Barber et al., 2020; Monarrez et al., 2022).

These practices (and notions) have been cemented in the structure and culture of the modern society, therein creating power imbalances manifested in inequality and discrimination in the recruitment, retention, and participation of Black people in academia. This systemic inequality creates eventual workplace disparities that privilege the White race over other persons of color, as alluded above. Mirza's (2018: 7) citation of the Sir Macpherson (1999: para 6.34) report captures this issue of structure leading to systemic exclusion evident in academia as the

> … collective failure of an organization to provide an appropriate and professional service to people because of their color, culture, or ethnic origin. It can be seen or detected in processes, attitudes and behavior which amount to discrimination through unwitting prejudice, ignorance, thoughtlessness, and racist stereotyping which disadvantage minority ethnic people.

In this case, Fricker's (2017) other type of epistemic injustice, referred to as hermeneutical injustice, manifests itself due to this historical configuration and practices. In this sense, hermeneutical injustice occurs when the systemic structure creates a situation of undue disadvantage for some people within the social structure, leading to the exclusion of and discrimination against others (Kidd & Carel, 2017; Posholi, 2020).

The implications of epistemic injustice due to epistemic exclusion and academic racism in the production and propagation of knowledge within the discipline of African Studies cannot be overemphasized. As the brief theoretical discussion above suggests, the need to probe the racial configuration and affiliation of the producer and disseminator of knowledge on African Studies vis-à-vis the historic epistemic structure of the western tradition and society is paramount. In this vein, the chapter attempts to present the stark picture of the dearth of Black agency in a field whose subject matter focuses on Black histories, experiences, and futures. It also points to institutionalized structures and the systemic racism that sustain pedagogical practices which exclude diverse voices and perspectives.

Methods of Data Collection

The research presented in this chapter adopts the exploratory pilot study technique as a research design. As Hallingberg et al. (2018) opined, the exploratory pilot study is a systematic review process designed to assess the feasibility and significance of embarking on a research endeavor. Therefore, the research design adopted for this chapter is aimed at assessing the configuration and representation of color and whiteness in the production and dissemination of knowledge within the African Studies discipline in the Global North as a prelude to a much in-depth future research program. The aim is to explore the state of representation as well as provoke policy discourse and solutions to epistemic exclusion and injustice in knowledge creation within the African Studies discipline.

This study followed three phases. In the first phase, Webometrics' rating of the top 100 colleges and universities for 2021 was used to determine which institutions offer African Studies programs (Webometrics, n.d.). Since the study is designed to examine the representation of African Studies in European and North American Universities, focusing on the United Kingdom (U.K.), Canada, and the United States (U.S.), the scope was subsequently redefined because most of the 100 leading universities are located in the U.S., leaving other countries with unequal representation. Thus, 20 leading universities in the U.S., U.K., and Canada were respectively surveyed (see Table 4.1) in order to provide a relatively equal sample of institutions across the three countries. This phase helped us to identify universities and colleges in the selected countries that offer African Studies, either at the undergraduate or at graduate level ("n/a" in Table 4.1 below means that either the University does not offer such program or there was limited information available at the time the search was conducted).

The study's second phase involved gathering respective African Studies syllabi from the selected universities (see Table 4.2) by retrieving course syllabi from the program or department websites or, if not accessible online, emailing the program coordinator although the latter option was not fully explored due to the time constraints of the pilot study.

Table 4.1 Top 20 universities surveyed in the United Kingdom, United States, and Canada

United Kingdom	*Canada*	*United States*
Oxford University	University of Toronto	Harvard University
University of Cambridge	University of British Columbia	Stanford University
Imperial University London n/a	McGill University	Massachusetts Institute of technology n/a
University of Edinburgh	University of Alberta n/a	University of California, Berkeley
University of Manchester n/a	University of Waterloo n/a	University of Michigan
Kings College London n/a	University of Calgary n/a	University of Washington
University of Leeds n/a	McMaster University n/a	Columbia University n/a
University of Nottingham n/a	University of Montreal n/a	Cornell University
Warwick University n/a	Simon Fraser University n/a	University of Pennsylvania
London School of Economic and Political Science n/a	Western University n/a	Princeton University
Cardiff University n/a	University of Ottawa n/a	University of Los Angeles n/a
University of Liverpool n/a	Queen's University n/a	Yale University
University of York n/a	Dalhousie University n/a	University of San Diego
University of Glasgow n/a	University of Victoria n/a	University of Wisconsin
University of Exeter n/a	York University	University of Minnesota
Queen Mary University n/a	Laval University n/a	Duke Trinity College of Arts & Sciences
Newcastle University n/a	University of Manitoba n/a	Pennsylvania State University
University of Bristol n/a	University of Saskatchewan n/a	Northwestern University
University of Sheffield n/a	University of Guelph n/a	New York University
	Carleton University	University of Texas at Austin

Source Authors' compilation from the Webometric 2021 university ranking

Hence, most of the information was gathered from readily available online resources. Overall, one syllabus for an African Studies core course was retrieved (where available) from each of the universities as a sample of their African Studies offering.

Table 4.2 Universities offering African studies (including Africana or African and American studies) in the United Kingdom, United States, and Canada

Institution	*Degree*	*Institution*	*Degree*
University of Toronto	B.A.	Harvard University	B.A., Ph.D.
University of British Columbia	B.A. (minor)	Stanford University	B.A.
McGill University	B.A.	University of California, Berkeley	B.A., Ph.D.
Carleton University	B.A. (minor)	University of Michigan	Certificate
York University	B.A.	University of Washington	B.A. (minor)
Oxford University	B.A. (minor)	Cornell University	B.A., Ph.D.
University of Cambridge	B.A. (minor)	University of Pennsylvania	B.A., Ph.D.
University of Edinburgh	B.A.	Princeton University	B.A., M.A.
New York University	M.Sc.	Yale University	B.A., M.A.
University of Texas at Austin	M.Phil.	University of San Diego	B.A. (minor)
Northwestern University	M.A.	University of Wisconsin	B.A., Ph.D.
Duke Trinity College of Arts & Sci	B.A., Ph.D.	University of Minnesota	B.A.
Pennsylvania State University	B.A., Ph.D.		

Source Authors' compilation from the universities' websites

The last phase of the pilot study involved reviewing the core African Studies syllabi collected from the selected universities' websites. The objective was to identify how the selected universities use African scholars, languages, and literature to convey African experiences and stories to students. The essence of this search was to examine who is telling the African story, the content of the message, and the source of information used in delivering the narrative. For representation of African scholars, we counted the number of scholars of African (Black) origin who are affiliated with the respective African Studies programs examined. As earlier argued, whiteness in the context of this chapter implies the absence of any ancestral, ethnic, or geographical connection to Africa (i.e., links with the historical African root and 'Africans' as a non-homogenous race). More specifically, while 'African' is used mostly for those born or raised on the continent, 'Black' is used holistically in reference to all persons of African descent or ancestry but not necessarily those born or raised on the continent. These specifications will become more pertinent below when examining the case of U.S. In terms of our pilot methodological strategy, such background information on origins was deduced from a combination of biographical information on program website and elsewhere. The purpose of this phase of work was to arrive at some summative understanding of common characteristics in African Studies programming across a number of leading institutions in North America and Europe—as a way to gauge past, current, and possible future trends in representational diversity in this field of study.

Discussion of Findings

Our findings indicate that 5 (25%) of the 20 leading universities in Canada teach African Studies and the U.K. has only 4 (20%) of its top 20 universities offering an African Studies program. The U.S., however, has one of the highest numbers of universities offering African Studies as a major or minor, with 17 (85%) out of the top 20 universities in the country offering such programs (see Table 4.1). Thus, it is important to note that North American universities generally (at least those in the U.S.) appear quite committed to promoting the teaching and learning of African stories, cultures, histories, and perspectives through the field of African Studies.

Representation Dynamics in the United Kingdom

The review of the universities in the United Kingdom shows that Oxford University, the University of Cambridge, University College London, and the University of Edinburgh are the only 20 leading universities in the country that offer the program (see Fig. 4.1). The London School of Economic and Political Science, for instance, has a popular Africa Centre that serves as a hub for research and engagement but does not seem to have programming that directly results in the attainment of a degree at the undergraduate or graduate level. Also, the University College London appeared to have a master's program in African Studies during the initial search but there was limited information on the website, hence its exclusion in the figure below.

At Oxford University, we evaluated the representation of African scholars and found that only two out of the seven faculty members are Africans from Nigeria and Zimbabwe, respectively. Furthermore, we examined the number of African literary writings that are incorporated into African Studies core course (*Themes in African History and Social*

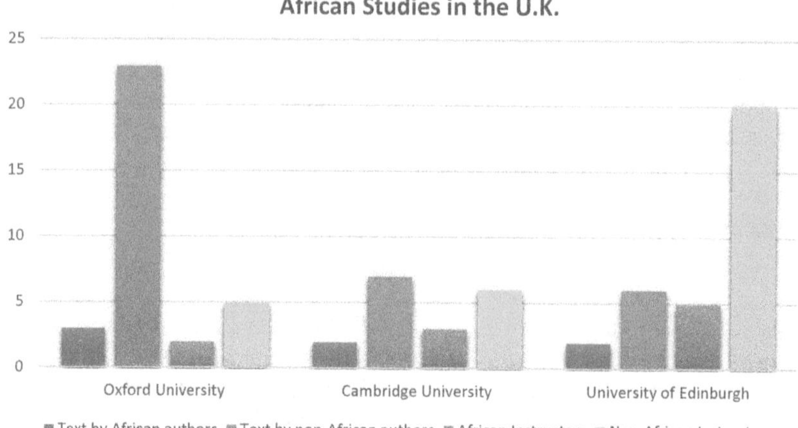

Fig. 4.1 African studies at U.K. universities

Sciences). In the course readings, three African scholars are listed as co-authors or lead authors while non-Africans wrote the other twenty-three works. The course presents students with issues pertaining to the contemporary study of Africa and attempts to situate these issues within their historical, social, and cultural contexts. It discussed key African issues, such as colonialism, resistance to colonialism, nationalism, and independence. Additionally, it discussed authoritarianism, patrimonialism, and the cold war (Oxford University, n.d.). The interesting thing is why only a handful of publications authored by African scholars are included in the reading list even though all these issues of focus represent the lived realities of people who have direct experience with the continent, which perhaps points to a historically informed and institutionally embedded racial hierarchy that sees the texts produced by White academics as superior to those by Africans themselves (Liu et al., 2021; see also Andrews & Odoom, 2021; Andrews, 2022). This superiority is augmented by the elite/privileged status of Oxford and how the university has been constructed over time as a pinnacle of higher education.

Three of University of Cambridge's nine African Studies faculty members are Africans, while the other six are not. This ratio of African and non-African faculty component is probably better than Oxford and Edinburgh but even in this case only two out of the nine readings selected for African core course (*Introduction to African Studies*) are works by African scholars. Despite the poor representation of African scholars and text assigned as core readings, the course content discusses issues pertaining to Africa, such as anxiety in and about Africa, media, and marginality in modern Africa, justice, citizenship, belonging, and political community in Africa. Having said that, representation cannot be downplayed because the way in which certain issues are approached differs from one author to another. For example, the discourse on neo-patrimonialism and the African state appears to be taken up much more by White scholars than by Black scholars.

At the University of Edinburgh, a total of five Africans and 20 non-Africans teach African Studies courses, including both permanent and visiting instructors. In reviewing the *Africa in the Contemporary World* syllabus, we found that only two of the eight suggested key readings were authored by African scholars. Yet, the content of the syllabus explores topical issues such as colonialism and post-colonialism, liberation struggles and nationalism, citizenship, ethnicity and identity, social movements and democratization, law and governance, conflict and civil war, poverty, and economic change (University of Edinburgh, n.d.). The numbers on representational diversity are quite telling especially given the global reputation of the University of Edinburgh's African Studies program. In line with Branch's (2018) argument, it appears Edinburgh's Centre of African Studies has largely preserved the dominance and superiority of White scholars.

Existing research has shown that Europeans have historically maintained ownership of knowledge created about Africa (see Ake, 1982; Falola, 2017; Mazrui, 1992; Ndlovu-Gatsheni, 2018), and this systemic marginalization of African contributions manifests in both the graph presented in Fig. 4.1 and the low representation of instructors who are of African origin. To be sure, such representational issues are part of historical legacies of institutions and they also capture the symptoms associated with the sheer ignorance or deliberate forgetfulness of the need to include diverse voices. However, Dotson (2012, 2014) has shown how the ignorance of epistemic agents in the maintenance of systems of both testimonial and hermeneutical injustices causes further epistemic harm to the agency of the knower. In other words, ignorance or forgetfulness is no excuse for the lack of diversity in a program that is meant to teach and study the African experience. In Europe where programs on European studies abound, it would be unlikely to find one where non-Europeans are over-represented. Yet, the reverse is true for African Studies, and this remains an issue worthy of critical examination.

Representation Dynamics in Canadian Universities

In Canada, the University of Toronto (Scarborough) has four out of seven African Studies faculty members being Africans. There is no information available online regarding course readings. However, the selected core course *Introduction to African Studies* syllabus addresses some relevant topics in Africa, such as pre-colonial, colonial, and contemporary African history, politics, African humanism, and Pan-Africanism (University of Toronto, n.d.).

At the University of British Columbia, three of the faculty members teaching African Studies are Africans, while the remaining eight instructors are not Africans. There is an unequal representation of Africans in the teaching of the program. Again, there is no online access to the selected literature for the courses. However, the syllabus of the selected core course *Perspectives in African Studies: A Social Science Approach* covers the histories of modern Africa, themes of African societies and statecraft in the nineteenth century, colonial conquest, collaboration, and resistance as witnessed in Nigeria, Algeria, Congo, Rwanda, Kenya, and South Africa (University of British Columbia, n.d.). As the reading list is not posted online, it is difficult to understand how the stories are being told and what materials are used to tell these African stories. African instructors are also underrepresented at McGill University where two out of the six faculty members teaching in the African Studies program are Africans. Again, the readings for the African Studies courses are not listed online but the *Introduction to African Studies* course discusses topics such as political conflict, governance, democratization, environment, rural life, urbanism, health, gender, social change, popular culture, literature, film, and the arts in Africa (McGill University, n.d.).

York University appears to have a full representation of African instructors in the African Studies Program with all four faculty members affiliated with the program being of African descent. The reading materials for the courses are not listed online. Meanwhile, the program features a selection of African languages, war, revolution, society in the twentieth century, and the experience of Africans in the Americas (York University, n.d.). Among the 20 leading universities in Canada, Carleton University offers a more comprehensive program of African Studies. The program has four full-time faculty members and numerous cross-appointed faculty and adjunct faculty members. Two of the four faculty members are Africans while the other two are not. Additionally, five out of the 17 cross-appointed and adjunct professors are Africans and the remaining 12 instructors are non-Africans. The *Introduction to African Studies* syllabus examines issues such as the African government from a global perspective and how Africa relates to human origin. Two of the recommended readings were written by Africans while seven other texts were written by non-Africans (Carleton University, n.d.).

Absence of diversity in the Canadian academy is visible across all fields of study and research has also pointed to the persistence of academic racism of different manifestations in Canada (see Daniel, 2019; Henry & Tator, 2009; Ibrahim et al., 2021) but the findings on African Studies is particularly interesting because of the subject matter (Fig. 4.2). In other words, and to reiterate an argument we made above, it is unlikely the faculty component of instructors teaching in a 'Canadian studies' program would be predominantly non-White. This is not to suggest that only White (Canadian) scholars can study or teach about Canada but it begs the question of why the reverse is the case for African Studies. This phenomenon speaks to the hermeneutical (yet taken for granted) injustice that is informed by dominant structures of power and unequal relations that result in the promotion of certain perspectives and valorization of others (see Fricker, 2017; Kidd & Carel, 2017). Such injustice "undermines subjects in their capacity as interpreters of their own social experiences," which then limits their ability to share their knowledge and experiences as part of "the collective shared pool of epistemic resources" (Posholi, 2020: 292; see also 'contributory injustice' in Dotson, 2012).

The evident lack of representation is leading to more cohort hires for equity-deserving groups (EDGs) such as Black people across Canadian higher education institutions. The University of Toronto, McGill University, and York University have recently undertaken such hiring of EDGs. However, the analysis for this chapter does not include an assessment of whether these positions, which are expected to be filled by people of African descent, directly contribute to African Studies programming. Yet, it is worth noting that such initiatives are meant to address the systemic racism that limits the opportunities of Black people to end up on the shortlists of academic search committees, let alone to be eventually

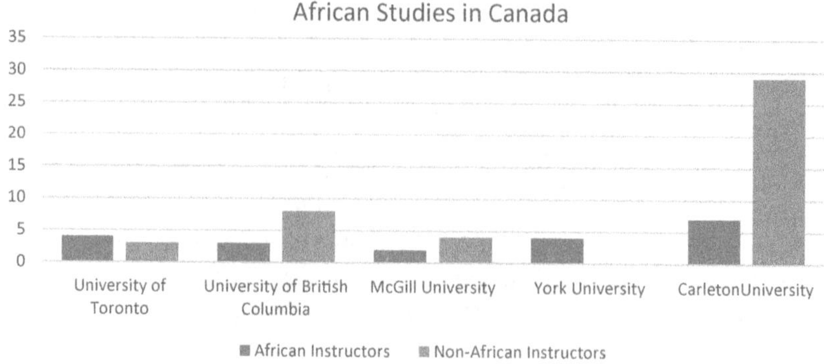

Fig. 4.2 African studies at Canadian universities

hired for permanent positions on an equal basis. Epistemic oppression, therefore, remains a function of this systemic inequality that leads us to continue questioning who is taking up spaces in academic fields of study as key instructors and thinkers and why others are excluded. York University is the only outlier in terms of full representation but this also reinforces the positionality and reputation of the institution as being more progressive than many of its Canadian counterparts.

Representation Dynamics in the United States

What may be considered as the field of African Studies has various names in the U.S., including Africana, African and African American Studies, and African Diaspora Studies among others. The general themes covered in core courses tend to mirror those elsewhere (U.K. and Canada, for instance) but there are notable differences in some cases. For instance, some programs are focused on studying the lives of people of African descent and their lived experience in the U.S. or elsewhere with little focus on life on the African continent whereas others focus on both or more directly on the African continent itself. Our emphasis in this pilot study was on the latter category. Also, the racial demographic characteristic of the U.S. is noteworthy here because it informed our simultaneous usage of 'African' and 'Black' with the latter representing persons of African descent or ancestry but not necessarily those born or raised on the continent. This demographic difference also manifests in the varied names of African Studies in respective institutions and the combination of issues that are African and those that are peculiar to the African American experience in the themes covered by respective courses.

Among the 49 faculty members affiliated with the African Studies program at Harvard University, 28 are Africans or Blacks. The syllabus of the selected core course (*Introduction to African Popular Culture*) explores the lives, interactions, and innovative practices of key figures in African music, television, fashion, dance as well as connections between African popular cultures and the rest of the world. The course further examines colonial and postcolonial class formations in Africa, the after-lives, cold war cultural circulation, and the specific works of African artists, including Fela Kuti, William Onyeabor, and Charly Boy as contemporary figures (Harvard University, n.d.).

At Stanford University, African languages such as Swahili, Yoruba, Igbo, Tigrinya, Twi, and Amharic are all studied under the African Studies program, which helps strengthen Africa's stories. Among the 65 faculty members in the department, nine are Blacks or people of African descent while the remaining 56 people are non-Africans. The syllabus of the selected course *(Literature and Society in Africa and the Caribbean)* explores African and Caribbean national and cultural identity, race and class, gender and sexuality, orality and textuality, transnationalism and migration, colonialism and decolonization, history and memory, and the politics of language. Among the 13 authors, filmmakers, and artists drawn upon in teaching the course, 10 people are Blacks or African (Stanford University, n.d.). Even though representational diversity is low in terms of number of permanent Black/African faculty, the reading list is one of the most diverse among the various programs included in this pilot study.

The language component at Stanford is important, which is also part of the African Studies program at the University of Wisconsin where Arabic, Yoruba, Hausa, Wolof, Swahili, and Zulu are included in the curriculum. The university seems to have a comprehensive African Studies program that cuts across fields, such as history, agriculture, language, African culture, law, engineering, and natural sciences. As such, its faculty members are drawn from different fields. Out of the 100 faculty members affiliated with the program (representing the largest number among the various programs in the U.K., Canada, and U.S., as can be seen in Fig. 4.3), only 14 are Africans or Blacks (University of Wisconsin, n.d.). This low number of African/Black representation does not measure up to the comprehensive nature of the program and its inclusion of African writers like Chinua Achebe, Ferdinand Oyono, Alex La Guma, and Nawal El Saadawi in the syllabus of the selected course *(The African Storyteller)* we examined.

At the University of San Diego, five African and 10 non-African faculty members are affiliated with the African Studies program. The syllabus of the selected course *(Fundamentals of Africana Studies I)* explores the story of Africa with a major focus on its struggle and relationship with the rest of the world (University of San Diego, n.d.). The readings for the selected course are not listed online, similar to programs at institutions such as the Duke Trinity College of Art and Science, New York University (NYU), Northwestern University, and the University of California Berkeley. Duke Trinity College has three non-African instructors and six African or Black members affiliated with the program while NYU has only one African or Black instructor out of seven in the department. Northwestern has eight African and 36 non-African faculty members teaching African Studies at the university whereas the program at the University of California Berkeley has 12 African and 83 non-African teaching faculty. Despite the deficit in the representation of Africans among the faculty,

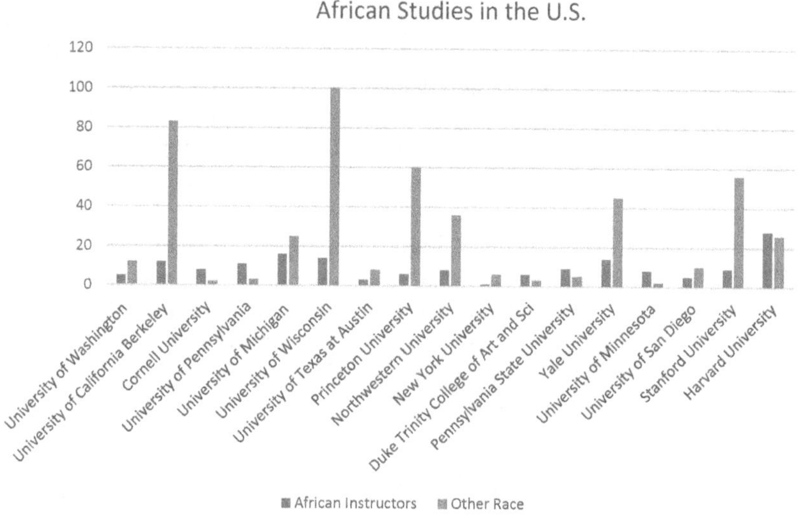

Fig. 4.3 African studies at U.S. universities

the program offers languages such as Amharic, Igbo, and Kiswahili as a way of promoting African culture and stories.

Again, African languages are well incorporated into many African Studies programs in the U.S., which is quite a distinct departure from programs in the U.K. and Canada. At Yale University, Swahili, Yoruba, Twi, Wolof, and Zulu are included although the component of faculty can be broken up into 14 African/Black and 45 White. At the University of Minnesota, African languages like Swahili, Somali, and Arabic are incorporated into the program and their *Introduction to African American and African Studies* course deals with issues such as political destabilization, social fragmentation, economic disruption, internal displacement, and international migration within African regions and in the global contexts (University of Minnesota, n.d.). Also, two of the five texts assigned are written by African or Black authors.

Some U.S. institutions appear to stand out for better representation of Africans or Blacks. Cornell University has eight African or Black faculty and the remaining two are non-African whereas eight out of the 10 faculty members affiliated with the African Studies program at the University of Minnesota are African or Black. At the Pennsylvania State University, nine Africans or Blacks and five non-Africans teach in the African Studies program. The University of Pennsylvania also has 11 Africans/Blacks and three non-Africans affiliated with the African Studies program. The same cannot be said for Princeton University where only six of the 66 faculty members affiliated African Studies are African/Black scholars. The program uses two texts authored by Africans (out of a total of six) for the selected course we reviewed (*Colonial and Postcolonial Africa*), which highlights the impact of European colonial rule on the traditional societies of Africa in the nineteenth and twentieth centuries (Princeton University, n.d.).

The remaining U.S. universities examined have a varied range of representational diversity. The University of Texas at Austin has three Africans and eight non-Africans teaching in the African Studies program while the University of Michigan has 16 Africans/Blacks and 25 non-Africans/Blacks core faculty members teaching African Studies. The program at the University of Washington has five African and 12 non-African direct faculty members, excluding graduate faculty members who are endorsed to chair doctoral supervisory committees and serve as a Graduate School Representatives. The selected course (*Africa Era Slave Trade*) uses the emerging evidence of historical, linguistic, and archaeological analysis to examine the lingering notions and racial stereotypes about Africa and its people (University of Washington, n.d.).

As noted above, it is refreshing to see that a few African Studies programs in the U.S. (e.g., Harvard, UPenn, Cornell, Penn State, Minnesota, Duke Trinity College) stand out for achieving or even exceeding representational parity for White and Black (African) scholars. This does not necessarily suggest these programs have dealt with racism or epistemic injustice but the growing representation matters in terms of the agency given to Blacks or Africans to remain central to knowledge creation and dissemination. Furthermore, the huge numbers in some of these programs with as many as 100 faculty members in the case of Wisconsin reflects the dominance of these well-resourced centers, their power to maintain structures that perpetuate whiteness, and their centrality in shaping the field itself (see Allman, 2019). Another aspect is that African Studies programs in the U.S. are also more expansive than their counterparts in the U.K. and Canada, even including language offerings (e.g., Arabic, Swahili, Yoruba, Twi, Wolof, Zulu, Igbo, Tigrinya, Amharic, Hausa)—which may be seen as part of the movement toward the decentering of the English language as a global lingua franca. Linguistic imperialism is linked with epistemic oppression (Phillipson, 1996, 2013) or what has been captured as testimonial injustice (Dotson, 2014; Fricker, 2017); thus, it is important to see more African languages becoming included in the African Studies curricula.

Further on the apparent representational parity in some U.S. schools, it is important to note that the programs with large numbers of African or Black scholars are mostly those that focus on Africana, diaspora, or African American Studies and the diversity could be explained by the high number of Black Americans or African Americans. For instance, Harvard and Minnesota have departments called "African and African American Studies" and Cornell's program is called "Africana Studies." A deeper look reveals that programs that are called 'African Studies' with a specific focus on the continent (e.g., Princeton or Wisconsin) tend to have much fewer faculty members who can be identified as African or Black. One implication is that because majority of African Americans or Black Americans focus their work on America (i.e., the experience of being Black in the U.S.), what this means is that the scholarship about Africa (i.e., the continent and people of Africa) ends up still being dominated by White non-African scholars. The point is that Black representation may not necessarily increase scholarship for and about Africa per se but, to counter persistent whiteness, an increased representation of any form for African/Black scholarship is still a move in the right direction.

Concluding Reflections

This chapter has shown that a critical engagement with the 'taught discipline' informs a robust understanding of where we are and where we are going in terms of the representation and agency of the knower and teacher within the discipline. As Monarrez et al. (2022) noted, the ability to understand and anticipate the present and future relies upon our collective knowledge of the past and how that shapes the present and the future. The result from this exploratory study supports the claim that the historical configuration of western society privileges the White race at the detriment of people of color, with significant ramifications for the epistemic agency and representation of people of color. Bearing in mind the reality of representation in the production and dissemination of knowledge within African Studies programs, it is worth reiterating that the issue of academic racism, exclusion, and implicit bias against people of color is a reality in which faculty in the Global North must not shy away from addressing (Acosta & Ackerman-Barger, 2017). In particular, a conscious shift in mindset and a deeper understanding of racial complexities is required to make necessary progress toward diversification within African Studies programs.

This chapter began with the following question: To what extent is the permanence of whiteness and epistemic exclusion or hegemony sustained in African Studies through institutionalized centers/programs of African Studies in North America and Europe? The evidence based on a preliminary examination of website content of respective African Studies programs in Canada, U.K. and the U.S. points to the persistent lack of representation of Africans (or other people of African ancestry). The presence of whiteness across majority of the programs—which manifests in who is teaching courses on Africa, who supervises students studying Africa, and who makes key decisions on African Studies curricula—is a function of the institutionalized hierarchies that have hindered the inclusion of others. Even for programs where there is some parity between White and non-White African Studies instructors, the key readings assigned are still primarily those authored by White people. This pedagogical practice reflects the academic racism and epistemic injustice that does not equally value the intellectual contributions of people have been historically written out of course syllabi.

The discussion above also showed that topics covered in the African Studies syllabi reviewed range from a selection of African languages to issues around (post)colonialism, imperialism, ethnicity and identity, rural life, African culture and media, democratization, independence, and human rights among others. It is important to note that knowledge production and dissemination in relation to these topics are likely to be distorted if we rely on an Anglo-American interpretation. There is the need for scholars who are well-positioned within the histories, lived experiences, and culture of Africa to be central to the creation and dissemination of such knowledge about the continent. This is not because only Africans can be experts on Africa; rather, it is because positionality matters a lot in determining the objects and subjects of knowledge. In line with this postulation, African scholars are arguably more inclined to write for Africa and to produce knowledge that can be used to advance African interests. In contrast, non-African scholars may interpret African phenomena for consumption by a non-African audience and, sometimes, in order to advance the political/ideological goals of their countries of origin. Writing *about* Africa and not *for* Africa produce a scenario where Africa (and Africans) becomes the object or recipient of knowledge rather than an agent that creates and distributes knowledge.

Again, the analysis does not seek to suggest that only Africans can teach in African Studies programs, as that would denote a sort of African exceptionalism that would not be meaningful. Rather, the point is that a field of study that truly deserves its name of 'African Studies' should have sufficient representation of 'Africans' not only as things or issues to study but also as teachers, thinkers, and even administrative leaders. Within this context, it makes sense to expect Africans to lead the narrative as a way of dismantling the prevailing whiteness and Eurocentric bias in African Studies pedagogy (Allman, 2019; Arowosegbe, 2014; Falola, 2017; Ndlovu-Gatsheni, 2018).

Being a pilot study, one obvious limitation of our analysis is the lack of depth with which we examined faculty representation and course content. Also, using only the formal African Studies center, department, or program as the unit of analysis is not entirely comprehensive since there are many faculty members who may be considered 'Africanist' but not located within such programs as well as African Studies courses taught in cognate disciplines like Political Science, Geography, and Sociology among others. Nonetheless, the preliminary analysis presented in this chapter still provides some useful insights about the state of representation in today's African Studies programs across some major institutions in North America and Europe. In particular, the findings provide an important basis for more detailed analysis of the pedagogical practices that surround the teaching of African Studies. For instance, within the context of representation, this chapter helps to partially address the questions of 'who' and 'how many' but does not adequately address the issue of why or even how such representational characteristics have been maintained over time. Future research on this topic can, therefore, explore answering such important questions by examining issues like the structural/systemic and program-level practices and constraints that perpetuate academic racism and epistemic imperialism.

To conclude, it is worth briefly discussing what the analysis in this chapter means for decolonization efforts in African Studies and higher education in general. To be sure, representation cannot be equated to decolonization, neither can we say increasing the count of texts written by African scholars on course readings necessarily contribute to the much deeper political issue of decolonization that many people who use this buzzword are probably not willing or able to engage with (see Sondarjee & Andrews, 2023). However, these efforts represent a starting point to imagining a field of study that pursues (pedagogical) practices that help to dismantle systemic racism. In other words, representational diversity is an intricate aspect of the epistemic or pedagogical decolonization needed to disrupt the coloniality of power that sustains whiteness. As recently noted by Posholi (2020: 280), epistemic decolonization requires "working 'outside' the Eurocentric paradigm, for the paradigm might be incapable of revealing and dismantling the epistemic oppression sustaining it." While it may be difficult to step fully 'outside' the Eurocentric paradigm—or, at least, that one cannot fully step outside the knowledge system created by Eurocentric thoughts especially when operating with the same lingua franca and within the existing capitalist rationality—an engagement into the dynamics of representation in relation to who and how the discourse of and about Africa is carried out is important. We hope this chapter, as well as the others in this volume, becomes part of efforts to dismantle whiteness and epistemic oppression without claiming to have completely succeeded in doing so.

Acknowledgements We are very grateful for the research assistance provided by Oliveth Anichebe Orjiocha, whose work involved collecting data and conducting the preliminary analysis that informs this chapter. We also thank Sally Matthews who provided detailed and constructive feedback on an earlier draft as well as participants of a panel at the 2022 Canadian Association of African Studies conference where a version of this chapter was presented. The usual disclaimer applies, however.

References

Acosta, D., & Ackerman-Barger, K. (2017). Breaking the Silence: Time to Talk About Race and Racism. *Academic Medicine, 92*(3), 285–288.

Ake, C. (1982). *Social Science as Imperialism: The Theory of Political Development*. Ibadan University Press.

Alatas, S. F. (2003). Academic Dependency and the Global Division of Labour in the Social Sciences. *Current Sociology, 51*(6), 599–613.

Allman, J. M. (2013). Kwame Nkrumah, African Studies, and the Politics of Knowledge Production in the Black Star of Africa. *The International Journal of African Historical Studies, 46*(2), 181–203.

Allman, J. M. (2019). #HerskovitsMustFall? A Meditation on Whiteness, African Studies, and the Unfinished Business of 1968. *African Studies Review, 62*(3), 6–39.

Andrews, N. (2020). International relations (IR) Pedagogy, Dialogue and Diversity: Taking the IR Course Syllabus Seriously. *All Azimuth: A Journal of Foreign Policy and Peace, 9*(2), 267–282.

Andrews, N. (2022). The Persistent Poverty of Diversity in International Relations and the Emergence of a Critical Canon. *International Studies Perspectives, 23*(4), 425–449.

Andrews, N., & Odoom, I. (2021). Outside the Orthodoxy? The Crisis of IR and the Challenge of Teaching Monocultures. In H. A. Smith & D. J. Hornsby (Eds.), *Teaching International Relations in a Time of Disruption* (pp. 49–61). Palgrave Macmillan.

Andrews, N., & Okpanachi, E. (2012). Trends of Epistemic Oppression and Academic Dependency in Africa's Development: The Need for a New Intellectual Path. *Journal of Pan African Studies, 5*(8), 85–104.

Arday, J., & Mirza, H. S. (Eds.). (2018). *Dismantling Race in Higher Education: Racism, Whiteness and Decolonising the Academy*. Palgrave Macmillan.

Arowosegbe, J. O. (2014). African Studies and the Bias of Eurocentrism. *Social Dynamics, 40*(2), 308–321.

Arowosegbe, J. O. (2016). African Scholars, African Studies and Knowledge Production on Africa. *Africa, 86*(2), 324–338.

Barber, P. H., Hayes, T. B., Johnson, T. L., Márquez-Magaña, L., & 10,234 signatories. (2020). Systemic Racism in Higher Education. *Science, 369*(6510), 1440–1441.

Bertocchi, G., & Dimico, A. (2014). Slavery, Education, and Inequality. *European Economic Review, 70*, 197–209.

Branch, A. (2018). Decolonizing the African Studies Centre. *The Cambridge Journal of Anthropology, 36*(2), 73–91.

Carleton University. (n.d.). *African Studies*. Retrieved from https://carleton.ca/africanstudies/

Daniel, B. J. (2019). Teaching While Black: Racial Dynamics, Evaluations, and the Role of White Females in the Canadian Academy in Carrying the Racism Torch. *Race Ethnicity and Education, 22*(1), 21–37.

Dotson, K. (2012). A Cautionary Tale: On Limiting Epistemic Oppression. *Frontiers: A Journal of Women Studies, 33*(1), 24–47.

Dotson, K. (2014). Conceptualizing Epistemic Oppression. *Social Epistemology, 28*(2), 115–138.

Dutt, K. (2020). Race and Racism in the Geosciences. *Nature Geoscience, 13*(1), 2–3.

Falola, T. (2017). *Africanizing Knowledge: African Studies Across the Disciplines*. Routledge.

Fricker, M. (2017). Evolving Concepts of Epistemic Injustice. In I. J. Kidd, J. Medina, & G. Pohlhaus (Eds.), *The Routledge Handbook of Epistemic Injustice* (pp. 53–60). Routledge.

Hallingberg, B., Turley, R., Segrott, J., Wight, D., Craig, P., Moore, L., & Moore, G. (2018). Exploratory Studies to Decide Whether and How to Proceed with Full-Scale Evaluations of Public Health Interventions: A Systematic Review of Guidance. *Pilot and Feasibility Studies, 4*, 1–12.

Hammett, D. (2010). Political Cartoons, Post-Colonialism and Critical African Studies. *Critical African Studies, 2*(4), 1–26.

Harvard University. (n.d.). *African Studies*. Retrieved from https://aaas.fas.harvard.edu/

Hawkins, D. F. (2021). A Racism Burnout: My Life as a Black Academic. *Race and Justice, 11*(3), 301–317.

Henry, F., & Tator, C. (Eds.). (2009). *Racism in the Canadian University: Demanding Social Justice, Inclusion, and Equity*. University of Toronto Press.

Ibrahim, A., Kitossa, T., Smith, M. S., & Wright, H. K. (Eds.). (2021). *Nuances of Blackness in the Canadian Academy: Teaching, Learning, and Researching While Black*. University of Toronto Press.

Kessi, S., Marks, Z., & Ramugondo, E. (2020). Decolonizing African Studies. *Critical African Studies, 12*(3), 271–282.

Kidd, I. J., & Carel, H. (2017). Epistemic Injustice and Illness. *Journal of Applied Philosophy, 34*(2), 172–190.

Liu, H., Martinez Dy, A., Dar, S., & Brewis, D. (2021). Anti-Racism in the Age of White Supremacy and Backlash. *Equality, Diversity and Inclusion: An International Journal, 40*(2), 105–113.

Macpherson, W. (1999). *The Stephen Lawrence Inquiry, Cm 4262-I*. The Stationery Office. Retrieved from https://assets.publishing.service.gov.uk/government/uploads/system/uploads/attachment_data/file/277111/4262.pdf

Mazrui, A. A. (1992). Towards Diagnosing and Treating Cultural Dependency: The Case of the African University. *International Journal of Educational Development, 12*(2), 95–111.

McGill University. (n.d.). *African Studies*. Retrieved from https://www.mcgill.ca/islamicstudies/undergraduate/african-studies

Mendonça, S., Pereira, J., & Ferreira, M. E. (2018). Gatekeeping African Studies: What Does "Editormetrics" Indicate About Journal Governance? *Scientometrics, 117*, 1513–1534.

Mirza, H. S. (2018). Racism in Higher Education: What then, can be Done? In J. Arday & H. S. Mirza (Eds.), *Dismantling Race in Higher Education: Racism, Whiteness and Decolonising the Academy* (pp. 3–23). Palgrave Macmillan.

Monarreza, P. M., Zimmt, J. B., Clement, A. M., Gearty, W., Jacisin, J. J., Jenkins, K. M., & Thompson, C. M. (2022). Our Past Creates Our Present: A Brief Overview of Racism and Colonialism in Western Paleontology. *Paleobiology, 48*(2), 173–185.

Ndlovu-Gatsheni, S. J. (2018). *Epistemic Freedom in Africa: Deprovincialization and Decolonization*. Routledge.

Noda, O. (2020). Epistemic Hegemony: The Western Straitjacket and Post-colonial Scars in Academic Publishing. *Revista Brasileira De Política Internacional, 63*(1), 1–23.

Odoom, I., & Andrews, N. (2017). What/Who is Still Missing in International Relations Scholarship? Situating Africa as an Agent in IR Theorising. *Third World Quarterly, 38*(1), 42–60.

Oxford University. (n.d.). *African Studies Center*. Retrieved from https://www.africanstudies.ox.ac.uk/

Phillipson, R. (1996). Linguistic Imperialism: African Perspectives. *ELT Journal, 50*(2), 160–167.

Phillipson, R. (2013). *Linguistic Imperialism Continued*. Routledge.

Posholi, L. (2020). Epistemic Decolonization as Overcoming the Hermeneutical Injustice of Eurocentrism. *Philosophical Papers, 49*(2), 279–304.

Princeton University. (n.d.). *African Studies*. Retrieved from https://piirs.princeton.edu/afs

Sondarjee, M., & Andrews, N. (2023). Decolonizing International Relations and Development Studies: What's in a Buzzword? *International Journal* (forthcoming).

Stanford University. (n.d.). *African Studies Programs*. Retrieved from https://africanstudies.stanford.edu/

Summerhill, W. (2010). Colonial Institutions, Slavery, Inequality, and Development: Evidence from São Paulo, Brazil. *Slavery, Inequality, and Development: Evidence from Sao Paulo, Brazil*. MPRA Paper No. 22162, 1–58. Retrieved from https://mpra.ub.uni-muenchen.de/22162/

University of British Columbia. (n.d.). *African Studies*. Retrieved from https://www.ubc.ca/search/?q=African+studies#gsc.tab=0&gsc.q=African%20studies&gsc.page=1

University of California San Diego. (n.d.). *Africana Studies*. Retrieved from https://catalog.ucsd.edu/curric/AFRI.html?_ga=2.197307049.768522776.1650304017-1851027485.1650304017

University of Edinburgh. (n.d.). *Africana Studies*. Retrieved from https://www.ed.ac.uk/studying/undergraduate/degrees/index.php?action=search&searchString=African+Studies

University of Minnesota. (n.d.). *African and American Studies*. Retrieved from https://cla.umn.edu/aaas

University of Toronto. (n.d.). *Africana Studies*. Retrieved from https://www.utsc.utoronto.ca/dgds/african-studies

University of Washington. (n.d.). *African Studies*. Retrieved from https://jsis.washington.edu/africa/

University of Wisconsin. (n.d.). *Africana Studies Program*. Retrieved from https://africa.wisc.edu/

Vanjani, R., Pitts, A., & Aurora, P. (2022). Dismantling Structural Racism in the Academic Residency Clinic. *New England Journal of Medicine, 386*(21), 2054–2058.

Webometrics. (n.d.). *Universities Ranking*. Retrieved from https://www.webometrics.info/en/world

York University. (n.d.). *African Studies*. Retrieved from https://www.yorku.ca/laps/sosc/afrs/

CHAPTER 5

Constructing Knowledge About Africa in a South African University Classroom: Living Creatively with the Colonial Library

Sally Matthews

Introduction

To effectively represent Africa for what it truly is, requires the experience of being African … as this presents the view of an insider and relays the story in its most authentic way.

Ideally, decolonized African Studies would involve African Studies and African literature dominantly produced by African people in their unfiltered voices.

A decolonized African Studies would be curated by African scholars and would not be contested by any outside opinion. African Studies would be a system of education that caters for the true experience of Africans first-hand and not based on western hegemony as the colonialists and imperialists'

S. Matthews (✉)
Department of Political and International Studies, Rhodes University, Makhanda, South Africa
e-mail: s.matthews@ru.ac.za

N. Andrews and N. E. Khalema (eds.), *Decolonizing African Studies Pedagogies*, Political Pedagogies,
https://doi.org/10.1007/978-3-031-37442-5_5

views are more aimed at their superiority rather than the true meaning of African Studies and the experiences of black people in Africa.

These quotes are adapted from undergraduate students' responses to the exam question "What would a decolonized African Studies look like?"[1] I begin with these quotes as they illustrate a viewpoint I frequently encounter in my classroom. This viewpoint is premised on two key assumptions: firstly, that western authors, perhaps deliberately, distort African realities and, secondly, that African authors can easily access and express accurate and authentic views on Africa.

The course in which these views were expressed is an African Studies course in which students are encouraged to think critically about the politics of knowledge production and the representation of Africa in scholarly writing. We begin the course by looking back on the history of African Studies and the implications of this history. African Studies arose as a scholarly discipline in the west and initially entailed non-African authors writing about Africa for a non-African audience. In our African Studies course, we look at why African Studies began this way and at how this way of writing about Africa has been contested. My classes are large (usually over 100 students take the course) and students respond to this section of the course in a variety of ways. Some students adopt a view like the one I describe above in which they argue that in order to decolonize knowledge production on Africa, we need to replace western authors (who they believe write falsehoods on Africa) with African authors (who they think will be able to write truths). As I will show below, I think this is an oversimplification. The challenge for me as an educator is how to respond to it in the classroom.

A couple of years ago, during a postgraduate course on African writing on Africa, I encountered a different but also worrying response to the politics of knowledge production from some of my postgraduate students. The course I was teaching introduced students to V. Y. Mudimbe's (1988) book *The Invention of Africa* and spent some time debating his concept of the colonial library. Mudimbe uses this concept to refer both to the texts produced by colonial writers on Africa and to the broader system of knowledge and meaning that these texts created. Here, and in other writing (such as Mudimbe, 1991, 1994), Mudimbe suggests that even attempts to challenge and reject the colonial library are in some ways

[1] All three are slightly edited extracts from student essays submitted in November 2021.

structured by the concepts and system of meanings inaugurated by the colonial library. For example, he controversially declares that "Modern African thought seems somehow to be basically a product of the west" (Mudimbe, 1988: 185) and that even the most rigorous challenges to the colonial library "are possible and thinkable only insofar as they actualize themselves within those same intellectual fields" (Mudimbe, 1991: 8). For the most part, my postgraduate students found Mudimbe's arguments convincing but also devastating. Here are two examples of postgraduate students' responses to Mudimbe's argument:

> I agree with Mudimbe that escaping the colonial library is difficult ... Thus, accepting being othered is the proper approach to the colonial library ....
>
> No matter how correct or efficient an African response [to the colonial library] might be, it tends to still be within the confines of western discourse. It makes me wonder if the colonial library can really be escaped.[2]

The students feared that the colonial library could not be escaped and, therefore, that African scholars may have no choice but to participate in colonial forms of knowledge production on Africa.

These different responses to my attempts to get students to think about the politics of knowledge production pose significant pedagogical challenges. In this paper, I explain what I think these pedagogical challenges are and reflect, very tentatively, on how we might respond to them. The discussion in this chapter is intended to complement other chapters by exploring some of the questions that arise when we try to rethink pedagogy in the context of decolonizing the study of Africa. Much of the debate on decolonization focuses on the content of research and teaching about Africa, with less attention being given to pedagogy. We cannot just change the books we prescribe and the scholars we revere while keeping our pedagogical practices unchanged. This chapter, like the book as a whole, reflects on the complex and difficult project of trying to change our pedagogies as part of the process of rethinking African Studies as a whole. While those teaching in different contexts may not experience the same challenges, I suspect that my students' responses to the politics of knowledge production are shared by others and, therefore, I hope that my reflections may be helpful beyond my immediate context.

[2] These examples come from blogs written by the students as part of the course.

What is Worrying About My Students' Views?

I need to begin by explaining what I find worrying about the views my students express. As mentioned above, I am concerned that some students misunderstand and underestimate the nature of the problem of knowledge production on Africa. Some students believe that western scholars, sometimes deliberately, produce knowledge about Africa that is false, and that a true account of African realities can easily be accessed and expressed by African scholars who are not motivated to distort such realities. This is an oversimplification of the problem of the politics of knowledge production in that it does not consider the possibility that African scholars may share the same epistemological framework as western scholars and, therefore, produce very similar accounts. Furthermore, this kind of view implies a form of essentialism whereby one's identity determines one's perspective such that non-African scholars are unable to see and understand what African scholars, by virtue of their Africanness, can apparently easily see.

The postgraduate students I discuss above came to different, but no less worrying, conclusions. These students accepted that addressing the problem of knowledge production is not so easy and that one cannot simply substitute African scholars for western scholars and think that we will then have decolonized African Studies. An understanding of the complexity of the politics of knowledge production led some students to despair because of the impossibility of producing knowledge on Africa which fully escapes the colonial library. They feared that because African scholars are constrained by the colonial discourses that have historically shaped scholarship on Africa, it is impossible to overcome the coloniality of knowledge production.

These two sets of responses are quite different, but underlying them is a shared assumption. Both responses suggest that what is needed is for African scholars to step outside the colonial library and produce authentic African knowledge untainted by the colonial library. The undergraduates are more confident than the postgraduates that this can be done, but both sets of students suggest that the goal for African scholars is to shake off the chains of colonial discourses and to produce African knowledge uncontaminated by any traces of the colonial library. In the rest of this chapter, I intend, firstly, to argue against this view and, secondly, to reflect on how to respond to it in the classroom. In so doing, I will draw particularly on the scholarship of V.Y. Mudimbe, whose influential texts reflect carefully and critically on the politics of knowledge production on Africa.

Escaping the Colonial Library

The politics of knowledge production on Africa is receiving considerable attention as part of broader calls to "decolonize" university spaces (see, e.g., Andrews & Okpanachi, 2012; Branch, 2018; Kessi et al., 2020; Ndlovu-Gatsheni, 2018, 2020; Nyamnjoh, 2019). However, such contestation is not new. As Desai (2001), Grovogui (2006) and Zachernuk (2000) demonstrate, African intellectuals were already engaging with and challenging colonial discourses during the colonial era. Contestation around knowledge production continued and intensified after the formal end of colonialism. Postcolonial scholarship has played an important role in exposing the Eurocentrism that distorted scholarship on former colonies. For example, Edward Said's (1978) *Orientalism* reveals the Eurocentrism in scholarly work on the non-west, and V. Y. Mudimbe's (1988, 1991, 1994) work details how Africa was "invented" through western scholarship. In more recent years, writing on coloniality and decoloniality is also highlighting how coloniality persists even in a supposedly postcolonial era due in part to the persistence of colonial epistemologies (Grosfoguel, 2011; Maldonado-Torres, 2016; Mbembe, 2016; Mignolo & Walsh, 2018; Ndlovu-Gatsheni, 2018, 2020).

Critics of Eurocentrism and coloniality call on African scholars to escape the shackles of the epistemological framework which has governed how Africa has been represented. Like many of my students, scholars who have reflected on how mainstream scholarship misrepresents the non-western world, want to think and write about Africa (and other parts of the Global South) in ways that are not subject to the constraints of the colonial library. Yet such scholars' lengthy engagement with the colonial library (and its critics) has led them to recognize the impossibility of fully escaping the constraints of the colonial library. For example, in a key text within the decolonial school of thought, Grosfoguel (2007: 18) tells us that to develop decolonial knowledge "we need to go 'outside' our paradigms, approaches, disciplines and fields". A few pages later, however, he laments that "There is no absolute outside to this system" (Grosfoguel, 2007: 24). Another influential decolonial scholar, Mignolo, calls us to "to delink (to detach) from [the colonial] structure of knowledge in order to engage in an epistemic reconstitution", but also says that it cannot be denied that "there is no outside [the colonial matrix of power]: we are all in it" (Mignolo, 2017).[3] Writing specifically on Africa, Ndlovu tells us that a decolonial perspective is not possible "without first transcending the current colonial knowledge production system", (2018: 96) but also stresses that we must reject the idea of "some form of mythical indigenous knowledge that is untouched by western modernity" (Ndlovu, 2018: 110). Similarly, Wai (2015: 287) talks about the need to imagine an African system of knowledge that is "no longer contaminated by the power-knowledge regimes of the [colonial] library" but also laments that "the ghost of the modern colonial gaze and its epistemic and representational schemas is always lurking in the shadows of attempts at looking back or speaking back" (Wai, 2020).

These scholars all help us see the difficult position that African scholars occupy: given the harm that the colonial library has wrought on Africa, they must try to escape its constraints. However, reflection on the nature of the colonial library shows how difficult such an escape is. V. Y. Mudimbe's careful, thoughtful engagement with this challenging situation helps us think through whether and how we can produce knowledge that is not complicit with coloniality (see Mudimbe, 1988, 1991, 1994). A key feature of Mudimbe's work is his careful, critical but sympathetic engagement with the writing of scholars who try in some way to present Africa differently to the way it was presented in the prevailing scholarship of the time. In such engagement, he shows us both how such scholars fail to fully transcend the colonial discourses they challenge, but also—and perhaps more importantly—how their work nevertheless disrupts and unsettles such colonial discourses.

A brief note is needed regarding why I want to revisit V. Y. Mudimbe's work when there is so much newer writing on the coloniality of knowledge production. As Wai (2020) argues, Mudimbe's work has been sorely neglected and sometimes misinterpreted, but is profoundly relevant to current discussions around decoloniality. Therefore, it is useful to bring his decades-long reflections (and the work of others who have built upon these reflections) into the contemporary conversation about how African scholars ought to relate and respond to the colonial library.

[3] Mignolo's position is a complicated one as he argues that there is an "exteriority" to the colonial matrix of power, even while there is not "outside" to it. For a discussion of his position, see Escobar (2004: 218–219).

As mentioned earlier, one of Mudimbe's most well-known insights is his argument that there is a "colonial library" which has constructed Africa as Europe's inferior Other and that even the most robust attempts to challenge colonial discourses end up reiterating them in some way. According to Mudimbe (1994: xv) even authors who claim to be writing "Afrocentric" accounts of Africa use "categories and conceptual systems that depend on a western epistemological order". His analysis of the writing of a range of western and African scholars reveals the resilience of the colonial library, showing how the system of representations and epistemological grids introduced by the colonial library inform and constrain attempts to challenge and evade it (Mudimbe, 1988, 1991, 1994). However, this analysis is not as negative and critical as the above description suggests, for Mudimbe shows both how various texts reiterate aspects of the colonial library *and* how they challenge and disrupt it. Mudimbe (1988, 1991, 1994) engages with the thinking of a range of different scholars, each of whom tries in some way to challenge or transform the prevailing discourses on Africa. For example, he explores various twentieth-century Christian African intellectuals, highlighting how their attempts to domesticate Christianity form an epistemological break with earlier missionary discourse on Africa (Mudimbe, 1988: 44–64). While Mudimbe believes that Christian African intellectuals have questioned and disrupted missionary discourse on Africa, he concludes his discussion by asking (but not quite answering) the question of whether or not they have really achieved an "epistemological rupture". As I read Mudimbe, his suggestion is that such discourses do indeed pose a challenge to colonial discourses on Africa, but at the same time, they express this challenge using epistemological "grids" which only make sense from the perspective of these colonial discourses. Thus, they pose a meaningful epistemological challenge to colonial discourses, but do not completely escape them.

Mudimbe (1988: 64–97) makes similar points when he looks at the ways in which African thinkers have engaged with anthropology and with Marxist ideology. Again, Mudimbe shows awareness both of the limits of various attempts to respond to the "othering" of Africa and of their great potential. Mudimbe's position is never a simplistic one: he resists contrasting one set of completely false claims about Africa (say, for example, colonial discourses) with another set of completely different and supposedly true claims about Africa (produced, for example, by critical African scholars). Rather, he painstakingly shows how the movements of resistance to colonial discourses (such as *négritude* and African interpretations of Christianity or Marxism) are produced by scholars who are steeped in colonial thinking and who do not fully escape the constraints of such thinking, but who nevertheless do cause epistemological shifts and ruptures. He also resists a neat dichotomy in which all European thinkers perpetuate colonial discourses while all African thinkers disrupt them. Instead of such a simplistic dichotomy, he shows us how some European thinkers participate in destabilizing colonial discourses and how African thinkers reiterate aspects of colonial thinking, even while they also resist them. He also makes it clear that scholars can simultaneously repeat and challenge aspects of colonial thinking. For example, Mudimbe says that E. W. Blyden's thinking shares with colonial discourses a belief in the need for a civilizing mission and for racial segregation, but at the same time unsettles colonial assumptions so profoundly that his thought can be called "an annunciating sign of [an epistemological] rupture" (Mudimbe, 1988: 80–81).

Mudimbe's work is helpful in challenging simplistic responses to the realization that much knowledge on Africa misrepresents Africa. As Mudimbe (1988, 1994) shows, the very idea of Africa is an invention of colonial discourses and the various forms of resistance to colonial discourses only make sense in relation to these colonial discourses. For example, he shows how the *négritude* movement has multiple influences including the Bible, French literature and various anthropological texts and that its principal proponents are "drawn from among those first and best assimilated to western culture and thought" (Mudimbe, 1988: 87–88). But this does not mean, argues Mudimbe, that *négritude* was a failed and false attempt to disrupt colonial thinking. In the light of the challenges to colonial discourses made by *négritude* and other African responses to colonial knowledge production, "[a] shift has occurred" whereby scholarship on Africa must now take seriously African systems and experiences (Mudimbe 1988: 89). Therefore, *négritude* and other attempts to challenge colonial discourses have succeeded in unsettling and shifting colonial thinking, even if they have not fully escaped the constraints of the colonial library.

One possible way to respond to Mudimbe's demonstration of the intransigence of the colonial library is to argue that while the various thinkers he discusses fail to escape the colonial library, thinkers who are more distant from the world of formal education (such as "traditional" leaders and other indigenous knowledge bearers) may be able to produce knowledge that escapes the colonial library. This response suggests that there is a world untouched by colonialism that can be drawn upon to produce untainted alternatives to the colonial library. But is there such a space? Even the most remote spaces in Africa have been influenced in some way by ideas and technologies that come from "outside" and, as the anthropological debate around the "invention of tradition" shows, seemingly precolonial traditions are often colonial inventions or distortions (Ranger, 1983; Spear, 2015). Thus, while rethinking knowledge on Africa requires us to be attentive to marginalized African thinkers and concepts, seeking out "traditional" and "indigenous" thinkers and concepts does not ultimately represent an escape from the colonial library. As Mudimbe (1988, 1994) demonstrates, even the very idea that it is possible to talk of something like an "African" perspective is itself an invention of the colonial library. The haunting presence of the colonial library means that rather than trying to escape it, we need to think about how to engage critically, creatively and subversively with it.

To do so, we need to think beyond the two alternatives suggested by some of my students. We need to acknowledge the impossibility of replacing faulty, Eurocentric thinking with a truthful, African alternative, as some of my undergraduate students long to do, while also not succumbing to the despondency shown by some of my postgraduate students when confronted by the structuring power of the colonial library. I propose that Mudimbe's work (and the work of scholars he inspired) offers us a better way in that he rejects the idea that there are two distinct knowledge systems: a Eurocentric one which generates untruths and an African one which correctly understands and represents the African condition. The picture Mudimbe presents is more complicated and creative. A further noteworthy feature of Mudimbe's position is that his preoccupation is not with dislodging "false" representations and replacing them with "true" ones. Rather than treating Eurocentric representations of Africa as falsehoods, Mudimbe prefers to describe them as "inventions" or "myths" or "fables" (see Fraiture, 2013; Wai, 2020). By using words like this, Mudimbe is not saying something like "European scholars made up fables about Africa. I, on the contrary, will write the truth". Indeed, as Wai (2020) points out, Mudimbe says "My own text might be only a fable or a parable about other fables" (Mudimbe, 1991: xxi). Thus, he is not trying to contrast Eurocentric lies about Africa with African truths about Africa. Rather, by using this kind of language, he is saying that

Africa is "never given, but constituted through the ideological and epistemic gazes of colonial modernity" (Wai, 2020: 65). He is also suggesting that the way to respond to this invention of Africa is through counter-invention, through creative reappropriation of the myths and fables which have produced Africa's alterity, and through a "postcolonial re-fashioning that opens up different avenues" (Wai, 2020: 65). Therefore, Mudimbe's position is a complex and nuanced one (unlike a mis-guided position which simply seeks to replace falsehoods on Africa with truths), and is a potentially optimistic one (unlike a reductive position which despairs at the thought of the inescapability of the colonial library).

I suspect that some will find this kind of position unsatisfactory as it seems to create an equivalence between two sets of myths—one in which colonial thinkers create an African "other" and another whereby African thinkers try to create a more empowering alternative. Critics might feel that describing both as "myths" devalues African challenges to colonial discourses. For example, Mudimbe (1988: 97) says that Cheikh Anta Diop's rewriting of African history might be a useful "mobilizing myth" which could bring about a new political order, while Amadiume (1998: 2), in contrast, sets out to use Diop's work to "establish an authentic narrative of African history" with which to counter European falsehoods. Unlike Amadiume, Mudimbe is sceptical of the possibility of slaying falsehoods and replacing them with truths. Indeed, he is openly sympathetic to the claim that all history is myth (Mudimbe, 1988: 192). But Mudimbe's position should not be misunderstood as a relativist and nihilistic position which ultimately gives us no grounds for choosing between various competing "myths" about Africa. He does not sit on the fence cynically surveying different fables about Africa. Rather, he celebrates and seeks to advance the emergence and increased prominence of African intellectuals, but what he celebrates is not their supposed ability to replace European falsehoods with African truths. Rather, he celebrates their very existence, their agency and their ability to disrupt European insistence on Africa's alterity by confronting it with their own concepts and interpretations. Thus, Mudimbe concludes *The Invention of Africa* by proclaiming that there is "good news" in the existence of the African thinker who has "the passion of a subject-object who refuses to vanish" and who has acquired "the freedom of thinking of himself or herself as the starting point of an absolute discourse" (Mudimbe, 1988: 200). What is worth celebrating is not the replacement of Eurocentric lies with Afrocentric truths, but the agency of Africans who are insisting on shaping the discourse on Africa and are not willing to be "objects" interpreted by others.

This conclusion shows that Mudimbe's position does not need to lead us to the despair that was the response of some of my postgraduate students when confronted with his arguments about the intransigence of the colonial library. The inability of African thinkers to fully extricate themselves from the web of colonial discourse does not need to close off the possibility that such thinkers can produce creative and regenerative alternatives. Colonial discourses have indeed been unsettled and ruptured by various critical engagements with them and, through such critical engagement, African scholars are changing the politics of knowledge production in all kinds of important ways. They might not fully escape the constraints of the colonial library and we should not imagine that their perspective is a "true" one that should not itself be questioned, but we can see that the Eurocentric invention of Africa is being robustly challenged and that the epistemological framework through which Africa has been interpreted is being unsettled and ruptured.

While it is, I believe, possible to interpret Mudimbe's project as an optimistic rather than despairing one, his discussion of the intransigence of the colonial library suggests that such optimism has to be tempered with vigilance. Precisely because the colonial library is so intransigent—we labour, says Wai (2020) "under the suffocating 'odeur' of an omnipresent father-figure: European colonialism and its epistemic and ideological gazes"—we cannot afford a naïve optimism about our attempts to produce knowledge that disrupts or evades colonial discourses. Therefore, we have to adopt a kind of epistemological vigilance whereby we continually interrogate our own and other scholars' representations of Africa (see Wai, 2015: 287). We cannot assume that we have been able to produce an alternative African epistemology which we can triumphantly wield against any Eurocentrism we may encounter, but must rather move forward with caution and humility subjecting each attempt to produce new knowledge to careful scrutiny.

Back to the Classroom—Responding to Exclusionary Forms of Essentialism

As the foregoing discussion makes clear, my views on the politics of knowledge production on Africa are different from at least some of my students. I do not share the view, held by some of my undergraduate students, that by promoting the work of African scholars, we will automatically be able to produce "true" knowledge about Africa rather than the falsehoods produced by Eurocentric scholars. I also do not share the despair expressed by some of my postgraduate students about the seeming impossibility of escaping the colonial library. This means I need to think carefully about why many of my students, over the years, have expressed the views I summarize earlier and what the appropriate pedagogical response to these views is.

The first pedagogical challenge I would like to touch on is the challenge of how to respond to the essentialism that informs some of my students' approaches to knowledge production on Africa. This essentialism allows them to be optimistic about the possibility of changing knowledge production on Africa by replacing western authors with African ones. When discussing the politics of knowledge production on Africa, many students make claims which suggest that western writers are incapable of understanding African realities and that, by contrast, African writers can authentically represent these realities. Students thus make claims like "Only an African can truly understand what it is like to live in Africa" or "Only black women can authentically represent black women's experiences". Such claims are premised upon essentialism which Gandhi (2015: 156) defines as the assumption that "a group or category of objects/people share some defining features exclusive to the members of this particular group or category". In the case of knowledge production, an essentialist may think that only members of a particular group can authentically and fairly represent it. The problem with this view is that it homogenizes and stereotypes the group it essentializes (Eide, 2016; Gandhi, 2015: 156). Essentialist accounts of group differences present such differences as if they are "natural" and fail to account for the way in which essentialist accounts construct and perpetuate such differences rather than simply reporting on them (Narayan, 1998). Essentialist thinking elides differences between people and sets up dichotomies whereby one can distinguish between "true believers and belongers on the one hand and outsiders on the other" (Kurzwelly et al., 2020). If we are to be really attentive to the diversity and complexity of human existence, we cannot accept the idea that members of particular groups share an "essence" which makes them all fundamentally similar. However, while I do not endorse the essentialist positions some of my students apparently favour, I have struggled to find a pedagogically responsible way to respond when students express these kinds of views. Furthermore, I think it unsurprising and understandable that students express such views. As they come to see the extent to which white scholars have dominated scholarship on Africa and have misrepresented African realities, it makes sense for students to assume that African scholars will be able to write more responsibly and fairly about Africa.

A very useful resource in thinking through how to respond to essentialist claims in the classroom is bell hooks' (1994: 77–92) engagement with Diana Fuss's (1989) discussion of essentialism. Fuss (1989) critiques essentialism, summarizing the various problems with the view that only people from a certain group can authentically produce knowledge about that group. In her response to Fuss, Hooks (1994: 77–92) recognizes the limits and dangers of essentialism but argues that Fuss's discussion presents marginalized students' embracing of essentialism as a "problem" to be solved, while not being attentive to the conditions which result in this embracing of essentialism. Hooks (1994) points out that dominant groups also promote essentialism, although they might not make explicitly essentialist claims. For example, the confidence with which members of dominant groups express their views is often founded on a kind of essentialism in that it is assumed that white westerners can write on any topic in a neutral and scholarly way. Therefore, essentialist claims do not only emerge in the classroom when a black student insists that their experience gives them authority of some kind. Essentialist beliefs about who can speak with authority lurk in the background even when they are not named. Hooks (1994: 84) further suggests that students who feel marginalized in classroom spaces might use essentialist claims as a way of "asserting voice". According to Hooks (1994: 88), "it is in a context where the experiential knowledge of students is being denied or negated that they may feel most determined to impress upon listeners both its value and its superiority to other ways of knowing".

My students cannot be assumed to feel and act similarly to students in classrooms in the United States several decades ago. Their context is very different. One significant difference is that my students are in classrooms where most of their fellow students are black and almost all African citizens. While the teaching staff at my university remain disproportionately white, in recent years, my students will have been taught by both black and white academics. This is different to the American students taught by Fuss and hooks, whose classmates and lecturers were almost all white. However, for reasons relating to the nature of desegregation in South African schools and universities, many of my black students are likely to have been in learning spaces where they felt marginalized.[4] Furthermore, my students are very aware that academic knowledge production remains overwhelmingly dominated by white western scholars as most of the texts they read as university students are written by white scholars based in the west. Therefore, it is likely that some of my students' enthusiasm for essentialist claims to authority is rooted in an attempt to grasp at authority in a context where they feel marginalized and in which they see that the knowledge of people like them has been denigrated and ignored.

This means that if I respond critically or dismissively to such essentialist claims, I risk silencing students who already feel marginalized. This risk is further intensified by my race—I am white—in that such criticism could be experienced as one more instance of a white person in power discrediting African claims to authoritative knowledge production. Furthermore, as one of the goals of my course on African Studies is precisely to get students to think about how to challenge western dominance of knowledge production on Africa, there is something ironic and counterproductive going on when I shut down attempts by black students to insist upon the authority of Africans to dominate knowledge production on Africa. Hooks (1994: 84) suggests that if we want to avoid students' putting forward exclusionary essentialist claims, we can "circumvent this possible misuse of power by bringing to the classroom pedagogical strategies that affirm their presence, their right to speak, in multiple ways on diverse topics". I do not know whether and to what extent I have been able to do this (and I suspect there are particular challenges that arise when trying to do this as a white person), but I think that Hooks' (1994) proposed way of engaging such students is preferable to a response that criticizes or undermines such students' views. My current strategy is to

[4] For example, many of my students come from former white schools in which the student body is now mostly black, but the teaching staff remain overwhelmingly white. Racist incidents happen with depressing regularity at such schools as reported in various recent news articles—see Joorst (2019) and Xaso (2021) for examples.

seek to affirm students' presence and right to speak by foregrounding peer discussion and interaction as a learning tool in class.[5] This has the advantage of displacing my authority as a white person and allowing students to work their own way to potentially rejecting exclusionary forms of essentialism through attending to the views of others. However, a potential disadvantage of such a strategy is that it does not disrupt other hierarchies in the classroom and so some students may silence others. Furthermore, such a strategy is not relevant when it comes to assessment—how does one assess an essay full of essentialist claims? Sometimes students' desire to challenge and reject Eurocentric approaches to Africa leads them to make some rather essentialist claims about who can produce "authentic" knowledge on Africa. One limited way I am seeking to address this challenge is to ask quite specific and focused questions which encourage students to engage thoughtfully and critically with key thinkers' ideas (such as "Compare and contrast the arguments of Author X and Y in relation to the decolonization of African Studies") rather than asking more general questions (such as "How can African Studies be decolonized?") which tend to invite vague and essentialist claims.

Engaging Creatively with the Colonial Library in the Classroom

Expressions of exclusionary essentialism are not, however, the most challenging aspect of the way in which some students respond to the politics of knowledge production on Africa. I find a bigger and more intractable issue to be the broader question of whether and how we might produce knowledge on Africa differently. As I indicate earlier, some of my students suggest that authentic and accurate knowledge about Africa could be produced through a simple substitution of African scholars for western scholars. However, other students are less confident that such substitution addresses the problem. Such students are concerned that the intractability of the colonial library (as demonstrated by Mudimbe) means that all attempts to produce knowledge about Africa are at risk of "conceptual contamination" by the colonial library (Wai, forthcoming). This conclusion can lead to a feeling of despair and disillusionment.

[5] I should note that the shift to online learning due to the COVID-19 pandemic disrupted my attempts to foreground peer interaction and discussion, and, as we move back to classroom teaching, I will need to revisit the earlier strategies I had been using.

As I argue above, I do not think that awareness of the apparent inescapability of the colonial library needs to lead us to despair. Mudimbe's work suggests that resistance to the colonial library will tend to be contaminated, at least to some extent, with aspects of that library, but that this does not mean that such resistance does not produce epistemological shifts and ruptures. We cannot neatly step outside of colonial discourses and produce a different, completely independent African alternative. But we can find creative and potentially liberating ways to engage with the colonial library. We can appropriate aspects of the colonial library for our own ends, we can turn its assumptions upside-down, we can unsettle its foundations. Mudimbe shows us that this is what African scholars (as well as critical western scholars) have been doing even during the height of colonialism. While such attempts are not purified of all traces of the colonial library, they are also not simply new iterations of colonial discourses, nor do they leave the colonial library unchanged.

The question, from the perspective of the classroom, is how to get this idea across to students. In the past, I think I have often gone about it the wrong way: I have often presented students with a "mainstream" text about Africa (usually authored by a western scholar) and then contrasted it with a critical text (usually authored by an African scholar). So, for example, I would present a prominent article on statehood in Africa (such as one by Clapham, 2001; Jackson, 1993) and then contrast it with a critique by an African scholar (such as one by Grovogui, 2002; Wai, 2012). We would then proceed to the next topic, again subjecting mainstream scholarship to African critiques.

My intention with this structure was to get students to approach knowledge critically, to be aware of the shortcomings of much mainstream scholarly writing on Africa, and to recognize the importance of promoting African authorship. However, by pitting western discourses against African responses in this way, I could be creating the impression that the politics of knowledge production is a kind of sparring match between two separate bodies of knowledge, one produced mostly by western scholars and the other by African scholars. In so doing, I have unintentionally invited students to make the mistakes I decry above: to assume that we can easily differentiate between colonial and decolonized texts and to assume that scholars' identities determine what kind of knowledge they produce. This course structure works very well in some ways and is easy for students to navigate. However, a messier, more complicated structure might better enable students to appreciate how resisting colonial discourses on Africa is complex but possible. By presenting students with a range of different views from authors positioned in various ways, I may encourage them to see the complex way in which knowledge is created and contested. They might then be able to see that each critical engagement with previous writing on Africa can help to unsettle some assumptions or open up some fresh insights or rupture a few lazy misrepresentations and, in so doing, can shift the representation of Africa. Students would then be invited to be both sympathetic to and critical of each text they read. Perhaps they might then adopt a similar attitude to that of Mudimbe who, as discussed earlier, engages with a broad range of scholars in a way that avoids sorting them into two neat piles: evil colonial discourses to the one side, perfect anticolonial alternatives to the other. Instead, each text is taken seriously and interrogated carefully both to learn from the text and to go beyond it. If we can encourage students to adopt this kind of attitude, then they will not make the mistake of being over-confident about the ability of African scholars to produce non-Eurocentric alternatives. Furthermore, this approach may also help students not to despair when they realize that a favoured text is "contaminated" in some way by the colonial library, as they will not then imagine that such a text needs to be relegated to the "evil Eurocentric discourses" pile of texts. Rather, they can both learn from and try to move beyond each text they encounter.

Conclusion

This reflection is an attempt to think through how we can best facilitate the creation of better knowledge about Africa in university classrooms. In my South African context, students are very keen to contest the way in which knowledge about Africa has been produced. They are eager, we could say, to challenge and try to dismantle the colonial library which has constructed Africa as Europe's other. However, as I show above, my students' critical orientation towards colonial discourses on Africa can lead them to think that what is needed is to produce a kind of pure, untainted African alternative to Eurocentric discourses and that, if this is not possible, there is no way to defeat the colonial representation of Africa. In this paper, I have tried to draw attention to Mudimbe's approach to the colonial library to map out a different way of thinking about decolonizing the curriculum. I suggest that Mudimbe's approach is one that recognizes the intransigence of the colonial library, but that celebrates

African authors' ability to challenge and disrupt existing discourses about Africa. This approach accepts that we cannot neatly step outside the colonial library to produce a completely decolonized alternative, but at the same time cautiously celebrates the emergence of an African thinker who, today, has "the freedom of thinking of himself or herself as the starting point of an absolute discourse" (Mudimbe, 1988: 200). The second half of the paper tentatively reflects on how such an approach could be worked out in the classroom by discussing some of the pedagogical strategies I have attempted to use in the classroom. While there is much enthusiasm, and likewise some ideological and reactionary resistance, to the idea that our university classrooms need to be "decolonized", university lecturers can often feel at a loss when trying to think about specific pedagogical strategies that can be used to achieve such decolonization. Honest discussion of the pedagogical strategies we are attempting (whether successful or not) can help us come up with new ideas. Furthermore, policymakers who are seeking to encourage less Eurocentric university curricula need practical illustrations to build on if they are to rework education policy. The examples described above are illustrations of possible pedagogical strategies that can be used in re-imagining Africa in the university classroom. I offer them up here in the hope that they, along with the insights from the other chapters in this book, can make a small contribution to ongoing conversations about how to generate creative new engagements with existing thinking on Africa and open up new ways to write and teach about the continent.

References

Adeleke, T. (2009). *The Case Against Afrocentrism.* University Press of Mississippi.

Amadiume, I. (1998). *Re-inventing Africa: Matriarchy, Religion and Culture.* Zed Books.

Andrews, N., & Okpanachi, E. (2012). Trends of Epistemic Oppression and Academic Dependency in Africa's Development: The Need for a New Intellectual Path. *Journal of Pan African Studies, 5*(8), 85–104.

Asante, M. K. (1987). *The Afrocentric Idea.* Temple University Press.

Asante, M. K. (2007). *An Afrocentric Manifesto: Towards an African Renaissance.* Polity.

Branch, A. (2018). Decolonizing the African Studies Centre. *The Cambridge Journal of Anthropology, 36*(2), 73–91.

Clapham, C. (2001). Rethinking African States. *African Security Review, 10*(3), 7–16.

Desai, G. (2001). *Subject to Colonialism: African Self-Fashioning and the Colonial Library*. Duke University Press.

Eide, E. (2016). Strategic Essentialism. In N. A. Naples, R. C. Hoagland, M. Wickramasinghe, & W. C. A. Wong (Eds.), *The Wiley Blackwell Encyclopedia of Gender and Sexuality Studies*. Wiley.

Escobar, A. (2004). Beyond the Third World: Imperial Globality, Global Coloniality and Anti Globalization Social Movements. *Third World Quarterly, 25*(1), 207–230.

Fraiture, P. P. (2013). *V.Y. Mudimbe: Undisciplined Africanism*. Liverpool University Press.

Fuss, D. (1989). *Essentially Speaking: Feminism, Nature and Difference*. Routledge.

Gandhi, K. (2015). The Politics of Strategic Essentialism: A Study of Spivak's and Butler's Feminist Theory. *Phenomenal Literature: A Global Journal Devoted to Language and Literature, 1*(2), 156–165.

Gilroy, P. (1983). *The Black Atlantic: Modernity and Double Consciousness*. Verso.

Grosfoguel, R. (2007). The Epistemic Decolonial Turn. *Cultural Studies, 21*(2–3), 211–223.

Grosfoguel, R. (2011). Decolonizing Post-colonial Studies and Paradigms of Political-Economy: Transmodernity, Decolonial Thinking, and Global Coloniality. *Transmodernity: Journal of Peripheral Cultural Production of the Luso-Hispanic World, 1*(1), 1–38.

Grovogui, S. N. (2002). Regimes of Sovereignty: International Morality and the African Condition. *European Journal of International Relations, 8*(3), 315–338.

Grovogui, S. N. (2006). *Beyond Eurocentrism and Anarchy: Memories of International Order and Institutions*. Palgrave MacMillan.

Hooks, B. (1994). *Teaching to Transgress: Education as the Practice of Freedom*. Routledge.

Jackson, R. H. (1993). *Quasi-States: Sovereignty, International Relations and the Third World*. Cambridge University Press.

Joorst, J. (2019, January 24). Racism is Still Rife in South Africa's Schools. What Can Be Done About It? *The Conversation*. Retrieved from https://theconversation.com/racism-is-still-rife-in-south-africas-schools-what-can-be-done-about-it-110195

Kessi, S., Marks, Z., & Ramugondo, E. (2020). Decolonizing African Studies. *Critical African Studies, 12*(3), 271–282.

Kurzwelly, J., Rapport, N., & Spiegel, A. D. (2020). Encountering, Explaining and Refuting Essentialism. *Anthropology Southern Africa, 43*(2), 65–81.

Maldonado-Torres, N. (2016, October 23). *Outline of Ten Theses on Coloniality and Decoloniality*. Frantz Fanon Foundation. Retrieved from http://frantzfanonfoundationfondationfrantzfanon.com/IMG/pdf/maldonado-torres_outline_of_ten_theses-10.23.16_.pdf

Mbembe, A. (2016). Decolonizing the University: New Directions. *Arts and Humanities in HigherEducation, 15*(1), 29–45.

Mignolo, W. D. (2017, January 21). Interview Walter Mignolo/Part 2: Key Concepts. Interview by Alvina Hoffman. *E-International Relations*. Retrieved from https://www.e-ir.info/2017/01/21/interview-walter-mignolopart-2-key-concepts/

Mignolo, W. D., & Walsh, C. E. (2018). *On Decoloniality: Concepts, Analytics Praxis*. Duke University Press.

Mudimbe, V. Y. (1988). *The Invention of Africa*. Indiana University Press.

Mudimbe, V. Y. (1991). *Parables and Fables: Exegesis, Textuality, and Politics in Central Africa*. The University of Wisconsin Press.

Mudimbe, V. Y. (1994). *The Idea of Africa*. Indiana University Press.

Narayan, U. (1998). Essence of Culture and a Sense of History: A Feminist Critique of Cultural Essentialism. *Hypatia, 13*(2), 86–106.

Ndlovu, M. (2018). Coloniality of Knowledge and the Challenge of Creating African Futures. *Ufahamu: A Journal of African Studies, 40*(2), 95–112.

Ndlovu-Gatsheni, S. (2018). *Epistemic Freedom in Africa: Deprovincialization and Decolonization*. Routledge.

Ndlovu-Gatsheni, S. (2020). *Decolonization, Development and Knowledge in Africa: Turning Over a New Leaf*. Routledge.

Nyamnjoh, F. B. (2019). *Decolonizing the university in Africa. In Oxford Research Encyclopedia of Politics*. Oxford University Press.

Ranger, T. (1983). The Invention of Tradition in Colonial Africa. In E. Hobsbawm & T. Ranger (Eds.), *The Invention of Tradition*. Cambridge University Press.

Said, E. (1978). *Orientalism*. Pantheon.

Spear, T. (2015). Invention of Tradition. *Oxford Bibliographies: African Studies*.

Wai, Z. (2012). Neo-Patrimonialism and the Discourse of State Failure in Africa. *Review of African Political Economy, 39*(131), 27–43.

Wai, Z. (2015). On the Predicament of Africanist Knowledge: Mudimbe, Gnosis and the Challenge of the Colonial Library. *International Journal of Francophone Studies, 18*(2–3), 263–290.

Wai, Z. (2020). Resurrecting Mudimbe. *International Politics Reviews, 8*(1), 57–78.

Wai, Z. (forthcoming). *Thinking the Colonial Library: Mudimbe, Gnosis, and the Predicament of Africanist Knowledge*. Routledge.

Walker, C. E. (2001). *We Can't Go Home Again: An Argument about Afrocentrism*. Oxford University Press.

Xaso, L. (2021, June 5). Institutional Racism: The Real Price of Admission to 'White Schools' Too High for Black Kids. *Daily Maverick 168*. Retrieved from https://www.dailymaverick.co.za/opinionista/2021-06-05-institutional-racism-the-real-price-of-admission-to-white-schools-too-high-for-black-kids/

Zachernuk, P. S. (2000). *Colonial Subjects: An African Intelligentsia and Atlantic Ideas*. University Press of Virginia.

CHAPTER 6

"Dem European Teachings in My African School": Unpacking Coloniality and Eurocentric Hegemony in African Education Through Burna Boy's *Monsters You Made*

Savo Heleta and Sakhile Phiri

Introduction

In *Monsters You Made*, a song that is part of his 2020 album *Twice as Tall*, Nigerian singer Burna Boy, whose real name is Damini Ebunoluwa Ogulu, highlights historical and contemporary socio-economic, political

S. Heleta (✉)
Durban University of Technology, Durban, South Africa
e-mail: sheleta@gmail.com

S. Phiri
Department of Development Studies, Nelson Mandela University, Gqeberha, South Africa
e-mail: sakhile.phiri@mandela.ac.za

N. Andrews and N. E. Khalema (eds.), *Decolonizing African Studies Pedagogies*, Political Pedagogies,
https://doi.org/10.1007/978-3-031-37442-5_6

and educational challenges in Nigeria. The song's relevance stretches beyond Nigeria and resembles similar experiences of colonial racism, exploitation and dehumanization across the African continent, as well as the marginalization, injustices and corruption after independence. *Monsters You Made* is an "indictment of miseducation, historical injustice and systemic racism" (Pareles, 2020) that the African continent has faced since the Europeans began with the slave trade and then followed with colonialism, neocolonialism and coloniality. The song links post-independence challenges to colonial conquest, subjugation, oppression and looting and the ongoing exploitation through global coloniality. Burna Boy shows that while the formal colonial rule has ended in Africa, "colonialism, in its many disguises as cultural, economic, political and knowledge-based oppression, lives on" (Sardar, 2008: xix). He highlights the persistence of Eurocentric hegemony in African education as one of the ever-present challenges on the continent.

Burna Boy explains that the song "comes from a lot of anger and pain, and me having to witness firsthand what my people go through and how my people see themselves" (qtd. in Pareles, 2020). He grew up in southern Nigeria's Port Harcourt, in the Niger Delta region, which after the end of colonial rule has seen decades of unrest, human rights abuses and conflict. This has in part been linked to the environmental degradation and exploitation of the region's oil reserves for the benefit of foreign oil corporations and Nigeria's political elites (Ajodo-Adebanjoko, 2017). For decades, the Niger Delta has been a "sacrifice zone"—a place heavily exploited and contaminated by the oil industry, while the successive Nigerian governments allowed this to happen (United Nations Human Rights Council, 2022). When discussing the song, Burna Boy stresses his goal was to paint a picture of the struggles and challenges many Nigerians and other Africans across the continent face on a daily basis (qtd. in Perry, 2020). He also sings about the inevitability of resistance to the post-independence oppression and the status quo. His emotion and anger, expressed in the song and particularly evident in the music video, echo the anger that anti-racist and anti-colonial thinkers such as Frantz Fanon, Walter Rodney and Steve Biko have expressed in their writings about the savagery and ruthlessness of European colonialism, white supremacy and racism. The anger, furry and resentment, as pointed out by Sardar (2008: vi) in his foreword to Fanon's *Black Skin, White Masks*, are about poverty, marginalization and oppression rooted in colonial exploitation, coloniality and post-independence failures. It is also the anger of Africans and other formerly colonized peoples "whose cultures, knowledge systems and ways of being... [have been and continue to be] ridiculed, demonized, declared inferior and irrational, and, in some cases, eliminated."

Monsters You Made is part of the long list of songs that address injustice, inequality, oppression and racism in the world. Burna Boy thinks that the global success he has had over the years has given him a platform and has brought a responsibility to speak out against injustices he sees in Nigeria, Africa and the world (qtd. in Pareles, 2020). The themes of colonial oppression, poverty, government corruption and brutality after independence, coloniality and Eurocentric hegemony in African education are all highlighted in the song. In this, Burna Boy follows in the footsteps of another Nigerian legendary musician, the pan-Africanist and father of Afrobeat, Fela Kuti. In the 1970s, Fela began challenging and exposing Nigeria's military dictatorships and their oppressive rule (Ngobili, 2021). He was inspired by the ideas of Malcolm X, Kwame Nkrumah and Frantz Fanon and this gradually took his music in a more radical direction, mixing pan-African messages with diatribes aimed at western multinationals and military dictatorships ruling his country (Pajon, 2021). An example of this is the song *Zombie* (1976) in which Fela sings about soldiers who enact violence against their own people at the command of government elites. *Monster You Made* also speaks about the government's brutality and violence against ordinary Nigerians. Similarly, in his 1977 song titled *Colonial Mentality*, Fela Kuti sings how the "oppressive tendencies through colonial education have long restrained Africans over the centuries" (Ogunyemi, 2021: 498). In *Monsters You Made*, Burna Boy critiques Eurocentric curriculum taught in Nigerian schools. Finally, both Burna Boy and Fela Kuti sing almost exclusively in Pidgin English, which constitutes a critique of European-centered notions of language.

In this chapter, we provide a critical analysis of Burna Boy's *Monsters You Made* and its engagement with socio-economic, political, educational and epistemic challenges and injustices the African continent continues to face. While our primary focus is on the challenges and possibilities of epistemic decolonization, we will unpack intersectional legacies of colonialism, as exemplified by Burna Boy, and highlight how colonial racism, white supremacy and racial capitalist exploitation are linked to the ongoing dehumanization of Africans through coloniality and neocolonialism. We will also show that coloniality and ongoing Eurocentric hegemonic influences in African education and within the African Studies field globally cannot be discussed in isolation, without a critical interrogation of the failures of Africa's post-independence elites to break away from colonial and neocolonial structures and systems and create an enabling environment for epistemic decolonization. This, in turn, has undermined the ability of African educational systems, institutions and scholars to develop and promote education and knowledge relevant for Africa and Africans (Mama, 2007).

The first part of the chapter will unpack the making of the "monsters" through post-independence neglect, repression and subjugation. The next section reminds that post-independence failures cannot be examined without a critical unpacking of colonial conquest, oppression and social and political engineering that the colonizers employed in Africa. The subsequent section touches on the "European teachings in my African school," which Burna Boy sees as one of the major failures in the delayed process of decolonization on the African continent. The last section focuses on the challenges and possibilities of epistemic decolonization and Africanization of education and pedagogy in Africa, and the implications of this for African Studies, in Africa and globally.

Post-Independence Failures and the Making of the "Monsters"

In *Monsters You Made*, Burna Boy sings about the socio-economic and political challenges in post-independence Nigeria. He argues that Nigerian governments have failed to develop the country and improve people's lives and that this has been the main reason communities have had to—time and again—resort to protest, resistance and rebellion. This is also highlighted by Ebikabowei "Boyloaf" Victor-Ben, the former commander of the Movement for the Emancipation of the Niger Delta, and is a reminder of the ongoing conflict and lack of development in this oil-rich region of Nigeria. The song opens with Boyloaf's short monologue:

> If the government refuse (sic) to develop the region and continue (sic) the marginalization and injustice, the youth, or the next people coming after us, I think, will be more brutal than what we have done. (qtd. in Burna Boy, 2020)

Burna Boy, who in the official music video for the song appears as a leader of a group of militants rebelling against repression, points out in the song that the corruption and nepotism in Nigeria, combined with the marginalization of many regions in the country, give people no choice but to resist oppression. Rather than addressing the failures of governance, post-independence governments have blamed the people and communities that resist marginalization and neglect for instability. He notes,

> It's like the heads of the state/Ain't comprehending the hate/That the oppressed generate/When they've been working like slaves/To get some minimum wage/You turn around and you blame/Them for their anger and rage/Put them in shackles and chains/Because of what they became/ We are the monsters you made. (Burna Boy, 2020)

Burna Boy highlights that the poor governance, looting and mismanagement of the economy by politicians will only lead to more rebellion. The resistance by communities in Nigeria and many other parts of Africa is an "attempt to survive, to breathe the air of liberty" that has been promised since independence, but for which millions are still waiting (Sardar, 2008: xii). Burna Boy argues that the marginalized in Nigeria will continue to fight for their rights and livelihoods despite the oppression by the state. He adds that the Nigerians will risk their lives for fundamental change in the country; they will either bring about the change or "smile in the grave" (Burna Boy, 2020).

The neglect of the masses by post-independence elites is not unique to Nigeria but has been a feature of governance across the African continent. Fanon (1963: 149) writes about the "intellectual laziness" among the African politicians to explain the failure to transform the oppressive and extractive structures and systems in their societies after the end of colonial rule. Rather than dismantling the status quo built by the colonial regimes in order to benefit the colonial capitals through the "parasitic exploitation" of the colonized lands and peoples (Rodney, 1972: 186), post-independence elites often only replaced the European colonizers at the helm. They continued to utilize the ruthless, divisive, exclusionary and corrupt structures, systems, institutions and forms of colonial governance and exploitation in order to enrich themselves while the majority of the African people continued to suffer.

Instead of bringing about fundamental transformation in their societies and economies, post-independence elites became mere intermediaries for the former colonial powers, other neocolonial powers and the global capital. Driven by Eurocentric individualism without social responsibility (Rodney, 1972) and lacking a genuine anti-colonial solidarity with the people they claimed to represent, they were only interested in staying in power and enriching themselves. Across the continent, African political elites continued to maintain the extractive practices introduced by European colonizers and capitalists, sending raw materials to Europe and North America, and later to China and elsewhere, rather than building capacity for processing raw materials at home, which would benefit their countries, economies and people. Nigeria, with its oil riches but without oil refineries for most of its independence, is a prime example of this, but not unique. Same challenges have been experienced since independence across the African continent regarding different riches and minerals. Thus, we argue that coloniality is an appropriate lens for analysis because it centers race and racism while also highlighting the interconnections between racialized ideological strategies, capitalist accumulation processes and the inter-state system of the core-periphery relationships on the world scale (Grosfoguel, 2006). We turn to this in the next section.

The Impact of Colonialism and Coloniality in Africa

In *Monsters You Made*, Burna Boy does not only blame Nigeria's post-independence elites for socio-economic and developmental failures. The song ends with the voice of Ama Ata Aidoo, a Ghanaian academic, author and the former minister of education in Ghana, who, in a 1987 interview with a European journalist, points out the following:

> Since we met you people five hundred years ago/Look at us, we've given everything/You are still taking/In exchange for that, we have got nothing/Nothing. (qtd. in Burna Boy, 2020)

In response, the journalist asks: "But don't you think that this is over now?" Here, the journalist seemingly refers to colonialism and its impact on the African continent, and suggests that colonialism has ended and that it, and the colonizers, cannot be blamed any more for Africa's challenges. To this, Aidoo replies: "Over where?/Is it over?" (qtd. in Burna Boy, 2020). Aidoo's words remind listeners that the post-independence challenges on the African continent cannot be examined in isolation, without a critical unpacking of the colonial conquest, looting, marginalization, oppression and social and political engineering that the colonizers employed while ruling over their colonial possessions. The exploitation of Africa through slavery, colonialism and racial capitalism has helped develop and enrich colonial European countries and their settler colonies such as the United States, while ravaging and impoverishing African societies (Maldonado-Torres, 2007; Rodney, 1972). This was done through ruthless oppression, looting and physical and emotional onslaught on African peoples (Aidoo, 1995).

The colonial rule included direct and indirect political and socioeconomic control, social engineering, redrawing of borders and exploitation by European colonial powers (Mamdani, 1996). Across the African continent, European colonizers brought different communities into the borders of new countries drawn by the European "robber statesmen" who met in Berlin in 1884–1885 "to decide who should steal which part of Africa" (Rodney, 1972: 135). While drawing new African boundaries, colonizers paid no attention to ethnic, cultural and linguistic realities on the ground. This way, they divided homogeneous groups and peoples, often separating communities; or, they put together groups which had no common history, culture or identity into the newly formed countries (Dowden, 2008). An example of this is the declaration of distinct Northern and Southern areas of what is today Nigeria as British protectorates in 1900, which were then joined by the colonizers into a political entity called Nigeria in 1914 (Ngobili, 2021). The people living in these territories had no say in any of this.

European colonizers propagated and entrenched "ethnic territories" across the African continent. These territories have "played a central role in colonial governability in diverse contexts, facilitating both the dispossession and the biopolitical management of colonized populations" (Anthias & Hoffmann, 2021: 218). The colonizers created patronage systems of governance in territories under their occupation, favored some ethnic groups over others and exploited African labor in order to extract natural resources to benefit colonial capitals (Dowden, 2008). All this has had a profound influence on the colonized and has left immeasurable marks on African societies and economies. Rodney (1972) stresses that the African post-independence challenges and underdevelopment are rooted in the centuries of European colonial exploitation. He adds that underdevelopment in Africa is a paradox as many countries are rich in natural resources but remain poor due to the past exploitation by the colonizers, and the contemporary global structures of power, control and capitalist exploitation, controlled by the countries and institutions in the global North, that keep them poor and dependent on foreign expertise and aid.

European colonialism was justified in part by the creation of the "other." This was done through the racialization of skin color, allowing for the dehumanization of colonized Africans in order to exploit them in the pursuit of profits. African people were considered subhuman based on the European racist ideas and worldviews which allowed for their dehumanization and exploitation. Quijano (2000) argues that the idea of race was used to justify and legitimize domination after the European colonial conquest. One of the ways that colonialism derived power was to propagate an idea that there is a natural difference between the colonizer and colonized based on race. The construction, classification and hierarchization of peoples and places in the colonial imaginary were key for domination and exploitation. Hidden in the European idea of modernity is the expendability of human lives for the sake of increasing wealth for the powerful, which was and still continues to be justified by the racial ranking of human beings (Mignolo, 2011). Burna Boy highlights the expendability and exploitation of some people for the benefit of the wealthy and politically connected when he sings about Nigerians being worked "like slaves/To get some minimum wage" (Burna Boy, 2020). While he is referring to the post-independence era, it is important to remember that the exploitation of Africa and Africans by the global capitalist system began with slavery and continued during and after the colonial times. As previously discussed, many African post-independence leaders have reproduced the exploitative economic and other systems brought by the colonizers.

Mamdani (1996) notes that colonial experiences, authoritarianism and brutality have shaped governance systems, structures and institutions that emerged across the African continent after independence. Many African countries have struggled to unify their populations due to social engineering, ethnic divisions and fragmentation left behind by the colonizers (Fenton, 2003). In the post-colonial context, "the nexus between ethnicity and territory remains powerfully shaped by the colonial legacy of racial segregation, dispossession, extraction, labor exploitation, repression and indirect rule" (Anthias & Hoffmann, 2021: 3). Despite the political independence, divisions that emerged during the colonial conquest and occupation continued to be entrenched and exploited by African political elites. Ochonu (2020: 508) argues that after independence, most African politicians continued to invoke the "colonial template of intra-African differences to secure their rule." This template was based on the divide-and-rule policies developed by European colonizers to undermine African solidarity, unity and revolt against colonial oppression. Mamdani (1996: 25) highlights that the only change in many African countries after independence was the move from the "decentralized despotism" through colonial indirect rule to "centralized despotism" by African political elites.

Ama Ata Aidoo's reply at the end of *Monsters You Made*, where she questions the European journalist's reference to colonialism and its impact being over, is a prime example of what decolonial scholarship refers to as coloniality. While colonialism has formally ended in Africa and elsewhere in the second half of the twentieth century, geopolitical, economic, social and educational structures that have been built and imposed over centuries of European colonial rule continue to shape the way the world works (Sardar, 2008). Coloniality is the residual structural and cultural presence of colonization, such as mental, emotional and agential dispositions and states of being, long after colonizers left (Maldonado-Torres, 2007). For Ndlovu-Gatsheni (2013a), coloniality is a global power structure built and entrenched to maintain unjust, unequal, asymmetrical and exploitative socio-economic, political and geopolitical systems, rooted in white supremacist ideas and the colonial conquest and aimed at the maintenance of neocolonial and Euro-American hegemony in all spheres of life.

By adding Aidoo's voice to *Monsters You Made*, Burna Boy frames the Nigerian and broader African post-independence challenges within the concept of coloniality. He leaves his listeners to ponder the causes of post-independence failures. In the song, he blames Nigeria's political elites for corruption, neglect, marginalization and oppression, and stresses that due to this, many communities have had no choice but to take up arms, resist and rebel. He also highlights, through Aidoo's words, that centuries of slavery, colonial conquest, divide-and-rule policies, brutality, exploitation and looting by European colonizers are to blame for many of Africa's post-independence woes. Most importantly, the song stresses that colonial power relations, hegemonic structures and systems did not end when African countries became independent, but have continued in different shapes and forms through coloniality and neocolonialism to this day. As Ndlovu (2018: 97) points out, the end of direct colonial rule, in Nigeria and elsewhere in Africa, was only a "performative episode within a prescriptive continuous historical structure of coloniality." By featuring Ama Ata Aidoo's questioning of the journalist's reference to colonial exploitation being over, Burna Boy reminds listeners that coloniality survives colonialism (Maldonado-Torres, 2007) and can be found in all spheres of life, including in education, which we discuss next.

Eurocentric Hegemony and African Education

In addition to the governance, socio-economic and security-related challenges linked to colonialism, coloniality and the failures of political elites, Burna Boy also sings about the Eurocentric hegemony in Nigerian education long after independence:

> I bet they thought it was cool/Probably thought we was (sic) fools/When we would break all the rules/And skip them classes in school/Because the teacher dem teaching/What the white man dem teaching/dem European teachings in my African school/So f*ck dem classes in school. (Burna Boy, 2020)

Here, Burna Boy puts Nigeria's education system under the spotlight, highlighting that despite the political independence from the British colonizers in 1960, Nigeria's education remains Eurocentric. Decades later, Nigerian youth are still taught white and Euro-American teachings and worldviews in their African schools and universities. In an interview, Burna Boy explains how schools and universities in Africa "don't really teach the truth about how we ended up in the situation we're in. They don't teach the truth about what's going on now and how to overcome it. And I believe that knowledge is power" (qtd. in Pareles, 2020). He compares his education in Nigeria to "brainwashing," arguing that the teachers taught him and other students other people's history and worldviews, while sidelining African knowledges, histories and worldviews (qtd. in Perry, 2020).

In *Monsters You Made*, Burna Boy gives an example of how the Nigerian youth are still taught that white colonizers and explorers "discovered" Nigeria and the rest of Africa. He focuses on Mungo Park, Scottish explorer who is credited with the "discovery" of the Niger River, and sings: "F*ck Mungo Park and the fool/That said they found river Niger/They've been lying to you/Ain't no denying the truth" (Burna

Boy, 2020). Burna Boy adds that he and his classmates preferred skipping school rather than being subjected to white and Eurocentric lies, propaganda and brainwashing during his schooling. He rejects the very notion of Mungo Park discovering the Niger River. Here, he follows in the footsteps of Walter Rodney (1972), who found it laughable that anyone could take seriously the claims of "discovery" of Africa by European colonizers and explorers. Yet, the fact that Burna Boy, who was born in 1991, identifies this as a problem that his generation encountered while going to school in Nigeria in the 2000s shows that, while laughable, these colonial, racist and hegemonic ideas, worldviews and notions continue to be recycled and propagated in Africa by African educators. Thus, Burna Boy highlights that colonial power and coloniality of knowledge are not confined to the past but remain enduring and pervasive realities that demand our critical attention here and now (Anthias & Hoffmann, 2021).

The idea that any part of Africa could be discovered by European colonizers—as if Africans have not known about them or that their knowledge about them does not matter—shows the disregard that the colonial powers and their educators and scholars have had for African people. Not acknowledging African knowledges, ways of knowing and thinking about the world has been and continues to be racist and deeply dehumanizing. As Zeleza (2006) points out, the origins of recorded knowledge development, scholarship and learning in Africa go back to the third century B.C., when the Alexandria Museum and Library was established in Egypt. This was followed by the development of educational institutions linked to monasteries and mosques in many parts of the continent, and the establishment of what today are considered higher education institutions in countries such as Tunisia, Egypt, Ethiopia and Mali, to name a few. All this, however, has been dismissed by the colonizers as irrelevant, and Africans were told that the only "objective," "scientific" and "true" knowledge is that which comes from the colonial centers.

The notion of white colonizers and explorers "discovering" Africa has served the colonial narrative of Africa as the "dark continent" in need of the "light," "civilization" and "discovery" that colonization by Europeans supposedly brought. Colonizers equated "discovery" with ownership, the rationale being: "If we discovered it, it's ours to do with it as we please." Similar "discoveries" are noted throughout the African curricula, such as the discovery of Mount Kenya or the Victoria Falls by white colonizers. The discovery of "new worlds" allowed for the commodification of Africa, assigning it a value to be exploited in the capitalist system that colonialism imposed. The imposition of Eurocentric knowledge, ideas and worldviews, and sidelining and dismissal of African knowledges, played a key role in this process. Another key component in this process was the introduction and imposition of the languages of the colonizers and the sidelining and suppression of the indigenous African languages. Wa Thiong'o (1993: 31) argues that through the suppression of African languages, "the culture and the history carried by these languages were thereby thrown onto the rubbish heap and left there to perish."

The purpose of colonial education in Africa was to develop a small number of local but "westernized" elites that would contribute to the maintenance of colonial rule and capitalist exploitation of the continent (Rodney, 1972; Wa Thiong'o, 1986; Woldegiorgis, 2021). In the process, colonial education created among African peoples who had access to it a "false understanding" of themselves (Biko, 1978: 57). Colonial educational institutions were modeled on the European institutions from the colonial centers (Mamdani, 2016; Zeleza, 2012). These institutions taught a Eurocentric curriculum that was designed for the European contexts, without any attempt to incorporate indigenous knowledges and perspectives. Wa Thiong'o (1986) explains how the "entire way of looking at the world, even the world of the immediate environment" in colonial education in Africa was Eurocentric, with Europe presented as the center of the world and source of all relevant knowledge. Rodney (1972) argues that the racist and Eurocentric education and the belief in innate superiority of whites that dominated European thinking during (and after) colonial times are to blame for the portrayal of Africa as a backward continent that cannot develop and progress in the same or similar way as the global North. He further stresses that "colonial schooling was education for subordination, exploitation, the creation of mental confusion and the development of underdevelopment" (Rodney, 1972: 241).

Through colonial education, Africans were forced to "see themselves through the hegemonic memory of the colonizing centre" (Wa Thiong'o, 2013). European colonizers "thoughtlessly applied their own curricula without reference to African conditions... with intent to confuse and mystify" (Rodney, 1972: 247). As Kessi et al. (2020: 274) argue, the purpose of colonial subjugation through education was to erase, sideline and dehumanize "African civilizational innovations, politics, and cultures in order to bring them into the 'universal' paradigm of European knowledge hierarchies." This was a deliberate policy choice with long-term domination and exploitation in mind. Subjugation through knowledge, scholarship, education and colonial languages has led to brainwashing and colonization of many African minds and the partial acceptance of Eurocentric and white supremacist ideas and notions as "normal." Sardar (2008: ix) notes that the colonizers had used education to propagate white supremacy and African "backwardness" in the colonies, leading some to internalize the "idea of the inherent superiority of the colonizing culture" and its knowledge systems and worldviews. Wa Thiong'o highlights how the suppression of African languages and the imposition of colonial languages enhanced this process:

> The second mode of captivation [after the colonial conquest] was that of elevating the language of the conqueror. It became the language of the elect. Those inducted into the school system, after having been sifted from the masses of the people, were furnished with new mirrors in which to see themselves and their people as well as those who had provided the new mirrors. (Wa Thiong'o, 1993: 32)

At independence, most African countries did not have any higher education institutions, and the ones that existed were modeled on the colonial institutions. The post-independence period saw an expansion of educational systems and institutions on the continent, including higher education (Zeleza, 2006). However, the much-needed epistemic decolonization did not take place in most countries and institutions in this period, and the African educators and academia largely continued to model themselves and their work on the Eurocentric scholarship and worldviews (Nyamnjoh, 2019). As Mama (2007: 9) points out, after independence, African educational institutions and universities continued to institutionalize Eurocentric disciplines, curriculum and pedagogies, with little attention given to "epistemological implications of importing paradigms and methodologies generated in very different historical and cultural contexts." Even the institutions that emerged after the political decolonization and independence in Africa have been shaped by the Eurocentric models, canon and curriculum. This took place even in Ethiopia, the only African country that was never colonized, with the Ethiopian political elites deciding to sideline and undermine country's indigenous knowledge systems and develop institutions and educational models—particularly on the higher education level—based on the Euro-American hegemonic models (Woldegiorgis, 2021). Nyamnjoh (2019: 3) highlights that African educational institutions and universities "have not been domesticated" since independence "through epistemological renegotiation informed by local languages, cosmologies and worldviews." Instead, they remain "trapped in the institutional and epistemic economies of Euro-American models" (Zeleza, 2012: 10) while conducting teaching and research using the languages of the former colonizers.

Apart from the challenges related to the colonial roots of many African educational institutions and the lack of epistemic decolonization after independence, the neglect, mismanagement and lack of investment in the education sector—and particularly in higher education—in the post-colonial period have resulted in substantial weakening of educational systems and institutions on the continent (Aina, 2010; Zeleza, 2006). In addition, violent conflicts and political instability in many African countries have led to destruction of educational institutions, exodus of educators, scholars and academics and widespread attacks on academic freedom (Aina, 2010; Mama, 2007). Structural adjustments and neoliberal impositions, promoted and imposed by international financial institutions, have since the 1980s contributed to further marginalization and impoverishment of African universities (Mama, 2007). Over a few decades, institutions such as the World Bank and the International Monetary Fund had pressured African governments to prioritize primary and secondary education at the expense of higher education and research. These policy prescriptions and impositions have led to the neglect of higher education across the African continent and brain drain in academia, directly undermining the ability of universities and research institutions to conduct research and develop new and relevant knowledge (Aina, 2010; Chelwa, 2021; Mama, 2007; Zeleza, 2012).

While Burna Boy sings about the Eurocentric and white curriculum in Nigeria's education system in *Monsters You Made*, this is a challenge facing the African continent. Continued Eurocentric hegemony in African education is another example of coloniality, which has been discussed earlier. As highlighted by Ndlovu (2018: 110), "coloniality of knowledge is a key lever in the structural system of colonial domination as a whole." Despite the rhetoric about Africanization and epistemic decolonization throughout the African continent since independence, education systems remain trapped in Eurocentric epistemologies, pedagogies and curriculum

(Nyamnjoh, 2019; Zeleza, 2012). Said (1989: 207) writes that through colonial education, coloniality and Eurocentric hegemony in education and knowledge production after independence, former colonies have been "fixed in zones of dependency and peripherality" and forced to mimic colonizers and their forms of knowledge. Maserumule (2015) points out that the majority of education leaders, administrators, scholars, educators and academics in Africa have been "schooled largely in the white [and Eurocentric] tradition." This has imprinted Eurocentricity among them, shaping their knowledge-related interests, pedagogical approaches and preferences.

Thus, African academia, scholarship, research and education continue to be shaped by white man's and Eurocentric teachings, perspectives and paradigms, as Burna Boy argues in his song, deriving their "impetus not from deep engagement with the real of the local, but from ritual obeisance to the theoretical and methodological fads" from the colonial and neocolonial centers (Zeleza, 2012: 16). Implicitly, Burna Boy (2020) highlights that "dem European teachings in my African school" are part of the neocolonial project that persists despite the formal end of colonialism decades ago. The questioning and rejection of Eurocentric knowledge, ideas, pedagogies and worldviews that continue to be taught in Africa are acts of resistance to colonization of the African mind and continued geopolitical, economic and knowledge-related coloniality. Burna Boy's song can be seen as a call to dismantle Eurocentric hegemony, decolonize and Africanize education in Africa and incorporate on all levels—from basic to higher education—"ways of knowing that transcend our epicolonial inheritance" (Kessi et al., 2020: 271). We unpack what this entails in the last section.

Challenges and Possibilities of Epistemic Decolonization in Africa

As we have shown earlier, Africa has faced complex systemic and structural challenges since independence. The challenges are linked to colonial socio-economic and political impositions, global power relations, coloniality, neocolonialism and continued Euro-American global epistemic hegemony. Ochonu (2020) highlights that most of the African post-independence elites have not been interested in dismantling colonial structures and binaries in politics, governance and economics. To this, we add the unwillingness of African politicians, university leaders, scholars, educators and academics to dismantle the Eurocentric hegemonic canon. Instead, many of them choose to remain "subservient to the orthodox western education forms and structures established by colonial authorities" (Afolabi, 2020: 94) and maintained through coloniality and Euro-American global hegemony in the post-colonial period. Burna Boy's *Monsters You Made* engages with and illustrates all this. He critically interrogates socio-economic, political, geopolitical and epistemic challenges and injustices the African continent continues to face, framing them within the experiences of colonial oppression and racism and the ongoing global coloniality.

Burna Boy highlights the persistence of Eurocentric hegemony in African education and the failure to "decolonize the mind" (Wa Thiong'o, 1986) as one of the greatest failures of the post-independence period. As highlighted by Biko, "the most potent weapon in the hands of the oppressor is the mind of the oppressed" (Biko, 1978: 74). European colonizers have known this since the beginning of the colonial conquest. Everything they did through colonial education was aimed at colonizing African minds. The results of this can be seen decades after independence across the continent. To this day, most of Africa's academia remains "cut from the cloth of western knowledge," the consequences of which have "imprinted the culture of whiteness in its making" (Maserumule, 2015). This continues to contribute to the maintenance of the Eurocentric hegemonic canon in African education. Instead of questioning and disrupting coloniality and Eurocentric hegemony, most of Africa's academia has "internalized the colonial world outlook" (Wa Thiong'o, 1986: 101–102) and continues to model education on the continent on the Euro-American models, practices, pedagogies and curriculums. As Mpofu and Steyn (2021: 11) point out, African academia has done little to transform and decolonize the "westernized university in Africa" after political independence. By and large, African academics have used their intellectual and scholarly positions to promote the Eurocentric canon and worldviews, contributing to the ongoing epistemic injustices, stereotyping and dehumanization of Africa and Africans.

Maserumule (2015) argues that Africa needs academics, educators and scholars with a "decoloniality posture" if the continent is to make progress on epistemic decolonization. Decolonial posture and thought offer new ways of understanding and thinking about the relations between the rich constellations of radical, Pan-African, progressive, feminist and internationalist thought outside and beyond the colonial logics. Epistemic decolonization can lead to a creation of knowledge that is contextually relevant and grounded in African indigenous knowledges, pedagogies, perspectives, beliefs, values, worldviews and experiences (Fomunyan, 2017). Epistemic decolonization is part of the broader project of dismantling the structures of coloniality, as well as an emancipatory project, what Ndlovu-Gatsheni (2013b: 51) calls the "redemptive epistemology, a liberatory force and an ethical-humanistic project gesturing toward pluriversalism in which different worlds fit." This, according to Nyoni (2019: 2), requires "liberation and de-caging of the colonized, caged mind" and unlearning and learning anew how to engage with ideas, worldviews and knowledges from and about Africa and the rest of the world "beyond the distorted cultural and/or historical imaginary and impoverished subjectivity of the modern horizon of thought where everything is hierarchically ranked according to Eurocentric concepts, standards and assumptions." For wa Thiong'o, this is part of decolonizing the mind and the "quest for relevance" of African education and knowledge. He argues that epistemic decolonization is a "search for a liberating perspective within which to see ourselves clearly in relationship to ourselves and to other selves in the universe" (Wa Thiong'o, 1986: 87). Likewise, Ochonu describes epistemic decolonization as follows:

> ... one of the most potent discursive challenges to the enduring epistemological legacies of colonialism, defined broadly as Euro-American systems of historical and contemporary oppression. Decoloniality is also a tool of Africa-centred analysis, which seeks to retrieve Africa from the margins of global sociopolitical, economic and epistemic formations and inscribe it at the centre of such configurations. Decoloniality insists on Africa's ontological sovereignty, and constructs its epistemological boundaries in broad pan-African geographic strokes. (Ochonu, 2020: 514)

Keet (2014) stresses that the decolonial project in Africa must tackle Eurocentric hegemony and epistemic injustices, but also critically question, rethink and transform Euro-American disciplinary templates and pedagogies that continue to be replicated on the African continent. Wa Thiong'o (1986) adds that epistemic decolonization is not only about the scholarship and materials that are taught or researched, but also about the attitudes and critical approaches to the materials and their interpretation.

Mpofu and Steyn (2021: 20) argue that African educators, scholars and academics must first delink from the Euro-American canon, decolonize their minds and their academic fields and then re-link with the world's scholarship, knowledges and worldviews, including the Euro-American-centric ones, but continue to see them as "one aspect of the thought that human beings have produced in the world, and not as the totality of world knowledge." Apart from this, decentring of colonial languages and inclusion and centering of African languages in all levels of education and scholarship has the potential to expand ways on knowing and being and make education and knowledge production more inclusive and relevant on the continent (Shaik & Kahn, 2021).

The challenges facing African educators, scholars and educational systems and institutions are not only pedagogical and epistemic, but are also linked to the broader structural and systemic failures since independence. Zeleza (2006) notes that African education sectors and institutions—and particularly universities—have faced a myriad of structural, systemic and pedagogical challenges, from the language used for tuition, relevance of educational models, global dynamics of knowledge production and the lack of support from governments. The lack of investment in African universities, combined with significant enrolment increases over the past few decades, has created a situation where African higher education systems and institutions have been fragile, understaffed, underfunded and unable to contribute to development of knowledge relevant for Africa and Africans (Mama, 2007). This has also created a dependency on foreign donors and funders. The dependency of external funding often forces African institutions and academics to align their research priorities to those of the donors (Beaudry et al., 2018). This has also led to a situation where African academics collaborate primarily with their counterparts from outside the African continent, while intra-Africa research collaboration that results in production of new knowledge remains negligible (Mouton & Blanckenberg, 2018). The expansion of intra-Africa research collaboration will be key for the continent's future. For this to happen, however, African governments have to deliver on their unfulfilled commitment to invest in, expand and revitalize higher education and research in their countries in order to be able to meaningfully and comprehensively address the challenges facing Africa and the world (African Union, 2016).

Many of the historical, systemic and structural challenges that were discussed in this chapter—all linked to colonialism and coloniality—have also plagued African Studies. African Studies globally has been part of the colonial and neocolonial projects, dominated by white and largely male scholars from Europe and North America. Similarly, the Euro-American epistemic hegemonic canon and worldviews have dominated and shaped the field, with African and Afro-diasporic knowledges, voices, worldviews, languages and scholars largely sidelined and dismissed. As such, African Studies has been part of dehumanization of the colonized and the propagation of colonial and neocolonial epistemic violence through education, research and knowledge production. The global socio-economic structural inequalities, rooted in colonialism and reinforced through coloniality and capitalism, have contributed to this through the impoverishment of African education systems and institutions, leaving African scholars dependent on the extractive interests and paternalistic whims of foreign donors and Euro-American "Africa experts" (Kessi et al., 2020).

Epistemic decolonization has the potential to positively impact the pedagogical practices in terms of how Africa is portrayed in teaching, research and writings, both within the continent and within African Studies globally. If we do not stop to reflect on the decolonization of African Studies and African higher education in general, we will perpetuate coloniality and help further entrench the Eurocentric epistemic hegemony. As argued by Mamdani (1993), few scholars in or of Africa have questioned enough the theories, concepts, pedagogies, practices, methodologies and assumptions shaped by the dominant Eurocentric epistemologies. The dominant canon, methods, pedagogical approaches and the disciplines—rooted in colonial racism and oppression and maintained through coloniality—must be challenged and disrupted. Illustrative of this is the curriculum in African education, as critiqued by Burna Boy in *Monsters You Made*. Africanization or indigenization of the curriculum in African education, and within African Studies globally, are merely a start of the decolonization process, not an end in itself. Decoloniality, as noted above, aims to dismantle the Euro-American epistemic hegemony and center Africa and Africans in African education. In the same way, African Studies must center Africa, Africans and African diaspora at its core. Unless it "centers Africa as a home for theory-making, and Africans [and diaspora scholars] as theory-builders" (Kessi et al., 2020: 273), it will only reinforce coloniality, Euro-American epistemic hegemony and white domination of the field.

Conclusion

In this chapter, we have unpacked Burna Boy's song, *Monsters You Made*, engaging with its critical takes on post-independence failures, the impact of colonialism and coloniality and persistence of Eurocentricity in African education. We did this—instead of only focusing on the section of the song discussing coloniality of knowledge and education—because all this is interlinked and influenced by the same colonial histories and neocolonial policies, systems and structures that continue to shape the world. Another key reason for looking at a bigger historical and contemporary picture and then zooming in on epistemic decolonization on the African continent and within African Studies globally is that dismantling Eurocentric hegemony and decolonizing knowledge cannot happen in isolation, without broader global and continental, social, economic, political and geopolitical decolonization. As highlighted by Mukoma Wa Ngũgĩ (2020), decolonizing the mind and knowledge must go hand-in-hand with material decolonization and breaking down of political, geopolitical and economic structures and systems that maintain and enable coloniality and neocolonialism. Chelwa (2021) argues that one of the failures in the struggle against colonialism on the African continent was the primary focus on political decolonization and independence. While this was the first and key step toward freedom, it failed to tackle other colonial remnants, such as the exploitation of African economies and resources along colonial patterns, the replication of colonial authoritarianism in post-independence governance and Eurocentric education. What the African continent needed at independence, and what it still needs, is "wholesale decolonization. Wholesale breaking down and building anew" (Chelwa, 2021).

Coloniality of knowledge and the struggle to decolonize African education and African Studies as a field are not only academic and scholarly concerns and priorities. Yet, as Mamdani (2016) points out, debates and work on epistemic decolonization have since independence remained largely removed from public debates and involvement across the continent. If Africa is to see any progress on this, the work, engagements and debates on epistemic decolonization cannot remain within the ivory towers, disconnected from the broader societies where the universities operate. Given the lack of a "decoloniality posture" among most of Africa's scholars and academics (Maserumule, 2015), Nyamnjoh (2019) believes that looking beyond the academia and engaging with ordinary

Africans and their experiences and stories is critical in the process of making knowledge and education representative of African worldviews. Burna Boy's *Monsters You Made* is an important critical contribution to the engagements, debates, theorizing, storytelling and charting the way forward by decolonial movements, activists and scholars in Africa and elsewhere in the world, who are struggling and pushing against the oppressive status quo in their settings, communities and institutions. The song takes the debate about coloniality, epistemic violence, Eurocentric hegemony and the need for decolonization outside the ivory towers and scholarly circles and places them into the public space. This is key if we are to keep the struggle alive and inclusive of all spheres of African and other formerly colonized societies.

References

Afolabi, O. S. (2020). Globalisation, Decoloniality and the Question of Knowledge Production in Africa: A Critical Discourse. *Journal of Higher Education in Africa, 18*(1), 93–109.

African Union. (2016). *Continental Education Strategy for Africa: 2016–2025*. African Union.

Aidoo, A. A. (1995). An Interview with Ama Ata Aidoo. Interview Conducted by Anuradha Dingwaney Needham. *The Massachusetts Review*, *36*(1), 123–133.

Aina, T. A. (2010). Beyond Reforms: The Politics of Higher Education Transformation in Africa. *African Studies Review, 53*(1), 21–40.

Ajodo-Adebanjoko, A. (2017). Towards Ending Conflict and Insecurity in the Niger Delta Region: A Collective Non-Violent Approach. *African Journal on Conflict Resolution, 17*(1), 9–27.

Anthias, P., & Hoffmann, K. (2021). The Making of Ethnic Territories: Governmentality and Counter Conducts. *Geoforum, 119*, 218–226.

Beaudry, C., Mouton, J., & Prozesky, H. (2018a). Lack of Funding. In C. Beaudry, J. Mouton, & H. Prozesky (Eds.), *The Next Generation of Scientists in Africa* (pp. 71–88). African Minds.

Biko, S. (1978). *I Write What I like*. Picador Africa, 2004.

Burna Boy. (2020). *Monsters You Made*. Featuring Chris Martin. Twice as Tall. Spaceship, Bad Habit, Atlantic Records and Warner Music. Apple Music. Retrieved from https://music.apple.com/za/album/monsters-you-made-feat-chris-martin/1527475833

Chelwa, G. (2021). 'We Need Wholesale decolonization': A Conversation with Grieve Chelwa. Interview by Bhakti Shringarpure. *Los Angeles Review of Books*. 25 October 2021. https://lareviewofbooks.org/article/we-need-wholesale-decolonization-a-conversation-with-grieve-chelwa/

Dowden, R. (2008). *Africa: Altered States, Ordinary Miracles*. Portobello Books.
Fanon, F. (1963). *The Wretched of the Earth*. Grove Press.
Fenton, S. (2003). *Ethnicity*. Polity Press.
Fomunyan, K. G. (2017). Decolonising the Future in the Untransformed Present in South African Higher Education. *Perspectives in Education, 35*(2), 168–180.
Grosfoguel, R. (2006). World-Systems Analysis in the Context of Transmodernity, Border Thinking, and Global Coloniality. *Review (fernand Braudel Center), 29*(2), 167–187.
Keet, A. (2014). Epistemic 'Othering' and the Decolonization of Knowledge. *Africa Insight, 44*(1), 23–37.
Kessi, S., Marks, Z., & Ramugondo, E. (2020). Decolonizing African Studies. *Critical African Studies, 12*(3), 271–282.
Maldonado-Torres, N. (2007). On the Coloniality of Being. *Cultural Studies, 21*(2–3), 240–270.
Mama, A. (2007). Is it Ethical to Study Africa? Preliminary Thoughts on Scholarship and Freedom. *African Studies Review, 50*(1), 1–26.
Mamdani, M. (1993). University Crisis and Reform: A Reflection on the African Experience. *Review of African Political Economy, 58*, 7–19.
Mamdani, M. (1996). *Citizen and Subject: Contemporary Africa and the Legacy of Late Colonialism*. Princeton University Press.
Mamdani, M. (2016). Between the Public Intellectual and the Scholar: Decolonization and Some Post-Independence Initiatives in African Higher Education. *Inter-Asia Cultural Studies, 17*(1), 68–83.
Maserumule, M. P. (2015, November 25). Why Africa's Professors are Afraid of Colonial Education Being Dismantled. *The Conversation*. Retrieved from https://theconversation.com/why-africas-professors-are-afraid-of-colonial-education-being-dismantled-50930
Mignolo, W. D. (2011). Geopolitics of Sensing and Knowing: On (De)coloniality, Border Thinking and Epistemic Disobedience. *Postcolonial Studies, 14*(3), 273–283.
Mouton, J., & Blanckenberg, J. (2018). African Science: A Bibliometric Analysis. In C. Beaudry, J. Mouton, & H. Prozesky (Eds.), *The Next Generation of Scientists in Africa* (pp. 13–25). African Minds.
Mpofu, W., & Steyn, M. (2021). The Trouble with the Human. In M. Steyn & W. Mpofu (Eds.), *Decolonising the Human: Reflections from Africa on Difference and Oppression* (pp. 1–24). Wits University Press.
Ndlovu, M. (2018). Coloniality of Knowledge and the Challenge of Creating African Futures. *Ufahamu: A Journal of African Studies, 40*(2), 95–112.
Ndlovu-Gatsheni, S. J. (2013a). Why Decoloniality in the 21st Century? *The Thinker, 48*, 11–15.

Ndlovu-Gatsheni, S. J. (2013b). Decolonising the University in Africa. *The Thinker, 51*, 46–51.

Ngobili, C. (2021). Close to a Century of Popular Music Practices and Experiences in Nigeria (1922–2020) and a Brief History of Their Socio-Political Background. *Muziki: Journal of Music Research in Africa, 18*(1), 34–58.

Ngũgĩ, M. W. (2020, January 17). The Pitfalls of Symbolic Decolonization. *Africa Is a Country*. Retrieved from https://africasacountry.com/2020/01/the-pitfalls-of-symbolic-decolonization

Nyoni, J. (2019). Decolonising the Higher Education Curriculum: An Analysis of African Intellectual Readiness to Break the Chains of a Colonial Caged Mentality. *Transformation in Higher Education, 4*(0), a69, 1–10.

Nyamnjoh, F. B. (2019). *Decolonising the university in Africa*. In Oxford Research Encyclopedia of Politics. Retrieved from https://doi.org/10.1093/acrefore/9780190228637.001.0001/acrefore-9780190228637-e-717

Ochonu, M. E. (2020). South African Afrophobia in Local and Continental Contexts. *Journal of Modern African Studies, 58*(4), 499–519.

Ogunyemi, C. B. (2021). Fela Kuti's Black Consciousness: African Cosmology and the Re-Configuration of Blackness in 'Colonial Mentality.' *African Identities, 19*(4), 487–501.

Pajon, L. (2021, June 28). *Nigeria: Fela Kuti's 'Zombie' – A Struggle That Lives On*. Africa Report. https://www.theafricareport.com/94838/fela-kuti-zombie-a-struggle-that-lives-on

Pareles, J. (2020, August 5). Burna Boy Has the Whole World Listening. *The New York Times*. https://www.nytimes.com/2020/08/05/arts/music/burna-boy-twice-as-tall.html

Perry, K. E. G. (2020, August 7). *Burna Boy: 'A Revolution is Needed. I Want to Inspire It.'* NME. https://www.nme.com/big-reads/burna-boy-cover-interview-2020-twice-as-tall-afrobeats-african-giant-2723141

Quijano, A. (2000). Coloniality of power and Eurocentrism in Latin America. *International Sociology, 15*(2), 215–232.

Rodney, W. (1972). *How Europe Underdeveloped Africa*. Pambazuka Press, 2012.

Said, E. W. (1989). Representing the Colonized: Anthropology's Interlocutors. *Critical Inquiry, 15*, 205–225.

Sardar, Z. (2008). I Think It Would Be Good If Certain Things Were Said: Fanon and the Epidemiology of Oppression. Forward in Fanon, F. *Black Skins, White Masks* (pp. vi–xx). Pluto Books.

Shaik, A., & Kahn, P. (2021). Understanding the Challenges Entailed in Decolonizing a Higher Education Institution: An Organizational Case Study of a Research-Intensive South African University. *Teaching in Higher Education, 26*(7–8), 969–985.

United Nations Human Rights Council. (2022). *The Right to a Clean, Healthy and Sustainable Environment: Non-toxic Environment*. Report of the Special

Rapporteur on the Issue of Human Rights Obligations Relating to the Enjoyment of a Safe, Clean, Healthy and Sustainable Environment. A/HRC/49/53. United Nations Human Rights Council.

Wa Thiong'o, N. (1986). *Decolonising the Mind: The Politics of Language in African Literature*. James Currey.

Wa Thiong'o, N. (1993). *Moving the Centre: The Struggle for Cultural Freedoms*. James Currey.

Wa Thiong'o, N. (2013). *Consciousness and African Renaissance: South Africa in the Black Imagination*. 4th Steve Biko Memorial Lecture, 12 September 2013. University of Cape Town, South Africa.

Woldegiorgis, E. T. (2021). Decolonising a higher education system which has never been colonised. *Educational Philosophy and Theory, 53*(9), 894–906.

Zeleza, P. T. (2006, August 30). Beyond Afropessimism: Historical Accounting of African Universities. *Pambazuka News*. Retrieved from https://www.pambazuka.org/governance/beyond-afropessimism-historical-accounting-african-universities

Zeleza, P. T. (2012). *Internationalization in Higher Education: Opportunities and Challenges for the Knowledge Project in the Global South*. Keynote address. Southern African Regional Universities Association (SARUA) Leadership Dialogue on Building the Capacity of Higher Education to Enhance Regional Development, Maputo, Mozambique, 21–22 March 2012.

CHAPTER 7

Is Sub-Saharan Africa a Knowledge Society or Economy?

Nelson Casimiro Zavale

Introduction

From 1990s onwards, a new socio-economic model emerged, the so-called knowledge-based economy or society. While the term "knowledge-based economy" was first coined in the 1960s (Godin, 2006) and its roots can be traced back to the period of Enlightenment and the subsequent Industrial Revolution (Mokyr, 2002), the core features of this socio-economic model, as known today, have occurred from 1990s onwards. From 1990s onwards, the economy or society has witnessed five major changes that are thought to differ from earlier periods. First, the relevance of intangible capital (i.e., human capital and highly skilled workers)

N. C. Zavale (✉)
Eduardo Mondlane University, Maputo, Mozambique
e-mail: nelson.casimiro.zavale@gmail.com

Käte Hamburger Kolleg: Cultures of Research, RWTH Aachen University, Aachen, Germany

CSHE, University of California, Berkeley, CA, USA

N. Andrews and N. E. Khalema (eds.), *Decolonizing African Studies Pedagogies*, Political Pedagogies,
https://doi.org/10.1007/978-3-031-37442-5_7

for economic growth and development has outweighed tangible capital (e.g., natural and physical capital). Second, the speed at which knowledge is created, accumulated and depreciated has unprecedentedly accelerated, intensifying the pace of scientific and technological progress and innovation. Third, the information and communication technologies have facilitated the storage, access, sharing and usage of information and knowledge at global level. Fourth, the division and specialization of labor in and between organizations became flexible, so as to adapt to the constant changes in user's demands and other external factors. Fifth and last, knowledge producers and users have built alliances to be more effective in fueling innovation (David & Foray, 2003; Foray & Lundvall, 1998; Powell & Snellman, 2004).

The precursors of this debate do emphasize, despite their different disciplinary backgrounds and vocabulary (e.g., *knowledge economy/society, information economy/society, network society*), the key role played by information and/or knowledge for the functioning of contemporary economies and societies (Choong et al., 2021). Economists such as Fritz Machlup, Una Manscheld and Peter Drucker, sociologists like Daniel Bell and Manuel Castells and organizational theorists like Ikujiro Nonaka and Hirotaka Takeuchi, all have conceptualized the usefulness of knowledge for socio-economic systems and organizations (Bell, 1973; Castells, 1996; Drucker, 1969; Machlup, 1962; Nonaka, 1994; Nonaka & Takeuchi, 1995). Therefore, knowledge-based societies or economies are societies or economies whose functioning relies on the production, usage and dissemination of knowledge.

Inspired by these narratives, the African Union in 2015 adopted the so-called *Agenda 2063*, a set of socio-economic initiatives and plans intending to transform Africa into a knowledge-based economy by 2063. This timeline was not chosen at random. In 2063, the African Union will celebrate 100 years since its foundation in 1963, then known as the Organization of African Unity. The agenda years was adopted as plan for the next 50. One of the objectives of the *Agenda 2063* is to reposition the continent, from a supplier of unprocessed raw materials for export, into a knowledge society or economy, through improving the state and usage of (higher) education, science and technology in development. For example, in 2014, the African Union adopted the Science, Technology and Innovation Strategy for Africa, 2024 (STISA-2024), an initial 10-year framework for pursuing the goal of becoming a knowledge economy.

However, SSA is not and will unlikely become a knowledge-based economy or society by the defined deadline, particularly if only conventional western-rooted approaches of knowledge readiness and performance are used (e.g., knowledge index, index of knowledge societies, global knowledge index and global innovation index). Africa is and will likely continue to lag behind because the conventional measures of knowledge readiness tend to reflect (i) inequalities in levels of development between developed and developing countries and regions (Adu, 2014), (ii) a monolithic western-based view of science or knowledge (Kraemer-Mbula et al., 2019) (iii) and geopolitical inequalities in the world system of knowledge production (Demeter, 2020).

In this chapter, I seek to critically question the SSA's portrait displayed by these conventional approaches and metrics. My accounts draw from perspectives emerging from the Global South in defense of epistemic pluralism within knowledge production and the greater scientific community, as well as from calls for inclusivity and valorization of other types of (non-scientific) knowledges. I argue that epistemic justice is an important pre-requisite for transforming the epistemological debate into a pedagogical debate. Once all knowledges find their legitimate way into the educational realm in SSA, it would be much easier to revisit African pedagogical practices and discourses, namely to democratize them by incorporating non-western knowledges, non-western pedagogic traditions and unconventional approaches when doing research on SSA education systems. The reminder of this chapter is organized as follows: Sect. 7.2 discusses the commonly used metrics and indices of knowledge-based economy or society; Sect. 7.3 locates SSA within the commonly used metrics and indices of knowledge-based economy or society; Sect. 7.4 questions whether SSA is knowledge-based economy or society, arguing that the region might be a different kind of knowledge-based economy or society.

Knowledge Economy and/or Society: Commonly Used Metrics or Indices

Several metrics and indices have been devised by international organizations to measure performance, similarities and differences in development among and across countries and regions. Some indices measure economic performance (e.g., rates of economic growth; amount of GDP nominal and GDP per capita in US dollars; global competitiveness index). Other indices measure the quality of governments, governance and institutions (e.g., rule of law index, regulatory quality index, corruption perception index, political rights index). There are also metrics of people's well-being (e.g., human development index, Gini income inequality index), education (e.g., expenditures in primary, secondary and tertiary education) and innovation (e.g., global innovation index)[1,2]

Most of these metrics and indices often measure the political, social and economic factors enabling the production and use of knowledge, but not knowledge per se. Thus, some specific indices and metrics have been suggested to measure countries' performance and readiness for knowledge (e.g., knowledge economy index, knowledge index, index of knowledge societies, global knowledge index, digital economy and society index, state new economy index, web index; for further indices, see Ojanperä et al., 2019). In this chapter, I discuss two of such indices: Global Knowledge Index (GKI) and Global Innovation Index (GII). My rationale for selecting these indices is threefold. First, they are underpinned by a broader and multi-dimensional concept of knowledge (GKI) and innovation (GII) and, as a result, they have been devised to capture the main dimensions of the knowledge economy and society, including the enabling environment conditions. Unsurprisingly, these two indices often use similar pillars, variables and data to measure countries' capabilities and readiness for knowledge and innovation; in addition, these indices are drawn from and seek to perfect former discontinued indices (e.g., Knowledge Economy Index, Knowledge Index), and hence, they merge dimensions of knowledge economy with those of knowledge society. Second, the two indices have been devised by international organizations with the ambition of periodically (annually) comparing the performance of different countries and regions; this ambition has been met, as these two indices are calculated annually on regular basis. Last but not least, in their ambition of drawing international comparisons, the two indices include African countries, and this inclusion enables to situate SSA's standing vis-à-vis other regions.

[1] For a comprehensive list of commonly used indicators, metrics and indices at the international level, see the global economy site: https://www.theglobaleconomy.com/).

[2] https://www.theglobaleconomy.com/.

Global Knowledge Index

The GKI was jointly produced by the United Nations Development Programme (UNDP) and the Mohammed Bin Rashid Al Maktoum Knowledge Foundation (MBRF), to capture the multi-dimensional nature of knowledge through incorporating the components of both knowledge economy and knowledge society (UNDP & MBRF, 2017). GKI replaces Knowledge Economy Index (KEI), a World Bank's aggregate measure of knowledge economy, discontinued in 2012 (Chen & Dahlman, 2005). GKI breaks down knowledge concepts into their social and economic constituents and it links knowledge to developmental issues (e.g., the 2030 agenda for Sustainable Development Goals; GKI-2021, see UNDP & MBRF, 2021).

The GKI consists of seven sub-indices: six of them highlight the performance of six sectors, namely (i) pre-university education; (ii) technical and vocational education and training (TVET); (iii) higher education; (iv) research, development and innovation (RDI); (v) information and communications technology (ICT); (vi) and economy. These six sub-indices are complemented by a seventh, which measures the enabling social, political and economic context or environment. Each of these sub-indices aggregates pillars and each pillar comprises sub-pillars and measurable variables (for specific variables, see GKI, 2021 in UNDP and MBRF, 2021):

1. *The pre-university education* sub-index comprises the pillars of knowledge capital (three sub-pillars: enrollment, completion and outcomes) and educational enabling environment (four sub-pillars: expenditure, resources, early learning and equity and inclusivity);
2. *The TVET sub-index* consists of pillars of formation and professional training (three sub-pillars: continuous training and skilling; TVET structure; TVET's quality and qualifications) and features of the labor market (three sub-pillars: efficiency of the labor market; post-TVET employment; equity and inclusivity);
3. *The higher education sub-index* comprises the pillars of higher education inputs (three sub-pillars: expenditure, enrollment, resources), learning environment (two sub-pillars: diversity and academic freedom; equity and inclusivity) and outputs (three sub-pillars: attainment, employment, impact);

4. *The RDI sub-index* comprises the pillar of research and development, innovation's inputs (three sub-pillars: inputs of R&D institutions, of business enterprises and of societal innovation); outputs (three sub-pillars: outputs of R&D institutions, of business enterprises and of societal innovation) and of impact (three sub-pillars: quality, linkage and business development);
5. *The ICT sub-index* consists of pillars of infrastructure (three sub-pillars: coverage, quality, affordability), access (two sub-pillars: subscriptions; and skills and employment) and usage (two sub-pillars: services and outcomes);
6. *The economy sub-index* consists of pillars of economic competitiveness (two sub-pillars: infrastructure investment, business agility), economic openness (two sub-pillars: trade and diversification, financial openness) and financing and domestic value added (two sub-pillars: financing and taxes; domestic value added);
7. *The enabling environment sub-index* comprises three pillars: governance (two sub-pillars: political environment, quality of institutions), socio-economic (three sub-pillars: gender equality, social inclusion, standard of living) and health and environment (two sub-pillars: health, environmental performance).

Global Innovation Index

The Global Innovation Index (GII) is an annual composite metric launched in 2007 by the *Institut Européen d'Administration des Affaires* (INSEAD). It merges two formerly used indices, namely: the Index of Knowledge Societies, suggested by United Nations Department of Economic and Social Affairs (UNIDESA, 2005) to measure the properties of knowledge society; and the Knowledge-Based Index (KEI), suggested by the World Bank to measure of knowledge economy, discontinued in 2012 (Chen & Dahlman, 2005). During 2011–2020, GII was co-published by INSEAD, in co-authorship with Cornell University and the World Intellectual Property Organization (WIPO). In 2021, GII was published by WIPO in partnership with the Portulans Institute, various corporate and academic network partners and the GII Advisory Board. GII's objective is to evaluate and capture countries' performance in innovation. For its proponents, GII (2021) is important because (i) innovation is important for driving economic progress and competitiveness; (ii) the concept of innovation has broadened beyond R&D, scientific papers and patents; (iii) showcasing innovation in emerging economies is critical to inspire entrepreneurs and innovators. GII adopts a broad concept of innovation, inspired by the Oslo Manual: "*An innovation is a new or improved product or process (or combination thereof) that differs significantly from the unit's previous products or processes and that has been made available to potential users (product) or brought into use by the unit (process)*" (Oslo Manual fourth edition). Besides improvement of products, processes and radical innovation, GII's underlying concept also encompasses incremental innovation—the ability of new context (e.g., developing countries) to exploit new innovations produced elsewhere. Moreover, GII's concept goes beyond industrial innovations to cover innovations occurring in services and public administration. The GII relies on two sub-indices, the *innovation input sub-index* and the *innovation output sub-index*, each built around pillars. The *sub-index innovation inputs* are captured through five pillars that enable innovative activities: (1) institutions, (2) human capital and research, (3) infrastructure, (4) market sophistication and (5) business sophistication. The *sub-index innovation outputs* are captured through two pillars: (6) scientific outputs and (7) creative outputs. Each pillar is divided into sub-pillars, and each sub-pillar is composed of individual indicators.

SSA's Position in Knowledge Economy and/or Society: Commonly Used Metrics or Indices

How does SSA perform in these indices and metrics? Based on these indices, to what extent can SSA be considered knowledge economy or society? In this section, I address these questions. I start by summarizing the main pillars, sub-pillars and indicators of two indices currently used to measure countries' knowledge readiness, capabilities and performance: GKI and GII. Given that my focus is on knowledge, I take GKI as reference, and I compare it with GII.

GKI and GII use similar metrics to measure countries' readiness and performance in knowledge and innovation. This similarity is not surprising given that knowledge and innovation are associated with and dependent on each other—innovation is often seen as a way of creating, exploiting and adapting new knowledge—and both are equally thought to be core for the functioning of knowledge economies or societies. GII's pillars fit well into the seven sub-indices of the GKI, despite difference in terminologies and the fact that GII has more pillars and indicators than GKI. The GKI's sub-indices of *education* and *R&D* and their respective pillars, sub-pillars and indicators are similar to GII's pillars of *human capital and research, business sophistication, knowledge and technology outputs and creative outputs*; through these pillars, both indices measure the core elements of knowledge in a knowledge economy and society, namely the inputs, throughputs, outputs and impacts of education and R&D. The GKI's sub-index of *ICT* is also similar to GII's *infrastructure*, although GII has a broader concept of infrastructure which, in addition to ICT, includes energy, electricity and environmental performance. The remaining GKI' sub-indices, namely *economy* and *enabling environment*, albeit important, do not concern the core knowledge elements but rather the surrounding political, social and economic conditions for the production and usage of knowledge. The GII designates these conditions by the terminologies of *market sophistication* and *institutions*. In other words, the comparison of GKI and GII shows that the international conventional or mainstream wisdom assesses a country or region's readiness, capabilities and performance toward knowledge economy or society through three cluster of dimensions: the first cluster, core to knowledge, concerns inputs, throughputs, outputs and impacts of *education, human capital* and *R&D*; the second cluster, also core as it enables storage, access, sharing and usage of information and knowledge at the global level, concerns the availability, quality and access to *ICT*; the third cluster, also important but perhaps less core than the previous two, are the *surrounding socio-political and -economic conditions* facilitating or constraining the production, usage and diffusion of knowledge.

GKI and GII similarity suggests that the two suffice to assess how SSA stands or performs, as far as conventional or mainstream international conventional metrics are concerned, in its possibility or quest of becoming a knowledge-based economy or society. Unsurprisingly, SSA performs low in both indices. During the last 5 years (i.e., from 2017 to 2022), SSA remained low on the index rankings in comparison to other regions. In the GKI, from about 130 to 138 countries that are annually assessed, most Sub-Saharan African countries are in the bottom tier: for example, most of the last 25–40 low-ranked countries are from SSA, with only about 5–10 ten being non-African (mostly low-income), namely Venezuela, Bangladesh, Nepal, Tajikistan, Yemen, Pakistan, Syria, Yemen, Pakistan, Myanmar, Lao. Similar pattern is observed in the GII: from about 126–126 annually assessed countries, most of the last 25–40 low-ranked countries are from SSA, with only about 5–10 being non-African, namely the ones mentioned earlier plus El Salvador, Honduras, Bolivia, Guatemala. Countries like Seychelles, South Africa, Mauritius, Botswana, Cape Verde, Namibia and occasionally Kenya often perform better than their SSA counterparts, but these better-off countries also perform lower than developed countries and emerging economies.

Overall, SSA's low performance is also confirmed by specific research that assessed SSA's readiness to knowledge, in comparison with other regions (Amoah, 2014; Anyanwu, 2012; Asongu & Andrés, 2020; Asongu & Tchamyou, 2018; Asongu et al., 2020). This bulk of research shows that SSA lags behind, even if some countries are better-off (e.g., South Africa, Mauritius), or are better-off in some dimensions (e.g., South Africa in innovation; Mauritius and Botswana in institutional regime) (Asongu et al., 2020). Unsurprisingly, some literature suggests possible strategies, trajectories and policies for SSA to catch-up, often using South Korea as paradigmatic successful example (Asongu, 2017; Asongu & Andrés, 2020; Asongu & Tchamyou, 2018). However, even where SSA has caught up, like in primary education (from 1970 to 2008, enrollment in primary education increased from 23 to 129 million in SSA, i.e., 5.5 times; and during the same period, GERs [gross enrollment ratios] have increased from 52.5 to 101.6%, UNESCO, 2011), doubts persist as to whether increase in enrollments are translated into proportional learning. A recent study published in *Nature*, targeting 164 countries from 2000 to 2017, shows that SSA lags behind all regions in learning outcomes, apart from South Asia, the other poorest world region (Angrist et al., 2021).

Therefore, if looked from the perspective of conventional or mainstream international metrics and indices, SSA does not seem to embody or is far from having the key patterns of a knowledge economy or society. SSA lacks highly educated population and skilled human capital; produces little R&D products in high quantity and of high quality; lacks good quality ICT infrastructure that enables easy circulation of knowledge. Even worse, SSA lacks the necessary inputs, resources and capabilities, including favorable surrounding socio-political and economic conditions, to educate its population to be globally competitive as knowledge workers, and to invest in R&D that can produce globally competitive cutting-edge science and technology. This suggests that the possibility of SSA being considered a knowledge society or economy, or a region that is home to some kind of socially and economically useful knowledge, demands to look beyond conventional or mainstream international metrics and indices.

Sub-Saharan Africa: A Different Kind of Knowledge Society or Economy?

Adu (2014) has compared these conventional knowledge measures with commonly used measures of economic performance (e.g., GDP) and development (e.g., Human Development Index) at the international level. She found out that top and low performers are almost the same, with SSA countries occupying, again, bottom positions. In reality, as Adu (2014: 11) concludes, these measurements are simply "telling a well-known story of 'developed' and 'less developing', and the only difference is that they are just more complex way of measuring GDP or development". As Adu (2014) rightly points out, it is important to question the useful of these measurements to account for knowledge dimension of developing countries.

Adu (2014) is not unique to have suggested that knowledge might need alternative accounts in SSA. In their recently edited volume, several scholars have claimed that the way research excellence is conceived and measured in Global South should be revisited (Kraemer-Mbula et al., 2019). Overall, the editors and contributors in this volume suggest that the idea of research excellence, that is to say., of what counts as best, excellent or good science in Global South, and in SSA in particular, should not be strictly framed and measured in light of conventional approaches and metrics often used in Global North. In Global North, research excellence is often equated with publishing breakthrough research in top or high-impact journals and with being highly cited (in case of publications and authors) or highly ranked (in case of institutions and countries). While this concept is also contested in the Global North, the quest for simplifying the complexity of science for informing decision-making in research assessment, funding and policies makes the usage of conventional quantitative indicators more appealing, attractive and necessary (Ferretti et al., 2018). Publishing outstanding and highly citable research in top or high-impact journals is of course an important criterion to judge good science in Global South but it is not the unique or eventually not the most important one. Authors in the volume argue for a more pluralistic vision of research excellence, based on which the Global South may define and measure research excellence differently and better. Given Global South's specific conditions and challenges, particularly related to scarce resources and to the need to produce research that is both globally visible and capable of responding to pressing local and regional development issues, the meaning of excellent science in Global South should not solely rely on "blind" quantitative bibliometric indicators. Instead, good science should also be able to generate significant societal impact; should be both output-driven and impact-inspired; and both inclusive and locally relevant, that is also to say, what counts as good science should be able to equally reward all entities and individuals involved in the often team-based research endeavor and, in doing so, should open a dialogic, reflexive space from which recognition of the diversity of knowledge is possible. Likewise, a top scientist or researcher in Global South is not only the one who outperforms other researchers in publications and citations, but the one whose research impacts institutions and people's lives.

Calls for a more pluralist science are also made by authors who denounce Global North's dominance over Global South in global academic knowledge production (Demeter, 2020). This dominance takes several forms, such as overrepresentation of Global North's academics as editors, members of editorial boards and authors of top journals; dominance of English as the international scientific lingua franca; the academic but also geopolitical challenges facing authors from Global South to get their work published in top journals; overrepresentation of Global North's academic institutions in top of the ranking systems; and the dominance of Global North's publishing houses (Cummings & Hoebink, 2017). Given these geopolitical inequalities in the world system of knowledge production, calls for decolonizing or de-westernizing academic knowledge production and for promoting academic pluralism have been voiced.

As a result of criticisms against conventional measures of science and Global North's dominance in global knowledge production, alternative approaches, often labeled Southern perspectives or theories, have emerged to make visible Global South's knowledge systems. While the historical roots of these alternatives perspectives date back to the 1950s and 1960s' decolonization movements of the then called Third World (Asia, Africa and Latin America), it is over the past two decades that their theoretical foundations were established under diverse labels such as post-colonial (Chakrabarty, 2000), decolonial or decoloniality (Mbembe, 2016; Mignolo, 2009; Ndlovu-Gatsheni, 2015) and multiple modernities

(Eisenstadt, 2000). However, as remarked by Rosa (2014), their influence in epistemological debates became higher after they have been synthetized under the label of *Theories of the South*, notably by Santos (2009), Connell (2007) and Comaroff and Comaroff (2012).

In his *Epistemologies of the South*, the Portuguese social scientist Boaventura de Sousa Santos challenges the pretentious universality and superiority of the western science over other forms of knowledge, particularly those from non-western societies, which are often suppressed and rendered invisible. Santos coins the term "cognitive injustice" or "epistemicide" to refer to the failure to recognize the different ways by which people across the globe run and provide meaning to their lives. For Santos (2009), the possibility of global social justice and development requires a kind of "cognitive or epistemic justice", i.e., the valorization of the diverse world knowledge systems, including those from marginalized people from Global South. In this "ecology of knowledge", Santos argues that the plurality of knowledge should be recognized, and the conception of knowledge-as-intervention-in-reality should prevail rather than hierarchical continuum championed by the west. The search for epistemic justice is also present in Connell's (2007) *Southern Theory*. However, in contrast to Santos's search for dialogue between science and other forms of knowledge, Connell attempts to bring epistemic justice within the scientific community. Departing from the marginalization of academic knowledge produced in the peripheries, i.e., outside western Europe and North America, Connell unveils, in her extensive reviews of social theories from Global South, a wide range of powerful social thought from the colonized and post-colonial world. Comaroff and Comaroff (2012) are even more radical in their analysis about Global North–Global South relationship, by suggesting that, in the same way that Global South looked at the Global North as model for progress, Global North will likely move southward, or, put differently, the Global North will look at the Global South as a model and center for value production on issues such as democracy, personhood, liberalism and knowledge.

Therefore, the theories of the South claim for the recognition of all kinds of knowledge produced and/or shared in different geographical and cultural contexts. This recognition brings back African knowledge systems into the heart of developmental narratives and interventions. The concept of African knowledge systems encompasses, of course, indigenous and traditional knowledge, but it should not delve into inductive generalization and nativist decolonization. Inductive generalization is the fallacy of failing to recognize variations and diversities in African knowledge systems by thinking that all of them are equal or unique (Ndofirepi & Gwaravanda, 2019). Nativist decolonization is the exaggerated romanticization or unwarranted flattery of Southern scholarship, which may result in failing to subject this scholarship to rigorous epistemological vigilance and interrogation. Nativist decolonization can also take a puritanical and hegemonic stance, by distrusting the Northern scholarship just because it is Northern and by attempting to cleanse it at all cost and blindly and uncritically promoting *Southerncentrism* (Moosavi, 2020).

If these cautions are observed, the recognition and co-existence of different knowledge systems is important for enhancing the role of knowledge in development. As recently demonstrated in edited book by Ludwig et al. (2022) on politics of knowledge in inclusive development and innovation, the debate about knowledge for development should reconsider three dimensions. First, the recognition that knowledge, including academic or scientific knowledge, is never value-free and context-independent. The context surrounding knowledge (or ecology of knowledge) always matters in any account related to knowledge for development. Second, the diversity of different forms of experiential, indigenous, local and traditional knowledge, all beyond institutionalized academic knowledge, should be considered in development projects alongside the academic knowledge. This is because local communities are not only experts about local ecological and social dynamics, but their knowledge is also intertwined with practices, values and worldviews that often articulate different perspectives on the co-production of knowledge and social orders. Third, these different knowledge systems should be put in permanent interaction and negotiation. Ludwig et al. (2022) present relevant cases where the lack of recognition of local knowledge, or the lack of interaction between academic knowledge and local knowledge, has resulted in failures in implementation of agricultural projects. The over-emphasis of technocratic knowledge and the lack of consideration of local religious rituals about rice farming in Bali have changed local communities' knowledge about irrigation schedules, impacting negatively crop production. Likewise, the objective of improving goat keeping and marketing in the Inhassoro district in Mozambique was compromised by over-reliance on transfer of academic knowledge without recognizing or addressing the residual tensions between market-led thinking (promoted by academic knowledge) and indigenous values and practice such as mutual assistance and help (held by local communities). Both cases illustrate "how development projects produce hermeneutic injustices by imposing concepts and frameworks that exclude local perspectives and practices, such as those on irrigation as practiced through rituals in water temples in Bali and the entangled social and spiritual perspectives on mutual help that are commonplace among goat keepers in Mozambique" (Ludwig et al., 2022: 24).

Therefore, the theories of the South not only promote epistemic justice by recognizing all kinds of knowledge (e.g., both academic and non-academic, both produced in the center and in the peripheries); these theories also enable us to see SSA as a (different kind of) knowledge-based society and/or economy. Despite weighing little in conventional knowledge metrics (e.g., patents, indexed-publications), SSA is indeed rich in different kinds of knowledge, such as traditional indigenous knowledge and non-indexed (and hence not recognized by Global North's standard) academic knowledge. These kinds of knowledge are used on daily basis by Africans to solve their existential challenges, despite remaining invisible or difficult to measure and hence to valorize.

Epistemic Justice and Implications for African Pedagogies

The promotion of epistemic justice in narratives about knowledge society or economy in SSA challenges us to revisiting discourses and practices about African pedagogies. This is because the epistemological debate has inherently a pedagogical dimension: the educational system often selects, promotes and teaches knowledges that are considered to be valid in and by a specific society. Thus, the Southern perspectives' calls for democratizing knowledge—and the concept of knowledge society or economy—represent a starting point to revisit the discourses and practices in African pedagogies. Changing how one conceives knowledge is a starting point to change how ones teaches or acquires knowledge. As Takayama et al. (2016) pointed out, Southern Theory has implications for education scholarship, since Southern Theory is essentially a pedagogic project. Southern Theory challenges educators to broaden their epistemic horizons, by incorporating unfamiliar knowledges that are produced outside the "west", by incorporating rich non-western pedagogic traditions, and by incorporating unconventional approaches when researching education. Takayama et al. (2016: 4) make a significant claim in this respect: "Perhaps 'doing' Southern Theory might offer resources that help rearrange how educators (and education researchers) think about knowledge and the institutional and political practices that are involved in its production".

In SSA, some alternative decolonizing pedagogical approaches have been suggested. For example, drawing from Zimbabwean post-colonial educational policy reforms, Sigauke (2016) highlights efforts to incorporate the traditional African indigenous knowledge' into the school curriculum. Zimbabwe is not unique in so doing. Almost everywhere in Africa, indigenous knowledge has been to different degrees integrated into the curriculum as an effort to decolonize and Africanize education (Emeagwali & Dei, 2014). Similarly, Zembylas (2018) reflects on how decolonial project of social transformation in African higher education may shape the pedagogical praxis and discourse. Zembylas discusses three approaches for decolonizing post-apartheid South African higher education from western models. Firstly, the soft-reform, which emphasizes the need to increase access and inclusion of marginalized groups and to supplement existing curricula with non-western perspectives so as to enhance diversity in ways that do not significantly challenge existing power relations and structures. Secondly, radical-reform, an approach that takes seriously the need for fundamental changes because changes made through soft-reform are tokenistic, incomplete, insufficient and/or inadequate. Radical-reform grounds the decolonization of higher education as a consciousness that rejects the values, norms and worldviews imposed by the colonizers and a commitment to empower marginalized groups. Thirdly, beyond-reform, a set of approaches which recognize the fundamentally violent and unsustainable system within which the university is embedded. Zembylas (2018) then addresses the pedagogical challenges imposed by these three approaches, highlighting the need to go beyond humanizing critical or radical pedagogy as suggested by the Brazilian Paulo Freire, to embrace a decolonizing pedagogy, capable of (i) unveiling the epistemic violence of colonial knowledge and practices of knowledge; (ii) acknowledging the contribution of western knowledge but also providing intellectual and pedagogical spaces of decolonial praxis; and (iii) ethically addressing the complex and sometimes contradictory histories of different peoples in (post-)colonial settings, while enabling to change our relationship to colonial/colonized modes of signification and relationality. Zembylas's claims on decolonizing knowledge and pedagogy are repeatedly voiced in South Africa (Heleta, 2018) and across Africa (Morreira, 2017). Thus, in the same way that knowledge should be democratized and decolonized—to reimagine a knowledge-based economy or society in SSA—African educational realm and pedagogical discourses and practices should also open up their fences to include non-western knowledges, non-western pedagogic traditions and unconventional approaches.

Conclusions

In this chapter, I have argued that if only conventional western-rooted approaches of knowledge readiness and performance are used (e.g., knowledge index, index of knowledge societies, global knowledge index and global innovation index), SSA is not and will unlikely become a knowledge-based economy or society, even by 2063. Thus, while SSA might continue measuring its knowledge readiness through conventional metrics, alternative lens are also required in order to do (epistemic) justice to the several useful knowledge systems that co-exist in SSA. I have argued that Southern perspectives can offer such alternative lens. The importance of Southern perspectives is twofold: on the one hand, they enable us to re-conceptualize the possibility of an alternative model of knowledge society or economy, which could best fit the conditions and realities of SSA; on the other hand, Southern perspectives' defense of epistemic pluralism enables us to decolonize knowledge production and recognition inside the scientific community, as well as to promote inclusivity and valorization of other types of (non-scientific) knowledges that exist in developing contexts. Therefore, any debate about knowledge society or economy in SSA in general, would not be complete if it avoids considering the plurality of knowledge produced by SSA's academia, as well as the diversity of knowledge produced by different types of social actors. Epistemic justice is an important pre-requisite for transforming the epistemological debate into a pedagogical debate. Once all knowledges find their legitimate way into the educational realm in SSA, then it will be much easier to revisit African (studies) pedagogies, namely to democratize them by incorporating non-western knowledges, non-western pedagogic traditions and unconventional approaches when doing research on SSA education systems.

References

Adu, K. H. (2014). What Is the Opposite of a Knowledge Society? In L. G. A. Amoah (Ed.), *Impacts of the Knowledge Society on Economic and Social Growth in Africa* (pp. 1–19). IGI Global.

Amoah, L. G. A. (Ed.) (2014). *Impacts of the Knowledge Society on Economic and Social Growth in Africa*. IGI Global.

Angrist, N., Djankov, S., Goldberg, P. K., & Patrinos, H. A. (2021). Measuring Human Capital Using Global Learning Data. *Nature, 592*, 403–408.

Anyanwu, J. C. (2012). Developing Knowledge for Economic Advancement in Africa. *International Journal of Academic Research in Economics and Management Science, 1*(2), 73–111.

Asongu, S. A. (2017). Knowledge Economy Gaps, Policy Syndromes, and Catch-Up Strategies: Fresh South Korean Lessons to Africa. *Journal of the Knowledge Economy, 8*(1), 211–253.

Asongu, S. A., & Tchamyou, V. S. (2018). Human Capital, Knowledge Creation, Knowledge Diffusion, Institutions and Economic Incentives: South Korea Versus Africa. *Contemporary Social Science, 15*(1), 26–47.

Asongu, S. A., & Andrés, A. R. (2020). Trajectories of Knowledge Economy in SSA and MENA Countries. *Technology in Society, 63*, 101–119.

Asongu, S. A., Tchamyou, V. S., & Acha-Anyi, P. N. (2020). Who Is Who in Knowledge Economy in Africa? *Journal of the Knowledge Economy, 11*(2), 425–457.

Bell, D. (1973). *The Coming of Post-Industrial Society: A Venture in Social Forecasting*. Basic Books.

Castells, M. (1996). The Net and the Self: Working Notes for a Critical Theory of the Informational Society. *Critique of Anthropology, 16*(1), 9–38.

Chakrabarty, D. (2000). Subaltern Studies and Postcolonial Historiography. *Nepantla: Views from South, 1*(1), 9–32.

Chen, D. H., & Dahlman, C. J. (2005). *The Knowledge Economy, the KAM Methodology and World Bank Operations*. World Bank Institute Working Paper.

Choong, K. K., & Leung, P. W. (2021). A Critical Review of the Precursors of the Knowledge Economy and their Contemporary Research: Implications for the Computerized New Economy. *Journal of the Knowledge Economy, 13*(2), 1573–1610.

Comaroff, J., & Comaroff, J. L. (2012). *Theory from the South: Or, How Euro-America Is Evolving Toward Africa*. Routledge.

Connell R. (2007). *Southern Theory: The Global Dynamics of Knowledge in Social Science*. Polity.

Cummings, S. J. R. & Hoebink, P. (2017). Representation of Academics from Developing Countries as Authors and Editorial Board Members in Scientific Journals: Does This Matter to the Field of Development Studies? *The European Journal of Development Research, 29*(2), 369–383.

David, P. A., & Foray, D. (2003). Economic Fundamentals of the Knowledge Society. *Policy Futures in Education, 1*(1), 20–49.

Demeter, M. (2020). *Academic Knowledge Production and the Global South: Questioning Inequality and Under-Representation*. Palgrave Macmillan.

Drucker, P. F. (1969). The Knowledge Society. *New Society, 13*(343), 629–631.

Eisenstadt, S. (2000). Multiple Modernities. *Daedalus, 129*(1), 1–28.

Emeagwali, G., & Dei, G. J. S. (2014). *African Indigenous Knowledge and the Disciplines*. Sense Publishers.

Ferretti, F., Pereira, Â. G., Vértesy, D., & Hardeman, S. (2018). Research Excellence Indicators: Time to Reimagine the Making Of? *Science and Public Policy, 45*(5), 731–741.

Foray, D., & Lundvall, B. Å. (1998). The Knowledge-Based Economy: From the Economics of Knowledge to the Learning Economy. In T. Siesfeld, J. Cefola, & D. Neef (Eds.), *The Economic Impact of Knowledge* (pp. 115–121). Routledge.

Godin, B. (2006). The Knowledge-Based Economy: Conceptual Framework or Buzzword? *The Journal of Technology Transfer, 31*(1), 17–30.

Heleta, S. (2018). Decolonizing Knowledge in South Africa: Dismantling the 'Pedagogy of Big Lies'. *Ufahamu: A Journal of African Studies, 40*(2), 47–65.

Kraemer-Mbula, E., Tijssen, R., Wallace, M. L., & McClean, R. (2019). *Transforming Research Excellence: New Ideas from the Global South*. African Minds.

Ludwig, D., Boogaard, B., Macnaghten, P., & Leeuwis, C. (2022). *The Politics of Knowledge in Inclusive Development and Innovation*. Routledge.

Machlup, F. (1962). *The Production and Distribution of Knowledge in the United States*. Princeton University Press.

Mbembe, A. J. (2016). Decolonizing the University. New Directions. *Arts & Humanities in Higher Education, 15*(1), 29–45.

Mignolo, W. D. (2009). Epistemic Disobedience, Independent Thought and Decolonial Freedom. *Theory, Culture and Society, 26*(7–8), 159–181.

Mokyr, J. (2002). *The Gifts of Athena: Historical Origins of the Knowledge Economy*. Princeton University Press.

Morreira, S. (2017). Steps Towards Decolonial Higher Education in Southern Africa? Epistemic Disobedience in the Humanities. *Journal of Asian and African Studies, 52*(3), 287–301.

Moosavi, L. (2020). The Decolonial Bandwagon and the Dangers of Intellectual Decolonization. *International Review of Sociology, 30*(2), 332–354.

Ndofirepi, A. P., & Gwaravanda, E. T. (2019). Epistemic (In)justice in African Universities: A Perspective of the Politics of Knowledge. *Educational Review, 71*(5), 581–594.

Ndlovu-Gatsheni, S. J. (2015). Decoloniality as the Future of Africa. *History Compass, 13*(10), 485–496.

Nonaka, I. (1994). A Dynamic Theory of Organizational Knowledge Creation. *Organizational Science, 5*(1), 14–37.

Nonaka, I., & Takeuchi, H. (1995). *The Knowledge Creating Company: How Japanese Companies Create the Dynamics of Innovation*. Oxford University Press.

Ojanperä, S., Graham, M., & Zook, M. (2019). The Digital Knowledge Economy Index: Mapping Content Production. *The Journal of Development Studies, 55*(12), 2626–2643.

Powell, W. W., & Snellman, K. (2004). The Knowledge Economy. *Annual Review of Sociology, 30*(1), 199–220.

Rosa, M. C. (2014). Theories of the South: Limits and Perspectives of an Emergent Movement in Social Sciences. *Current Sociology, 62*(6), 851–867.

Sigauke, A. T. (2016). Ubuntu/Hunhu in Post-colonial Education Policies in Southern Africa: A Response to Connell's Southern Theory and the Role of Indigenous African Knowledges in the Social Sciences. *Postcolonial Directions in Education, 5*(1), 27–53.

Santos, B. D. S. (2009). Para Além Do Pensamento Abissal: Das Linhas Globais a um Ecologia dos Saberes. In B. D. S. Santos & M. P. Meneses (Eds.), *Epistemologias do Sul* (pp. 23–73). Almedina/CES.

Takayama, K., Heimans, S., Amazan, R., & Maniam, V. (2016). Doing Southern Theory: Towards Alternative Knowledges and Knowledge Practices in/for Education. *Postcolonial Directions in Education, 5*(1), 1–25.

UNESCO Institute for Statistics. (2011). *Financing Education in Sub-Saharan Africa: Meeting the Challenges of Expansion, Equity and Quality*. UNESCO.

UNIDESA. (2005). *Understanding Knowledge Societies*. United Nations.

United Nations Development Programme (UNDP) and Mohammed bin Rashid Al Maktoum Foundation (MBRF 2017). Global Knowledge Index 2017: Executive Report. Al Ghurair Printing and Publishing.

United Nations Development Programme (UNDP) and Mohammed bin Rashid Al Maktoum Foundation (MBRF 2021). Global Knowledge Index 2021.

Zembylas, M. (2018). Decolonial Possibilities in South African Higher Education: Reconfiguring Humanizing Pedagogies as/with Decolonizing Pedagogies. *South African Journal of Education, 38*(4), 1–11.

CHAPTER 8

The Perceived Universality of the West and the Silencing of "Africa" in Western Syllabi of International Relations

Maïka Sondarjee

Introduction

In the past few decades, western scholars of International Relations (IR) have been confronted to growing criticisms for perpetuating a colonial and often racist worldview (e.g., Anievas et al., 2015; Henderson, 2013; Zondi, 2018). These criticisms were led not only by Global South and racialized academics but also by social activists and students worldwide. For example, the social movement #RhodesMustFall in the late 2010s impacted academic circles beyond South Africa, including in IR. Students at the University of Cape Town rightfully criticized the colonial culture of their institution and the continuing devaluation of African-based scholarship and epistemologies. Similar mobilizations online, like

M. Sondarjee (✉)
School of International Development and Global Studies, University of Ottawa, Ottawa, ON, Canada
e-mail: maika.sondarjee@uottawa.ca

N. Andrews and N. E. Khalema (eds.), *Decolonizing African Studies Pedagogies*, Political Pedagogies,
https://doi.org/10.1007/978-3-031-37442-5_8

#BlackInTheIvory,[1] pointed at the coloniality and race-blindness of many of the programs in Global South and Global North universities. In the Mauritius island, students at the African Leadership University also mobilized and argued for the inclusion of open-source publications, and readings in native languages in syllabi. Scholars have also pointed to the silencing of the agency of African epistemic agents in African studies within IR (Odoom & Andrews, 2017). These movements have pushed scholars in the field to realize the coloniality of their concepts and practices.

While studying the marginalization of feminist and Global South approaches in Introduction to IR syllabi at the undergraduate level (Sondarjee, 2022, 2023), I realized that western IR syllabi are, well, *very western*. Influenced by social movements calling IR scholars out on epistemic inequalities, I quickly noticed the coloniality of power in teaching world politics in North America and Europe, especially when mentioning the African continent or African leaders. The field of IR has compartmentalized African studies in an area studies box, and systematically devalued African approaches and scholars. Teaching on IR, including teaching on Africa from an IR standpoint, is still often done through a western gaze. This gaze has promoted an "afropessimism" within how we present the history and actuality of the continent (Sarr, 2016). After more than ten years as a student, teaching assistant, guest lecturer, and professor in IR courses at three Canadian universities, in both French and English, I was forced to admit that student activists were right: we continue to teach not only a masculine gaze of IR (Tickner, 1988) but also a colonial one.

I participate in this edited volume as a middle-class, mixed-race ciswoman scholar from Malagasy and Canadian origins, but still a western one. Studying western pedagogical practices from within rather than from without, I adopt an insider position rather than an outsider one to break the "complicit silence" (de Jong et al., 2019: xxix; Van Milders & Toros, 2020: 119). I do not pretend to be an expert of African epistemologies or philosophies, nor should I become one. Following scholars like Michi Saagiig Nishnaabeg Leanne Simpson (2001), or Colombian-Canadian

[1] #BlackInTheIvory started as a hashtag and quickly became a social movement seeking to amplify the voices of Black academics on anti-black racism in higher education. It was created by Dr. Shardé M. Davis, an associate Professor in the Department of Communication and a faculty affiliate of the Africana Studies Institute at the University of Connecticut.

scholar Leila Celis (2022), I believe that we should study the relations of power wherein we are always implicated rather than marginalized populations per se. Celis emphasizes that if western academics should not become experts on Global South *people*, we should always study relations of power and processes of marginalization. Like Barbara Rogers (1989) also argued, an acceptable role for western scholars is to study *our* institutions to expose *our* ethnocentric biases. Studying biases in my community is what I aim to do with this chapter. While I aim to deconstruct the field of IR, I specifically focus on African studies within IR.

To embark on this task, this chapter first briefly presents the data collected from 50 "Introduction to IR Syllabi" from undergraduate courses in the United States and Canada. This state of the field will be useful to see how instructors present Africa and African Studies in western IR. This dataset has first been randomly selected through online search through Academia.Edu, ResearchGate, and Google. To increase representativity in terms of geography, gender, and race of instructors, as well as language representation (French and English), the original list was completed with targeted solicitations through social media and email. The second section develops the argument that western IR supports a coloniality of knowledge and epistemic racism. The third section explores how we can "provincialize" western knowledge in IR, that is, how we can value all types of knowledge on world politics. Specifically, I explore historicism in IR and Dipesh Chakrabarty's argument on challenging western knowledge's perceived universality. I conclude with some thoughts about what westerners can do about the coloniality of knowledge in IR pedagogy.

What is Western About Western IR[2]

The history and landmarks of world politics presented to western undergraduate students are strongly influenced by what Robtel Neajai Pailey (2020) calls the "white gaze," what Lilian Thuram (2020) sees as "white

[2] The data section of this chapter is partly based on two articles: Sondarjee, M. (2022) "We Are a Community of Practice, Not a Paradigm! How to Meaningfully Integrate Gender and Feminist Approaches in IR Syllabi," *International Studies Perspectives*, *22. 229–248* and Sondarjee, M. (2023) "Decentring the Western Gaze in International Relations. Addressing Epistemic Exclusions in Syllabi in the United States and Canada," *Millennium—Journal of International Studies* 1–24.

thinking," or what Ngũgĩ wa Thiong'o (2005) criticized as the colonization of the mind. The pedagogical choices made by western instructors perpetuate a western vision of IR, which actively places African events, epistemologies, and epistemic agents on the margins. Most visibly, events outside Europe or North America are rarely, if ever, addressed in western syllabi (Table 8.1). For example, events that happened in the west such as the Cold War or World Wars are respectively mentioned in 54% and 46% of syllabi, whereas empires, de/colonization, or slavery are respectively mentioned in 10%, 8%, and 6%. Similarly, indigenous politics within the western world are mentioned in only three syllabi.

Ironically, one U.S. syllabus which states the goal of "reflectively" introducing students to the History of IR starts with one session on "pre-twentieth century" History with a reading on the Peace of Westphalia, followed by sessions on World War I, World War II, the Cold War, the post-Cold War, and the period after 9/11, with no mention of decolonization processes. It has to be noted that these choices are not supported by the importance of the events or by chronological choices, where older events would not be covered in favor of more recent ones, as this syllabus does not mention decolonization processes spanning from 1804 (Haiti from France) to 1999 (Macau from Portugal), which had a tremendous *international* impact on both former colonizers and former colonies. This selective history-telling is akin to what Grosfoguel (2013)

Table 8.1 Historical topics in Western "Introduction to IR" syllabi[3]

Topics	*# of syllabi*	*% of syllabi*
Globalization (or International Political Economy)	32	64%
Cold War	27	54%
Westphalia/n system	25	50%
World wars	23	46%
Nuclear war/deterrence	14	28%
Empires	5	10%
Colonization/decolonization	4	8%
Indigenous politics	3	6%
Slavery	3	6%

[3] All data in tables are based on first-hand collection of 50 Introduction to IR syllabi in North America (Sondarjee, 2022; Sondarjee, 2023).

calls the colonial theft of history for countries of the Global South. Like many other Global South nations, African countries have been written out of the history of the international.

Similarly, based on the data collected for this research, theories covered in Introduction to IR syllabi are heavily skewed in favor of western (and masculine) epistemologies (e.g., realism, liberalism, or norm-oriented constructivism), de facto silencing the impact of race, patriarchy, or colonialism on world politics. On the 50 western syllabi of Introduction to IR studied, only 30% address postcolonialism and 14% discuss critical-race studies as standalone topics. Another 10% have a critical studies week including a reading on postcolonialism or race, but coupled with (white) feminist approaches, postmodernism, or other approaches considered "critical." In comparison, 92% mention realist or neorealist theories, 78% liberal or neoliberal approaches, and 62% constructivism (Table 8.2).

This erasure then translates in another problem: a need for more inclusivity of Global South scholars in reading lists (Knight, 2019), and in IR journals (Aydinli & Mathews, 2000; Medie & Kang, 2018). These two discrepancies (representation of non-white scholars vis-à-vis representation of post/decolonial/race theories) are different, as not all scholars of color study race, just like not all Global South scholar study North–South relations, and "there is no intellectual reason to expect that they all do so" (Zvobgo & Loken, 2020).

This lack of representation is also flagrant in textbooks. All textbooks assigned in the syllabi analyzed for this research were edited in western countries and tend to reproduce an ethnocentric bias in the conception of history and a marginalization of Global South authors (Acharya, 2021; Frueh et al., 2020; Powel, 2020). Western textbooks often implicitly

Table 8.2 Theoretical Approaches in Western "Introduction to IR" Syllabi

Theoretical approaches	*# of syllabi*	*% of syllabi*
Realism/Neorealism	46	92%
Neo/Liberalism	39	78%
Constructivism	31	62%
Gender, women, or feminism	25	50%
Postcolonial studies	15	30%
Race studies	7	14%
Critical theories week including postcolonialism or race	5	10%

perpetuate the idea that only western scholars can theorize the international. To palliate this problem, Arlene Tickner and Karen Smith (2020) edited an alternative IR textbook with contributions only from scholars in the Global South. Their book shows the heterogeneity and richness of learning about classical IR concepts and issues from other perspectives, not because they are exotic but because they enrich our knowledge of the world.

The biases in western textbooks go beyond the positionality of editors or publishing houses. They pertain to their structure and content. Pedagogical books produced in western countries for western audiences reproduce the western gaze by giving priority to North American and European historical events and theories, thereby "obscuring non-western significance" (Powel, 2020: 1). Textbooks are crucial for the reproduction of a western gaze in IR, as many instructors will replicate their structures to organize their courses (Frueh et al., 2020: 4), thereby reproducing their biases. According to a 2014 survey of IR professors, 40% organized their courses using traditional IR paradigms in which the recognized authors are mainly Eurocentric, western, male, and white (Zvobgo & Loken, 2020). Even when textbooks start with historical events that include the Global South, like globalization, they "do not substantively discuss non-western civilizations or IR concepts or contributions derived from them" (Acharya, 2021: 32). To determine if textbooks represent global IR, Amitav Acharya suggests asking if they cover national and regional IR theoretical developments in the Global South, if they channel postcolonialism, race, imperialism, or dependency approaches into the core narrative of the book, and if they address Global South agency in the development of international norms and practices (Acharya, 2021: 32).

Coloniality of Knowledge and Epistemic Racism

The marginalization of African approaches in western IR textbooks is not an unfortunate mistake; it flows from a colonial way to conceive the world and science. If Canadian syllabi studied for this research assign French or German texts, they do not assign Senegalese or South African Ones. If American syllabi present British and Canadian theories, they do not present Moroccan or Somalian ones. Coloniality of power refers not only to colonization as political and economic control but to epistemic processes of domination and to capitalist racial hierarchies (Lugones,

2011; Maldonado-Torres, 2007; Quijano, 1991). If colonization as direct political and economic control ended in most parts of the world (with notable exceptions such as indigenous populations in western countries or Palestine), the coloniality of power perdured in racialized institutions, cultural systems, the capitalist world order, self-representations, and epistemes. Aníbal Quijano (1991) coined the term "coloniality of power" to describe racialized hierarchies in the imaginaries of the colonizers and the colonized, and the dehumanization processes relating to racialized capitalism.

Because colonization, and its continuity through colonialism has "erased, suppressed, and demonized" indigenous modes of thoughts, histories, and epistemologies (Spivak, 1988; Tamale, 2020: 28), it led to a variety of epistemicides or destruction of ways of thinking, *epistemes* (Santos, 2014). From colonization on, humanity was deprived of multiple viewpoints coming from various time(s), space(s), and geopolitical sites of meaning-making. What western instructors present as (valid) knowledge mainly comes from one geographical center, that is, the western world (Andrews, 2020; Henderson, 2013; Sondarjee & Andrews, 2023). This is broader than formal colonization processes: "during the unfolding of imperialism and colonialism, colonial invaders did not only target the land and human resources, they also invaded the mental universe of those people they colonized" (Ndlovu-Gatsheni, 2018a: 137).

Some African thinkers have focused on epistemic aspects of power, or the colonization of the mind, defining knowledge as the "software" of colonialism (Ndlovu-Gatsheni, 2018a: 43; wa Thiong'o, 2005). Already in 1965, African thinker Kwame Nkrumah (1971) was talking about neocolonialism in those terms, as going beyond the control of a government, but as the persistence of colonial power in other forms, as the "last stage of imperialism." Coloniality of knowledge is what produced and sustained (often violently) a western gaze on the world, namely through the imposition of colonial language in learning spaces and academia in former colonies (wa Thiong'o, 2005). As Kenyan author reminds us, formal military and political colonization was followed by a colonization of the minds of the colonized: "Berlin of 1884 was effected through the sword and the bullet. But the night of the sword and the bullet was followed by the morning of the chalk and blackboard" (wa Thiong'o, 2005: 35). A few years ago, wa Thiong'o has even stopped writing in English, to counter the hegemony of the colonial language, from which follows a western superiority.

Coloniality of knowledge, as a perpetuation of colonialism through other means, was successful in homogenizing ways of thinking and violently imposing western epistemes as the "neutral" way to think about the world. This was also a very complex process of "deployment of global imperial technologies of subjectivation taking the form of translating and re-writing other cultures, other knowledges, and other ways of being, and presuming commensurability through western rationality" (Ndlovu-Gatsheni, 2013: 31). Coloniality of knowledge thus embodies the epistemic dimension of depreciation of certain population (Mignolo, 2011).

Epistemic racism sustains a coloniality of knowledge, a colonial hierarchy of knowledge whereas western subjects (both white and racialized) are considered superior to former colonial subjects. This amounts to a hierarchy attributing superiority and valid existence only to knowledge produced by western subjects (Grosfoguel, 2013). This hierarchy revolves around what Franz Fanon (1961) called zones of being and non-being, the latter being incapable of producing knowledge. For Fanon, this hierarchy of superiority and inferiority refers to the definition of humanness in terms of who has access to certain rights but also to subjectivity (Maldonado-Torres, 2007). This attributed subjectivity as *homo cogito* (and thus being-ness) enables a valid, potentially universal, viewpoint on the world. "Being" thus becomes intimately tied to the ability to "think." The lack of diversity in syllabi comes from the fact that women and men in the non-being zone (especially in Africa) are not considered as epistemic beings, beings endowed with reason, capable of thinking and producing adequate solutions to the problems of their existence. What is more, the coloniality of gender devalues even more women of the Global South as epistemic agents (Knight, 2019; Medie & Kang, 2018; Mohanty, 1988; Spivak, 1988).

For example, in the context of the COVID-19 crisis, epistemic racism was seen at two levels. First, international media and western institutions assumed the pandemic would be more damaging on the African continent than on the European continent. Second, when it came time to look for possible answers to the various health issues, these were mostly sought in western circles. If a solution is to be developed, it will be in the west, although the United States and Europe have managed the crisis first chaotically (by trial and error) and then selfishly (by appropriating vaccines) (Sondarjee & Rugira, 2020). However, the devaluation of African epistemic capacities in the COVID-19 crisis and in IR syllabi, does not come from a deficiency of the discourse itself or a cognitive incapacity, but from a "deficiency of available hermeneutical resources" (Mbonda, 2021: 25). The difficulty in bringing voices from what Fanon called the zone of non-being (Africa) to the zone of being (the west) comes from a self-attribution of epistemic superiority on the part of westerners. Non-experts, non-knowers, and thus non-whites often cannot be heard in the production of knowledge (Spivak, 1988).

Boaventura De Sousa Santos (2014) associates this imperial thinking with an indolent, lazy reasoning. This kind of reasoning perceives itself not only as superior but fundamentally unique. It does not consider that it needs to draw on the world's wealth to meet its needs, or to resolve crises. After five centuries of teaching the world from the height of its superiority, peoples in the zone of being now have difficulty learning from the rest of the world with humility. This constructed superiority deprives the world of rich knowledge and multiple imaginaries and prevents a decentering of knowledge and power. Thus, the west continues to view cultures outside of its own through the prism of superiority and prejudice (Sarr, 2016: 101). "International" experts too often deny African experts or governments on the continent the status of epistemic agents, capable of reasoning and building their proper solutions (Odoom & Andrews, 2017). This coloniality of power creates an entire colonial typology of crises based on epistemic racism.

Provincializing Western Knowledge

Critiques of the coloniality of power and the coloniality of being have been accompanied in Africa by calls for the decolonization of the mind, of knowledge, of identities, and for a rehumanization of the world (Mbonda, 2021; Ndlovu-Gatsheni, 2018b; Sarr, 2016; Tamale, 2020; wa Thiong'o, 2005). To understand how to deconstruct coloniality of knowledge in western syllabi, I would like to add to this already rich literature insights from Indian scholar Dipesh Chakrabarty (2000). His argument about provincializing Europe gives decolonial scholars the tools to bring down European epistemes at the level of other epistemes.

Historicism

On November 9, 2007, while still president of France, Nicolas Sarkozy stated: "the tragedy of the African man [sic] is that he has not yet entered history."[4] This statement perpetuates (in the western minds) the relegation of African countries to a state outside of history, outside the master narrative of history, which is inevitably European. African countries are not seen as having a *different* path: they are *ahistorical* or *prehistorical* (Glissant, 1999: 61). It is thus not accidental if less than ten percent of western IR syllabi studied for this research mention de/colonization, empires, or slavery, 46% mention one of the world wars, 54% the Cold War, and 64% globalization (Table 8.1). Some scholars have argued that western thinkers' perception of African countries' lack of history may come from the absence of written documents to prove it (Nabudere, 2012: 127). This emphasis on the written word to record the passing of time has unsurprisingly led to a depreciation of civilizations relying on oral traditions: "Africa had no history because history begins with writing and thus with the arrival of the Europeans. Therefore, their presence in Africa was justified, among other things, by their ability to place Africa in the 'path of history'" (Ogot, 1992: 71; Tamale, 2020: 7).

Felwine Sarr (2016) deplores what he calls "afropessimism," a perception that Africa is a "reservoir of misery." Of course, it is well-documented and widely reported that different countries on the continent are facing real socio-economic problems. Nevertheless, there is a posture in western discourse that always glorifies the worst regarding the African continent. This depreciation defines Africa as a series of lack, absence, and historical backwardness. Africa is still historically incomplete: "the African 'man' has not yet entered history," following Sarkozy. Sarr criticizes the expression "The future is African," because since "the African continent is the future and will be, this rhetoric says, in hollow, that *it is not*" (Sarr, 2016: 11).

In an article on the western gaze of IR, I argue that afropessimism is visible in how instructors present Africa to western students of IR. On the one side, 36 syllabi studied for this research mention the United States, and to do so, instructors underline concepts such as foreign policy, power, military strategies, leadership, and domestic policies (Sondarjee & Andrews 2023). On the other side, African countries or the African continent were mentioned in only 22 syllabi, and with concepts such as poverty, underdevelopment, HIV/AIDS, genocide, hunger, authoritarian governments, corruption, and foreign aid. If Europe is presented with references to the European Union, Africa is never linked to the African

[4] « Le drame de l'Afrique, c'est que l'homme africain n'est pas entré dans l'histoire» (2007, 9 novembre, Le discours de Nicolas Sarkozy, Le Monde), my translation.

Union or Pan-Africanism. Additionally, on the 22 syllabi mentioning Sub-Saharan Africa, nine of them do so in relation to the United States or France (so not as actors per se), and in six it is cast in a rather negative light around the Rwandan genocide. One syllabus assigns a reading on the Rwandan genocide that asks why the United States let the tragedy happen.

Seeing western knowledge as a "finished" intellectual product is based on a historicist vision of theoretical development, whereas Africa has not yet reached the level of epistemic complexity of Europe. Historicism, whether implicitly or explicitly, posits that Global South cultural differences with the west are based on historical time and thus are absent from modern time. Historicism is a western myth: it represents an attempt to universalize an enterprise that found its origin and its most accomplished degree of realization in the west, the historical culmination of which marks modernity. History, or historical development, is reinforced epistemically by academic institutions and research: Europe in historicism becomes the "master narratives," and all other histories are ones of subalternity, and "one can only articulate subaltern subject positions in the name of this history" (Chakrabarty, 2000: 27). Even how Karl Marx used the terms "capitalist" and "pre-capitalist" economies implicitly assumed that there was a world-historical or teleological path excused from the question of necessary historicity to explain cultural differences.

Chakrabarty (2000) draws on the example of India after its independence from Great Britain to explain how development is neither theological nor premised on the European path. He aims to show how historical and national context influences the formation and durability of political institutions. He underlines the western gaze of many European philosophers and criticizes their teleological ideas of how to mature from barbarity to civilization. He starts by explaining how John Stuart Mill speaks of self-rule in "On Liberty" and "On Representative Government," which argues against giving Indians and Africans self-rule because of their political immaturity. For Mill, Chakrabarty argues, "Indians or Africans were *not yet* civilized enough to rule themselves" (Chakrabarty, 2000: 8). According to the English philosopher, colonial rule and British education were prerequisites to enabling India's escape from backwardness. Having not yet achieved European standards, India, much like Africa, is presented as in the "waiting room of history ... We were all headed for the same destination, Mill averred, but some people were to arrive earlier than other" (Chakrabarty, 2000: 8). The decision to adopt a universal adult franchise despite a lack of education was thus in contradiction to Mill's theory, who argued that universal teaching had to precede universal enfranchisement. Two visions of the subject are thus opposed: "One is the peasant who has to be educated into the citizen and who therefore belongs to the time of historicism; the other is the peasant who, despite his or her lack of formal education, is already a citizen" (Chakrabarty, 2000: 10). Chakrabarty instead argued that Indian citizens could access democracy from another path.

From Chakrabarty to IR

How can we, then, provincialize Europe in western education about IR? In other words, this is to pose the question: how can we strip this master narrative from the teachings of world politics? Part of the answer is to write history from below and give value to those "minority histories" (Chakrabarty, 2000: 97). Minority here does not refer to a number of people but to active processes of marginalization and subalternization of African as well as Indian histories. Pasts that are "minoritized" are systematically marginalized in academic research, and pedagogical practices. Chakrabarty (2000: 100), for example, criticizes Immanuel Kant's term of human "immaturity" to qualify those histories, because, according to the Eurocentric, master narrative, given that "they are not based on the deployment of reason in public life," they are not modern. Chakrabarty elaborates on this historicizing task: "To attempt to provincialize this 'Europe' is to see the modern as inevitably contested, to write over the given and privileged narratives of citizenship other narratives of human connections that draw sustenance from dreamed-up pasts and futures where collectivities are defined neither by the rituals of citizenship" (Chakrabarty, 2000: 46).

In the end, the western gaze in IR syllabi is not only about the ignorance or silencing of African histories and epistemologies. Indeed, 72% of syllabi mention the United States, only 44% mention countries in Sub-Saharan Africa, and only 8% mention countries in North Africa. However, the former is presented with concepts such as foreign policy, hegemony, wars, military, or diplomatic strategy, or empires, and the latter are mostly considered through the prism of poverty, genocide, humanitarian interventions, humanitarian interventions, corruption, AIDS, and domestic conflicts. One outlier syllabus speaks of an African IR perspective. In the 50 syllabi studied, there are 32 mentions of United States state leaders, including two defeated presidential candidates (Al Gore and Mitt Romney) and two public servants (Michael Pompeo and Henry Kissinger). However, no syllabus mentions African leaders, not even the most influential ones for world politics, like Thomas Sankara, Nelson Mandela, Patrice Lumumba, or Jomo Kenyatta. This silencing gives the impression that only western leaders influence world politics because the "international" is, understood here, as being equivalent to the west.

The underlying argument in this chapter is that pedagogical choices are not incidental; they carry with them a worldview. This is not to deny that the United States currently has a lot of hard and soft power or that Europe has been the theater of important world wars. However, speaking of each region with a historicist mindset reinforces a pernicious racial and colonial hierarchy in students' minds. Nevertheless, some, albeit relatively scant, syllabi do address indigenous wars, decolonization struggles, state formation in Africa, or migration patterns in the Mediterranean, showing that it is possible to teach about "classically important"—and hence predominantly western—topics while speaking of other regions with depth and humility.

This chapter, in applying the important insights of Chakrabarty's work, insists the call to provincialize Europe or to "turn our back away from Europe" (Mbembe, 2010: 17) is not one of cultural relativism. The argument does not mean to reject single-handedly modernity as a referent nor does it refuse the importance of European events or epistemologies for the Global North or Africa. Provincializing Europe instead means to "write into the history of modernity the ambivalences, contradictions, the use of force, and the tragedies and ironies that attend it" (Chakrabarty, 2000: 43). The example of the Peace of Westphalia is an interesting one to support this point. The establishment of European principles of statehood, non-intervention, and national identity—all elements of the Treaty of Westphalia—are decisive historical conjunctures for European and non-European countries. However, this narrative in most IR courses currently silences the fact that the integration into the modern inter-state system was violently imposed, or that it served as a tool of "othering" between countries which moved to "end anarchy" (the civilized ones) and those who did not (the un-civilized ones) (Kayaoglu, 2010: 193). The history of Westphalia, for instance, is rarely thought to be linked to histories of "authoritarianism, theft, racism, and in significant cases, massacre and genocide," the consequences of which, political and otherwise, cannot be understated (Jones, 2006: 3–4).

Acharya (2021: 31) suggests understanding IR from a civilizational perspective to deconstruct Westphalian-centered biases. Going back thousands of years would give IR scholars a better view of the world and broaden the possibilities for conceptualizing world politics. This includes but is certainly not limited to: Chinese exploration of the rest of the world; ancient realms in Africa and Italy; international political economy through Ottoman imperial trade; civilizations in Latin America; and transnational politics among Indigenous Nations in what is now North America—to name just a few. Furthermore, the Westphalian narrative has led to a detrimental focus on states as the main actors of IR and on state-based institutions as case studies (Inayatullah & Blaney, 2004; Jones, 2006; Kayaoglu, 2010), giving less importance to non-governmental actors, epistemic power and institutions which were not founded by so-called international hegemons. In short, this focus on great powers is an "attempt to erase the work and life worlds of those who are at the 'margins'" (Agathangelou & Turcotte, 2016).

Like Chakrabarty for India, Senegalese philosopher and poet Sarr imagines a different path for the future of the "development" of the continent without rejecting modern tools and norms: "The path of African modernity would consist in the selective incorporation of modern technologies, discourses, and institutions of western origin into an African cultural and political universe, to give birth to a distinct and autonomous modernity" (Sarr, 2016: 33). Cameroonian philosopher Achille Mbembe also developed the concept of *déclosion,* of opening of the mind: "The idea of declosion includes that of hatching, of emerging, of the advent of something new, of blossoming. To *déclose* is therefore to lift the fences so that what was locked up can emerge and blossom" (Mbembe, 2010: 68). For Africa to "belong to the world," to inhabit and create this world is linked to decolonization not only formally but also of our mentalities (wa Thiong'o, 2005).

Conclusion: What Westerners Can Do About Coloniality of Knowledge in IR Pedagogy

As some of the chapters in this book demonstrate, teaching African Studies still needs decolonization. This need is true in African Studies departments but also within the field of IR, where Africa and African epistemic agents are portrayed with a lingering afropessimism. Western scholars are not passive transmitters of historical memory; they are active participants in its biased reproduction (Mbonda, 2021: 142). The a-historicity assigned to African populations must cease, and western IR instructors must deconstruct their ethnocentric biases when presenting the continent to students. Decolonization of the mind or epistemic decolonization is not limited to a critique of the existing world; they refer to a broader quest for epistemic justice and freedom (Tamale, 2020; wa Thiong'o, 2005). It is a matter of reviewing with greater lucidity those we listen to and those we choose to silence, to revise our relations to the world.

The decolonization of the western gaze will require a denunciation of the pretentious character of universal knowledge based in the west, a decentering of how we present Africa, and a more open, dialogic circulation of forms of knowledge outside the west (Mbonda, 2021). The fact that IR instructors teach from a western standpoint using western theories (e.g., realism, liberalism, constructivism, or mainstream feminism) means that instructors believe these are the theories that can explain the world, and by implication, explain the so-called "international." African theories and epistemic agents are marginalized as non-representative of valid knowledge (Odoom & Andrews, 2017). To challenge that assumption implies a decolonial engagement with existing knowledge: "The decolonial turn is the opening and the freedom from the thinking and the forms of living (economies-other, political theories-other), the cleansing of the coloniality of being and of knowledge the delinking from the spell of the rhetoric of modernity" (Mignolo, 2011: 48).

This perceived capacity to know the world from one standpoint leads to a western tendency to develop universal theories devoid of context. Universal knowledge is considered the appanage of western episteme, the only able to develop a universal truth beyond time, space, and subjectivity. This bias puts African approaches in the "area studies" box, far away from valid universal knowledge. While postcolonial theories (including many from an African standpoint) emphasize the importance of subjects' social positions and local context to understand the bigger picture (Agathangelou & Turcotte, 2016; Bhambra, 2014; Simmons & Zehfuss, 2013), no IR western undergraduate syllabi studied for this research mention the concepts of positionalities or interpretivism as integral to developing theories about the social world. Coupled with assigning mostly western authors, these tendencies lead to reproducing colonial hierarchies in modes of knowing. For example, a globalization perspective from the United States might be assigned as a approach of IR, while no indigenous perspective of globalization is assigned, or if it is, it is as an "indigenous perspective" or "African perspective" of IR (Odoom & Andrews, 2017; Sondarjee & Andrews, 2023). As already remarked, western research with western case studies is the most assigned and the most published, even in critical fields like feminist studies (Knight, 2019; Medie & Kang, 2018; Sondarjee, 2022). This argument does not suggest that we should only acknowledge other ways of doing research or other epistemic agents, especially from the peripheries, but to deconstruct this racial hierarchization of modes of knowing. African philosophies and African scholars are IR scholars in their own right.

Intellectual honesty invites us to ask about the ways in which "people outside a few countries that constitute the small group of societies we call the west imagine their world and interact with each other and with the living in their daily lives" (Bhargava, 2013: 41). Rohit Bhargava reminds us of our duty to help excavate the treasures of other traditions in order to nurture the world of different visions, just like Felwine Sarr begs us to reconsider our relationality to the world and the respect for all the world's cultures and epistemes (Sarr, 2017). This has important implication for western IR pedagogy, but also African pedagogies within the confines of IR.

Cognitive justice recognizes the right of different forms of knowledge to coexist. However, it adds that this plurality must go beyond tolerance or liberalism and advocate an active recognition of the necessity of diversity. This diversity requires recognizing knowledge not only as methods, but also as ways of life. Knowledge is seen as embedded in an ecology of knowledge where everyone has its place, its claim to a cosmology, its meaning as a form of life. In this sense, knowledge cannot be detached from cultures; it is connected to livelihoods, a life cycle, a way of life, and it determines life chances (Visvanathan, 1997). The idea of cognitive justice proposes a democratic imagination in a worldview without market and without competition, where conversation, reciprocity, and translation create and inform knowledge. This novel knowledge assemblage would be an amalgam of memories, heritages, and heritages, a plural problem-solving heuristic in which citizens take back power and knowledge into their hands.

References

Acharya, A. (2021). *Teaching Global International Relations*. Routledge.

Agathangelou, A. M., & Turcotte, H. M. (2016). Reworking Postcolonial Feminisms in the Sites of IR. In Steans, J., & Tepe, D. (eds.), *Handbook on Gender in World Politics*. Edward Elgar Publishing.

Andrews, N. (2020). International Relations (IR) Pedagogy, Dialogue and Diversity: Taking the IR Course Syllabus Seriously. *All Azimuth: A Journal of Foreign Policy and Peace*.

Anievas, A., Manchanda, N., & Shilliam, R. (2015). *Race and Racism in International Relations: Confronting the Global Colour Line*. Routledge.

Aydinli, E., & Mathews, J. (2000). Are the Core and Periphery Irreconcilable? The Curious World of Publishing in Contemporary International Relations. *International Studies Perspectives, 1*(3), 289–303.

Bhambra, G. K. (2014). Postcolonial and Decolonial Dialogues. *Postcolonial Studies, 17*(2), 115–121.

Bhargava, R. (2013). Pour En Finir Avec l'Injustice Épistémique Du Colonialisme. *La Nouvelle Revue Des Sciences Sociales, 1*, 41–75.

Celis, L. (2022). La Décolonisation Des Connaissances et Des Pratiques de Recherche. In Sondarjee, M. (ed.), *Perspectives Féministes En Relations Internationales : Penser Le Monde Autrement*. University of Montreal Press.

Chakrabarty, D. (2000). *Provincializing Europe: Postcolonial Thought and Historical Difference*. Princeton University Press.

de Jong, S., Rosalba Icaza, R., & Rutazibwa, O. (2019). *Decolonization and Feminisms in Global Teaching and Learning*. Routledge.

Fanon, F. (1961). *Les Damnés de La Terre*. Maspéro.

Frueh, J., Diehl, P. F., Li, X., Gokcek, G, Kalpakian, J., Vlcek, W., Bower, A., Espinoza, R. S., Carranco, S., de Matos Ala, J., Behera, N. C., & Acharya, A. (2020). *The Introductory Course in International Relations: Regional Variations. International Studies Perspectives, 22*(2), 153–159.

Glissant, E. (1999). *Caribbean Discourse: Selected Essays*. University Press of Virginia.

Grosfoguel, R. (2013). The Structure of Knowledge in Westernized Universities: Epistemic Racism/Sexism and the Four Genocides/Epistemicides of the Long 16th Century. *Human Architecture: Journal of the Sociology of Self-Knowledge, 11*(1), 73–90.

Henderson, E. A. (2013). Hidden in Plain Sight: Racism in International Relations Theory. *Cambridge Review of International Affairs, 26*(1), 71–92.

Inayatullah, N., & Blaney, D. L. (2004). *International Relations and the Problem of Difference*. Routledge.

Jones, B. G. (2006). *Decolonizing International Relations*. Rowman & Littlefield.

Kayaoglu, T. (2010). Westphalian Eurocentrism in International Relations Theory. *International Studies Review, 12*(2), 193–217.

Knight, S. C. (2019). Even Today, a Western and Gendered Social Science: Persistent Geographic and Gender Biases in Undergraduate IR Teaching. *International Studies Perspectives, 20*(3), 203–225.

Lugones, M. (2011). Methodological Notes Toward a Decolonial Feminism. In A. M. Isasi-Diaz & E. Mendieta (Eds.), *Decolonizing Epistemologies: Latina/o Theology and Philosophy* (pp. 68–86). Fordham University Press.

Maldonado-Torres, N. (2007). On the Coloniality of Being: Contributions to the Development of a Concept. *Cultural Studies, 21*(2–3), 240–270.

Mbembe, A. (2010). *Sortir de la grande nuit: Essai sur l'Afrique décolonisée. Cahiers libres*. Découverte.

Mbonda, E. M. (2021). *Une décolonisation de la pensée: études de philosophie afrocentrique*. Sorbonne Université Presses.

Medie, P. A., & Kang, A. J. (2018). Power, Knowledge and the Politics of Gender in the Global South. *European Journal of Politics and Gender, 1*(1), 37–53.

Mignolo, W. D. (2011). Epistemic Disobedience and the Decolonial Option: A Manifesto. *Transmodernity, 1*(2), 44–66.

Mohanty, C. (1988). Under Western Eyes: Feminist Scholarship and Colonial Discourse. *Feminist Review, 30*, 61–88.

Nabudere, D. W. (2012). *Afrikology and Transdisciplinarity a Restorative Epistemology*. Africa Institute of South Africa.

Ndlovu-Gatsheni, S. (2013). *Coloniality of power in postcolonial Africa: Myths of decolonization*. Codesria.

Ndlovu-Gatsheni, S. J. (2018a). *Epistemic Freedom in Africa: Deprovincialization and Decolonization*. Routledge.

Ndlovu-Gatsheni, S. J. (2018b). The Dynamics of Epistemological Decolonisation in the 21st Century: Towards Epistemic Freedom. *Strategic Review for Southern Africa, 40*(1), 16–45.

Nkrumah, K. (1971). *Neo-Colonialism: The Last Stage of Imperialism*. Panaf Press.

Odoom, I., & Andrews, N. (2017). What/Who Is Still Missing in International Relation Scholarship? Situating Africa as an Agent in IR Theorising. *Third World Quarterly, 38*(1), 42–60.

Ogot, B. A. (1992). *General History of Africa: Africa from the Sixteenth to the Eighteenth Century* (Vol. 5). University of California Press.

Pailey, R. N. (2020). De-centring the 'White Gaze' of Development. *Development and Change, 51*(3), 729–745.

Powel, B. (2020). Blinkered Learning, Blinkered Theory: How Histories in Textbooks Parochialize IR. *International Studies Review*, *22*(4), 957–982.

Quijano, A. (1991). *Colonialidad y Modernidad/Racionalidad. Peru Indigerna, 13*(29), 11–29.

Rogers, B. (1989). *The Domestication of Women: Discrimination in Developing Societies*. Routledge.

Santos, B. D. S. (2014). *Epistemologies of the South: Justice against Epistemicide*. Routledge.

Sarr, F. (2016). *Afrotopia*. Philippe Rey.

Sarr, F. (2017). *Habiter Le Monde: Essai de Politique Relationnelle*. Mémoire D'Encrier

Simmons, B., & Zehfuss, M. (2013). Critical Theory, Poststructuralism, and Postcolonialism. In W. Carlsnaes & T. Risse (Eds.), *Handbook of International Relations* (pp. 145–169). Sage.

Simpson, L. (2001). Aboriginal Peoples and Knowledge: Decolonizing Our Processes. *The Canadian Journal of Native Studies, 21*(1), 137–148.

Sondarjee, M. (2022). We Are a Community of Practice, Not a Paradigm! How to Meaningfully Integrate Gender and Feminist Approaches in IR Syllabi. *International Studies Perspectives, 23*(3), 229–248.

Sondarjee, M. (2023). Decentring the Western Gaze in International Relations: Addressing Epistemic Exclusions in Syllabi in the United States and Canada. *Millennium: Journal of International Studies*, 1–24. https://doi.org/10.1177/03058298231171615

Sondarjee, M., & Andrews N. (2023). Decolonizing International Relations and Development Studies: What's in a Buzzword? *International Journal*, 1–21. https://doi.org/10.1177/00207020231166

Sondarjee, M., & Rugira, J. M. (2020). COVID-19 : Apprendre de l'Afrique. *La Conversation*.

Spivak, G. C. (1988). Can the Subaltern Speak? In C. Nelson & L. Grossberg (Eds.), *Marxism and the Interpretation of Culture* (pp. 271–313). University of Illinois Press.

Tamale, S. (2020). *Decolonization and Afro-Feminism*. Daraja Press.

Thuram, L. (2020). *La pensée blanche*. Mémoire d'Encrier.

Tickner, J. A. (1988). Hans Morgenthau's Principles of Political Realism: A Feminist Reformulation. *Millennium: Journal of International Studies, 17*(3), 430–440.

Tickner, A. B., & Smith, K. (2020). *International Relations from the Global South: Worlds of Difference*. Routledge.

Van Milders, L., & Toros, H. (2020). Violent International Relations. *European Journal of International Relations, 26*(1), 116–139.

Visvanathan, S. (1997). *A Carnival for Science: Essays on Science, Technology and Development*. Oxford University Press.

wa Thiong'o, N. (2005). *Decolonising the Mind: The Politics of Language in African Literature*. James Currey.

Zondi, S. (2018). Decolonising International Relations and Its Theory: A Critical Conceptual Meditation. *Politikon, 45*(1), 16–31.

Zvobgo, K., & Loken, M. (2020, June 19). Why Race Matters in International Relations. *Foreign Policy*.

CHAPTER 9

The Façade of "Transforming" Post-apartheid Universities in South Africa: Towards African-Centred Practices and Processes of Redress

Nene Ernest Khalema, Blessings Masuku, and Phumelele Makathini Zakwe

N. E. Khalema (✉)
School of Built Environment and Development Studies, University of KwaZulu-Natal, Durban, South Africa
e-mail: Khalema@ukzn.ac.za

B. Masuku
School of Built and Environment and Development Studies, University of KwaZulu-Natal, Durban, South Africa

P. M. Zakwe
College of Humanities, University of KwaZulu-Natal, Durban, South Africa

N. Andrews and N. E. Khalema (eds.), *Decolonizing African Studies Pedagogies*, Political Pedagogies,
https://doi.org/10.1007/978-3-031-37442-5_9

Introduction

> *...the proof of success lies in a whole social structure being changed from the bottom up.* (Franz Fanon, 1963)

Perhaps it is fair to suggest that black South African-born academics schooled in the country during the dark days of apartheid (where the former state apparatus ensured his/her dehumanization and humiliation) dreamed of a day, if and when given an opportunity to lead, and knowing what they now know, where political will could finally realize a transformation agenda in post-apartheid South Africa towards equity, justice, and redress. Despite the climate of uncertainty about the future of higher education in contemporary South Africa, there is certainly a mishmash between the promise of liberation and the current realities for one to maintain feelings of hope one once had. This is particularly true of the current situation we find ourselves in following the failed transition to true liberation and decoloniality in higher education. For most, there were hopes for a better tomorrow, for better days to come, the horizons from which we could exercise our agency and talents and make the promise of our blood-earned liberty and emancipation really mean something and inspire future generations. For some of us, the new post-apartheid democratic dispensation has ushered a never-ending nightmare to our psyche and mental wellbeing. It is a moment of despair, disbelief, and reckoning that what our ancestors fought and died for may never be realized in our lifetime.

Of course, the promise of better days to come could have been but a fragment of our imagination which offered the opportunity to escape and even reimagine a better and brighter future. Perhaps the reality of everyday exclusions cemented in the fibre of most institutions of higher learning also speaks to what some have called the last battleground of the colonial project: the university (Ndlovu-Gatsheni, 2020). Do we really have a true African university some thirty or so years later since our political emancipation? What is clear however is that the post-apartheid experience of the university has meant (or means) different things to different people. For some, the memories of the suppression, subjugation, and trauma endured by our forbearers during the apartheid period must be addressed to build a new normal within the rising consciousness of democratic dispensation (Brahima et al., 2021; Hlatshwayo, 2020; Makhaye et al., 2023; Nyamnjoh & Jua, 2002).

For others, the promise of hope entrenched and cemented in the liberation pageantry decades after the struggle is quickly vanishing and thus is something worth fighting for (Assié-Lumumba, 2007; Badat, 2010, 2017; Mbembe, 2016; Bunting, 2006; Jansen, 2023). Inspired by the emancipatory spirit to bring dignity to the human condition and to do better and be better often drives the call for transformative universities. To these visionaries, the situation demands formal redress and with it the complete realization of justice. The idea of a transformed academe minted by equity and justice will, from this view, dethrone the architecture of colonial institutions and carve a future for a just society that is more open, more affirming, and more focused on human values of unity. The imagined post-apartheid academe will be equipped with tools to not only transform *ourselves* besides the trauma of colonialism and apartheid, but also be able to transform the ***knowledge***, the ***space***, ***practices***, and terms of engagement and interactions. Such a process would make a lasting contribution in producing responsible, emancipated, cultivated, and "woke" citizens.

Well, these assumptions are ambitious or better yet, perhaps naive. The idealism, however, is understandable given the status quo. The promise of the possibility of transformation in higher education is an attractive panacea given a myriad of challenges South African higher education institutions battles with. Studies by Frantz Fanon's (1963) "*The Wretched of the Earth*" and Pierre Bourdieu's (1964) *"Les Héritier"* (*The Heirs*) both highlight how by design institutions of higher learning reinforce, perpetuate, and transmit values of inequality, competition, and a specific intellectual heritage that renders privilege (in)accessible from generation to generation, despite differential entanglements to that heritage. Nearly thirty years after South Africa's transition to political democracy, South African higher education remains deeply fragmented and racialized in a web of neo-colonial and imperialist existence; it is intentionally fashioned to (re)produce and preserve white supremacy and enact whiteness. A short analysis of the state of higher education and current conditions reveals an inescapable reality of stark inequality, systemic exclusion of black bodies, and sophisticated forms of injustice and structural violence in university settings.

The subjugation of black African bodies, be they students, thought leaders, teachers, professional strategists, cleaning staff, security personnel, administrators, and so forth, continues to this day in both former "historically black universities" (HBUs) and "historically white universities" (HWUs) despite talk about transformation. In fact, nearly three decades after the demise of apartheid higher education, very little has been accomplished to epistemologically "transform" colonial practices, modes of engagement and relationality when it comes to black bodies, which according to scholars remains firmly entrenched in notions of exclusion, segregation, and marginalization of black bodies (Badat, 2004, 2017; Heleta, 2018; Khalema, 2018). South African higher education transformation is not divorced from broader challenges the country is facing with the transition to democracy. So, as we reflect on the context of educational transformation in higher education in South Africa, we cannot ignore the glaring façade of transformation itself, never mind the humanist hopes of all of us about the nature of higher education institutions. Universities are *supposed* to bring up cultivated, critical, and emancipated citizens. Today, however, in its practical administration, higher education has become a breeding ground for the performance of coloniality.

This chapter is informed by a decolonial approach that considers the convergences and divergences of varying institutional experiences and contexts of South African universities. We stand as bonified "students" and observers working and learning in one of South Africa's major universities with all the privileges (and curses) bestowed upon us by the roles we play (figuratively and epistemologically) of which we reluctantly observe and carefully affirm may assist in opening or closing conversations and possibilities in the advancement of the institution we are part of; yet at the same time we acknowledge that we are somewhat shackled to the status quo that constrains the possibilities of what we are able to do or say as a consequence of our roles. What is important and critical about these varied positionalities is that regardless of where one stands in the spectrum of debates, we are confronted by a myriad of difficulties within the ongoing decolonial project as we engage, relate, govern, and interact within the given contexts and negotiate our agency against these structures. The spaces we occupy are riddled not only with contradictions and tensions; but also, possibilities of igniting the hope we once had to do better and be better. Navigating this terrain requires an honest reflection of why and how institutions have managed contradictions, tensions, and possibilities. If we are to continue with the decolonial project of transforming our institutions, we ought to concede that a decolonized curriculum and its corresponding pedagogies require fertile soil to grow. If our institutions are not conducive to nurturing, affirming, and incubating decolonial seeds, little or no growth will occur.

In this chapter, we tilt the soil and expose what is underneath. We problematize and explore the contradictions, tensions, and possibilities within the context of transformation and the associated constraints therein. We adopt a decolonial viewpoint that interrogates the entrenched modes of colonial praxis in implementing transformation in South African universities. By acknowledging the fact that no South African university is the same, we can critically interrogate dominant modes of thinking that continue to suppress experiences, knowledges, voices, and positions of black African scholars and administrators in enacting transformational change in higher education. Although the implementation of employment equity over the past three decades since the transition to a new form of democratic governance promoted an African flare and widened the demographic representation of black African intellectuals and strategists with some success, the preservation of neo-colonial practices and processes of engagement in the governance of transformation consigns such developments to exclusionary tendencies that continue to alienate African-centred ways of doing and knowing.

The paper first discusses the higher education transformation discourse since the dawn of democracy. Subsequently, it discusses the implementation of transformation dimensions and their diverse outcomes, whilst offering a critique paper also assesses the achievements and continuing challenge of the higher education in terms of transformative change. Finally, the chapter explores possible theoretical interventions that can be pursued from the well of Ubuntu/Botho philosophy to address the vestiges of the legacies of untransformed higher education in South Africa. Thus, we assert that in order to advance decolonial alternatives in curriculum, post-apartheid institutions must also infuse and nurture African-centred philosophies that nurture healthy work environments and affirm anti-oppressive modes of engagement to adequately imagine a truly transformed African institution.

Trends in Transforming Higher Education in South Africa

The South African higher education context is replete with systemic changes since the dawn of democracy. Immediately after the end of apartheid in 1994, there were marked reforms that aimed at domesticating the otherwise colonial system of higher education. This was necessitated by the fact that the apartheid education system was skewed towards meeting aspirations of white minority. The country needed an education that aligned with its non-racist and non-sexist agenda, and which would prepare individuals to be trained for the relevant development and socio-economic needs of a transitioning country. To this effect, the ruling African National Congress (ANC) embarked on numerous educational reforms aimed at redressing the inequalities of the apartheid era.

The transformation of higher education was (and continues to be) seen as an urgent intervention to facilitate the transformation of society and to expediate social and economic redress. According to Van Schalkwyk et al. (2022) the articulation of transformation in South Africa's higher education discourse remains rigidly entrenched and dominated by what most institutions do and to an extent that for some, the term has become 'hazy and routine without uncritically assessing what is being done particularly if the "politics" and "conceptual lucidity" of doing transformation is aways shiftting. There is still a greater call for conceptual lucidity to shift from overly adulated belief of what really constitutes transformation in South Africa's universities (Van Schalkwyk et al., 2022). Thus, the talk about "transformation" in South African universities has a particular meaning related to the political transformation of society. In the South African context, transformation relates to societal change, not just overcoming apartheid but addressing broader economic and social change. As the *Green Paper on Higher Education Transformation* (Department of Education, 1996, Section 4) proposed:

> ...Transition and Transformation .... higher education policy in South Africa confronts two sets of challenges simultaneously... Successful policy will have to overcome an historically determined pattern of fragmentation, inequality, and inefficiency; it will have to increase access for black students and for women; and it will have to generate new models of learning and teaching to accommodate a larger student population.... Successful policy

> must restructure the higher education system and its institutions to meet the needs of an increasingly technologically oriented economy; and it must deliver the requisite research, the highly trained people, and the useful knowledge to equip a developing society with the capacity to participate competitively in a rapidly changing global context.

The idea of change is very important in this regard and as Eckel et al. (1998) suggest, a change process must alter the culture of the institution by changing the underlying assumptions and institutional behaviours, processes, and products. Furthermore, this transformative impulse must be "deep and pervasive," affecting the whole institution and be "intentional" to affect change over time. For Harvey and Knight (1996), this change involves shifting institutional cultures to enable learner transformation. Thus, institutions play a key role in providing the agents to nurture change, and it is through the transformative experience that they themselves can take a leading role in transforming their students and society. In essence, Harvey and Knight (1996) imply the necessity of institutions to become versatile if they are to successfully transform others. Educational transformation thus evokes ideas of institutional landscapes that uphold principles of inclusivity, a non-racial, non-sexist, and democratic societies as well as contribute to building human developmental capacities that have potential to alter the status quo (qtd. in Govinder et al., 2013). Thus, transformation in higher education is not only concerned with high-quality knowledge production as a base for the development of competent and skilled graduates who affirm themselves as generational agents actively pursuing social equity, but also how this knowledge sets into motion economic and social emancipation (Govinder et al., 2013). Transformations should be understood as a process of the disbanding existing set of social, economic, political, ideological, and cultural hegemonies and creating space for the co-creation of new modes of engagement that affirms *all* experiences (Chen & Taylor, 2011; Cloete, 2020; Harvey & Green, 1993; Mezirow, 2000; Levy & Merry, 1986).

The question of curriculum transformation was at the axis of the equity intervention; an agenda that continues today. The critique of institutional forms of knowledge production involves what Santos (2012) understands as the subversion of a dominant discursive intellectualism to show their lineage in Eurocentric epistemologies. Santos (2012) outlines the hierarchies that emerge within Eurocentric paradigms and calls for the pluralization of the knowledge field by bringing into presence epistemologies of the marginalized that have been made invisible. Although Eurocentric canons of knowledge proliferate in the curriculum, this did not mean that these bodies of knowledge are disconnected from other ways of knowing and doing. In fact, it is precisely through deliberate practices of silencing and erasure that epistemic privilege is acquired (Mignolo, 2000).

Following its transformation, the Vice Chancellor of the University of KwaZulu-Natal at the time, Professor Makgoba, embarked on designing a laundry list of reform initiatives aimed at advancing a decolonial and Africanized model. As a way of justifying the contested ratification, the Vice Chancellor introduced new governance structures and language policy accompanying new leadership and programs of study that were meant to advance the decolonial and Africanization agenda. For example, the meaning of a decolonial university achieved great public scrutiny, with debates questioning how the transformation agenda will account and balance diversity, internationalisation, and indigenization. There were also commentators who reflected on the matters of representativity capability, equity, research excellence, and administrative capacity. As Balintulo (2004: 3) argues, given the educational context of the time and characterized by vested interests, multiple stakeholder disagreements, tensions, and competing agendas were unavoidable. Such tensions were further fuelled by the role performed by external structures in monitoring institutional change in the implementation of transformation.

Of course, one could not ignore the impact of the "Fallist" student movement broke into the fray where demands for decolonization and free education took centre stage illustrative of the increased student presence in the transformation debate. The current and never-ending situation of student protests that call attention to pressing issues encompassing (but not limited to): scrapping off student's historic debts; financial exclusion of deserving students on government funding such as National Student Financial Aid Scheme (NSFAS); inadequacy of government funding to financially needy students which has left students stranded without accommodation and food; discrepancies in the registration processes with some students forced to pay registration fee regardless of them being funded by NSFAS; and other concerns for agency and accommodation that were no less symptomatic of a much deeper problem.

One might ask why after years of transformation taking shape, we are still struggling to address issues of inclusivity and transformative change (especially investing in future generations) in our institutions of higher learning. How is it that historically disadvantaged black students who are still excluded from economic transformation are further subjected to exclusion in higher education? Other demands made by the "Fallist" movement included the need to deal with the hegemonic institutional culture at higher education sector; the role of language, and in this particular case, the Afrikaans, an entrenched historical tool of linguistic oppression for historically marginalized blacks; the restructuring of the curriculum to reflect epistemic freedom centred on black excellence and indigenous languages and culture in celebrating of Africanity; and a desire to achieve epistemic justice in South African higher education (Hlatshwayo, 2020).

According to Kumalo (2018), the 2015–2016 student movement protests marked the genesis of ontological and epistemic struggles for black students and black academics in South Africa's higher education sector, who were demanding the complete dismantling of the remaining colonial canons in post-apartheid institutions of higher learning. As such, recent years have seen a palpable rise in decolonial engagement in South African universities by the student led "Fallist" movement that demanded total decolonization. Echoed across most campuses in the nation and expressed in the populist register: #RhodesMustFall; #FeesMustFall, #StatuesMustFall; #LiberateMyDegree. Subsequent testimonies further exposed inaction as a mode of deactivating the decolonization of curricula, pedagogy, knowledge production, university policies, campus climate, and the experiences of students, faculty, and communities were also motivating forces driving student protest activities. Institutions of higher learning wrestled with finding effective ways to enact and implement transformational change that both has an impact in terms of curriculum reform. These movements call out the Eurocentricity of academic curricula and provide a platform to otherwise silenced "decolonial" discourse. The students themselves, through their direct action, offer several resources, materially, culturally, ideationally, and otherwise, for institutions looking to transform their learning spaces and undo forms of coloniality in their classrooms, campuses, and curricula. In each of these campaigns, students have clearly pointed to the institutional and structural issues facing South African higher education, and much of this has come to coalesce around energies mobilizing for the decolonization of higher education in South Africa and abroad, drawing upon the frameworks of the progressive historical struggles against apartheid and colonialism in the global south (Bhambra et al., 2018; Khalema, 2018).

In the past three decades, South Africa's post-apartheid government has implemented regulatory policy framework and mechanisms to promote and transform the higher education sector with some success. The following cases are exemplary of this process:

i. The White Paper on higher education policy in 1998, which positions itself as "a vehicle for bringing transformation within the institutions of higher learning".
ii. National Working Group (NWG) in 2000, established to advise the Minister of Higher Education on the remodelling of the higher education terrain in South Africa in an attempt to improve equity and increase the participation of black students and staff and also improve the capacity and performance of institutions of higher learning.
iii. The establishment of a "Ministerial Committee on Transformation and Social Cohesion and Elimination of Discrimination in Public Higher Education" in 2008 with the aim of tackling racial discrimination and promoting social cohesion especially in public universities that had been historically disadvantaged (Department of Education, 2008).
iv. The 2010 Summit of Higher Education Transformation hosted by the current Minister of Higher Education, Dr. Blade Nzimande, Ph.D., gave mandate to all universities across the country to produce a transformation plan that shows an institutional roadmap and commitments to strengthening and achieving transformation in the higher education sector (Department of Higher Education and Training, 2010).
v. The Higher Education Amendment Act No. 9 of 2017 established to investigate the lack of transformation, and under-representation of black students and staff in historically white universities (Republic of South Africa, 1996) and
vi. The White Paper on Science, Technology and Innovation, aimed at improving representation and the participation of historically disadvantaged black and female students in the field of research and development (R&D), which to date remains too low.

These policy documents and legislative frameworks all aimed at "transformation" and "reformation" in their inclinations. However, they have essentially failed to adequately deconstruct the underlying deeply entrenched epistemology based on structural racism of apartheid which is still reflected in historically black institutions in South African higher education sector.

Apart from government attempts to beat the drum towards institutional transformation in the higher education sector, universities together with civil society also had to show commitment to transform their institutions into knowledge creation hubs. This is evident with the formation of Universities South Africa (USAf) which pledged a commitment to the development of Integrated Transformation Plans by establishing a *Transformation Barometer Framework* in 2017, which would serve as a yardstick and a self-regulatory tool for institutions of higher learning to set their own targets regarding formal transformation within their respective universities. However, to date, no final version of the draft of *Transformation Barometer* document has been constructively formulated by any university (qtd. in Van Schalkwyk et al., 2022). What is more, despite calls at the national level by the Department of Higher Education and Training (DHET) in its transformative agenda, this transformation has been grossly limited to those who are already enrolled at the university and does not really take seriously what kind of knowledge is produced and whose knowledge, teaching methods, and learning cultures are foregrounded and promoted in higher education sector (Heleta, 2021; Luqman, 2022).

Responding the 2015 Fallist student movement that highlighted the continued exclusion and alienation of black African students in the current teaching and learning spaces, the University of Cape Town (UCT) for example proposed the UCT' *Curriculum Change Framework* which centred its intervention around curriculum decolonization and putting decolonization into practice by asking key questions about the production of knowledge by whom, the need to produce it, for whom and why. This intervention assisted UCT's conversations about decolonization of curriculum, far beyond symbolic gestures of renaming building or removing colonial statues as a reaction to the fallist movement; nothing the significance and trauma of everyday exclusions that students and faculty of colour face in the institution. There is no doubt that fallist student movement has sparked contemporary scholarship that seeks to practically engender epistemological decolonization in South

African universities. Following the fallist movements of 2015–2016, there has been movements in universities around curriculum reform that centres bottom-up approaches to facilitate indigenous learning pedagogies (Luqman, 2022). Further, the increased representation and participation of black South Africans (notably women) in the academe has inspired a much-needed African feminist and womanist critique of transformation pointing to its vagueness and impracticality (Bunting et al. 2020 cited in Van Schalkwyk et al., 2022). Although evidence shows a significant rise in the enrolment of black students, representation, and participation of black and female students and staff in South Africa's public universities over the past decade, the ongoing absence of consensus, barometers, and outcomes on what constitutes transformation in higher education sector hinders the attainment of a transformed system in public universities in South Africa (Makhaye et al., 2023).

The Façade of Transformation, Transformers, and Being Transformed?

> In the first place, the rulers of neo-colonial States derive their authority to govern, not from the will of the people, but from the support which they obtain from their neo-colonialist masters. They have therefore little interest in developing education, strengthening the bargaining power of their workers employed by expatriate firms, or indeed of taking any step which would challenge the colonial pattern of commerce and industry, which it is the object of neo-colonialism to preserve. 'Aid', therefore, to a neo-colonial State is merely a revolving credit, paid by the neo-colonial master, passing through the neo-colonial State, and returning to the neo-colonial master in the form of increased profits. (Kwame Nkrumah, 1970)

The above quote by Nkrumah (1970) paints a very telling scenario of the neo-colonial condition that limits what one can do or say given the centrality and situatedness of power. To date, South African institutions of higher learning remain a colonial project modelled to serve white supremacy and its complementary western ethos that impedes transformation and equality amongst historically disadvantaged black Africans. Jansen (2023) contends that South African institutions of higher learning have become a breeding ground for chronic institutional dysfunction that includes never-ending violence, stakeholder conflicts, ongoing student protests, violent confrontations, occasional burning of buildings, police presence, campus closures and now chronic corruption rooted in a political economy framework. This has serious implications for the viability of the academic system as well as the functionality and prospects for transformation of universities as knowledge creation hubs necessary for bringing to life decoloniality discourses. The ongoing chronic dysfunction across South Africa's universities has resulted in the loss of teaching time, waiving of funding, research delays, the departure of top academic staff and students, reduction in the production of PhD graduates, and less government intervention with the appointment of university administrators leading to violent conflicts, dismissal, threats, and attempted murders of top university administrators in the country (Govender, 2018; Jansen, 2023).

Jansen (2023) sees an immediate power imbalance between limited resources and the interests of stakeholders. For Jansen (2023), the questions of who should lead, who gets what, and the reasons for these decisions have been exacerbated by what he frames as a chronic system of corruption that is deeply rooted in the political economy of the country. Jansen (2023) further describes the everyday realities and struggle for institutional resources. One of the core challenges that contributes to the institutional dysfunction in South Africa's universities is lack of governance and managerial capacity. According to Jansen (2023), the university councils and senates, which are the highest governing bodies in decision-making, have been in dispute with university management, and this has worsened over years with the recent events showing division within the institutions. For example, at the University of Cape Town, the former Vice Chancellor Professor Mamokgethi Phakeng in her attempt to address what she viewed as transforming the governance processes within the university found herself "retiring" early to avoid further friction within the UCT Council (Daily Maverick, 2023). This early exit was unprecedented since her contract as Vice Chancellor was recently renewed with a clear mandate to lead the institution for another five years.

In other universities, the alleged inefficiencies in managing funds were reportedly taking place whereby both internal and external players masquerade as concerned stakeholders who sell the message of commitment to addressing students' financial debts and historical disparities that continue to disadvantage black students, is crippling the functionality of these institutions. The reported attempted assassination of the current Vice Chancellor of the University of Fort Hare, Professor

Sakhela Buhlungu, following his appointment to the position and his expressed dedication to investigate the ongoing governance issues and corruption activities has created animosities from within the institution. Such revelations would mean exposing the inefficient processes and leadership that perpetuates a deep embedded dysfunctional system that had brought such a prestigious institution to its knees (Cloete, 2023).

Moreover, the alleged axing of the Vice Chancellor and Principal of the Vaal University of Technology (VUT) Professor Dan Kgwadi in February 2023, who barely lasted a year in his position since his appointment in February 2022, is another shocking example of how politicized, fragmented, and dysfunctional institutions of higher learning have become. Professor Dan Kgwadi was reported to have been put under special leave following his fourteen-day sick leave in which he was hospitalized for a knee injury. According to reports written by the *Inside Education* and *News 24* media channel, the Vice Chancellor allegedly challenged his suspension and took the university council to the labour court (Bhengu, 2023; Naidu, 2023). Jansen (2023) further writes that university senates have become increasingly politicized and used as a platform for imposing regulatory rules and a business culture that is amenable to the private interests of council representatives perhaps even at the expense of the wellbeing of students. Hence Jansen (2023) suggests that if institutions of higher learning must transform, there is need to depoliticize processes, and enable an ethic of care based on integrity to lead these fragmented institutions.

The above examples point to a plethora of challenges within institutions of higher learning with roots in governance uncertainty for those who attempt to reform or transform practices that have roots in apartheid educational governance. In fact the challenges point to the challenge of the preservation of neo-colonial practices and processes of engagement in the governance of transformation post-apartheid. The neglected preservation and continuation of colonial practices and processes of engagement have tragically demonstrated a move towards the institutional violence of the past, resulting in what Jansen (2023) calls a chronic dysfunctional system of institutions. Whether one agrees with Jensen (2023) or not, it is clear that redressing practices and processes cannot just be about changing the demographic face of universities but further requires an intentional questioning of what transformation really means with respect to decoloniality. If not, the discourse of transformation will inevitably tear at the seams as inefficiencies in the system widespread corruption impacts decision-making, devolves into the inconsistency of treatment, perpetuates inequalities of punishment and inequalities of privilege, entitles mimicking and virtue signalling of institutions to appear transformed, and as articulated above, targets and labels black academics who apply policies consistently as disruptive and bullies. In our view, underlying the pageantry are deep-seated microaggressions that are often racialized, gendered, and class-based, and these get to the root consequences for how we treat people. Also, the examples above point to a bigger problem. Black bodies are suspended more, investigated more, and are more likely to be on the receiving end of accusations of being corrupt. How we go about dealing with these governance flaws and how we treat each other in these spaces extends to what we can do in the classroom. How possible is it then to offer "African solutions to African problems?" This will remain one of the biggest challenges facing institutions, and the excuses that continue to ignore the practices and processes (i.e. what and how) of transformation will only conceal what we know to be happening behind the scenes. These are difficult questions facing committed Black African intellectuals and professionals who find themselves at the crossroads of the transformation coalface.

As Hlatshwayo (2020) asserts, black people are still struggling to deal with the colonial and apartheid logic that continues to underpin and anchor the higher academic sector. The curriculum is still dominated by what Kennedy (2017) and Pett (2015) call an "epistemology of dead white men" (quoted in Hlatshwayo, 2020). The English language remains a "lingua franca" in most of the institutions despite the movement of asserting indigenous languages into the mix. Hlatshwayo (2020) contends that like former colonies of Britain, South Africa uses the English language as an imperial semantic tool of oppression and petrification to marginalize non-white scholars. Douglas Ficek (2011: 76), writing on Fanon and petrification, reminds us that by "petrification," Fanon meant an excessively strong adherence to tradition in the face of the colonizer's culture, which brings about a kind of paralysis or "immobility" of the culture of the colonized. This socio-cultural "petrification" expresses itself as a commitment "to the old ways, to the superstitions and rituals that, however fantastic, offer outlets for their profound anger they effectively distract themselves from the hard realities of colonialism, and this ultimately benefits the colonizers, the architects of petrification" (Ficek, 2011: 76).

The point being made here is that as long as South African universities allow their educational and scientific agendas to be determined by neoliberalism, their cultural "petrification" would remain the status quo. Thus, the neo-colonial condition pushes people to go out of their way to guarantee that the post-colonial order benefits from the neo-colonial strategies. But more precisely, there is another side to petrification that Fanon alerts us to, namely the deliberate cultivation of such petrification on the part of the people by new leaders, which is designed to prevent criticism of their economically privileged position and effectively ensures the process of decolonization is stopped short of completion (Ficek, 2011: 83). In this way, petrification thrives on people's complacency and the lack of criticism for the new, "post-colonial" regime. In Fanon's words (quoted in Ficek, 2011: 83):

The break from neo-colonial impositions therefore involves a move towards relative autonomy rooted within and concomitant with a *living* cultural tradition, appropriating other knowledge traditions (including western and eastern ones) from a resolutely African perspective in terms of the African value placed on community (and, one may add, ecology), above that of the exploitation by capital. Because South Africa's institutions of higher learning have failed to dismantle western hegemony that is centred on western epistemological traditions of white knowledge supremacy, African epistemicide continues despite countless attempts made by the post-apartheid ANC government and the Department of Higher Education and Training (DHET) to bring about transformation in the higher education sector (see Heleta, 2021; Luqman, 2022).

The views espoused by Soudien (2010) have also been instructive in shaping our critique of the neo-colonial condition of the South African higher education. Soudien (2010) argues that there are two main approaches to transformation: (1) the first sees transformation as a demographic intervention around the imbalances of race, class, gender, and language; whilst (2) the second understands it to mean the nature of dynamics of privilege and power. Positions that side with the first viewpoint insist that numbers matter, and this is essentially the representativity approach to transformation. Positions based on the second viewpoint postulate that transformation is an ideological process that must engage with domination and its attendant forces and discourses. There is a focus on the distribution of political and economic power in society and the processes through which social inclusion and exclusion are affected (Soudien, 2010). Thus, transformation has different dimensions, all of which are important. It is therefore essential that the discourse on transformation should not be fixated on one or few dimensions only. We add that equally important is a critique of modes of engagement and governance of transformation as shown above.

Although the policy hardware enshrined in the transformation directives provides a sound and clear framework for how we ought to relate and engage, ethical governance and accountable leadership are still a challenge in most South African institutions. Thus, as Heleta (2016) suggests, there is a need for an "epistemological transformation" that consists in dismantling the apartheid knowledge system, which operated a curriculum that was modelled based on racialized grounds as a tool of subjugation and exclusion. The current epistemic logic in South Africa's higher education system lacks prioritization of the aspirations of historically disadvantaged groups notably black students of which the transformation efforts reflected in the form of policy documents and legislative frameworks have not "translated into any significant shifts in the structure and content of the curriculum" (Heleta, 2016: 3; see also Crossman, 2004). There is no doubt that despite the relative efforts made by both government and institutions of higher learning to transform the higher education sector, transformation remains relatively slow and imperceptible in most of the universities across the country as the inequality gaps between former white and former black universities continue to grow over the last decade (Kumalo, 2018).

Towards African-Centred Practices and Processes of Redress

The post-apartheid institutions require an infusion of African-centred practices and processes to animate redress. The *Ubuntu/Botho* concept, like many African philosophies, is not easily definable as many authors have posited (Brack et al., 2003; Cloete et al., 2015; Govender, 2018; Makhaye et al., 2023; Mezirow, 2000; and Mbembe, 2016). Various authors (Khoza, 1994; Makhudu, 1993; Maphisa, 1994) have interpreted *Ubuntu* in terms of the worthwhile, good, and valuable in human life, which is concerned with visions of happiness and fulfilment and ideas of how these might be realized (Prinsloo, 1998: 276). However, scholars who study *Ubuntu* maintain that its inherent focus relies on the importance of personhood, selfhood, and common humanness (Gade, 2012: 487–489; Lutz, 2009: 314–318; Mnyaka & Motlhabi, 2005: 215;

Mangena, 2016). Nussbaum (2003: 21) states that *Ubuntu* is the capacity to express compassion, reciprocity, dignity, harmony, and humanity in the interests of building and maintaining community. According to Woermann and Engelbrecht (2019), Metz (2012), and Gade (2012) *Ubuntu* embodies the following aphorisms:

> "I am because you are, and you are because I am"
> "A person is a person through others", and
> "I am because we are".

Fox (2010: 123–124) states that in *Ubuntu*, the emphasis is placed on the human aspect, and teaches that the value, dignity, safety, welfare, health, beauty, love, and development of the human being are to come first and should be prioritized before all other considerations, particularly in modern times, before economics, financial, and political factors are considered. In another sense, *Ubuntu/Botho* is about the art of being a human person (quoted in Fox, 2010: 122). Its characteristics are, ***amongst others***:

- An affirmation on one's humanness, which means that being human comprises values such as universal humanity and sharing and treating and respecting diversity of others and recognizing their humanity.
- The importance of valuing the human experience of positive relational capacity and treating people with dignity and respect; and
- A way of life contributing positively to sustaining the wellbeing and livelihoods of other people as equal members of your community or society.

In the context of transforming institutions of higher learning, the *Ubuntu/Botho* worldview proposes a much-needed opening which calls for an African-centred approach to transforming the relational capacity of valuing each other's humanity (including the talents, styles in leadership, and diversity we bring) within universities. According to Nzimakwe (2014) the ubuntu ethic of governance is to serve humanity in a practical way as equal contributors in building healthy environments regardless of difference. Thus, through positive and affirmative actions of being included, one is connected, linked, and bound to others. Evidently, a practical communal action in the praxis of Ubuntu is to alleviate human suffering and disconnection as the best way one can demonstrate one's contribution to society. We have to ask ourself how many of us are suffering because of us? It is an important principle in the form of additional support, where those who are in positions of power and influence make it their point to uplift others regardless of whether there are affiliated in other ways (i.e. economically, culturally, ethnically, racially, or otherwise). The *Ubuntu* ethic, thus addresses affirming others' views with compassion, empathy, and kindness thus humanizing them (Fox, 2010; Nzimakwe, 2014). Within the *Ubuntu/Botho* ethic of care there is a concerted effort and commitment to advance the interests, dreams, and hopes of others. These acts help to "bring sense not only to one's own life but also to the lives of others" (Mnyaka & Motlhabi, 2005: 228). In summary, Gildenhuys and Knipe (2000: 272) argue that to live and work by the principle of *Ubuntu* requires, *amongst others*:

- Providing hospitality in the workplace.
- Acknowledging the importance of gratitude by affirming the successes, contributions, and inputs from others.
- Celebrating equally and at all occasions the successes of others; and
- Providing prayers of thanks and taking into account the spiritual dimensions of the work.

Institutional leaders of higher education operating within an *Ubuntu* worldview stress and model the importance of respecting the individual, place value on working as a team, and support each other. In the case of universities, an ethics of relational connectivity should be in the service of values rooted in humanity itself. In order to effectuate such an ethics, *Ubuntu* embodies a tradition of consultation and decision-making by members of society. In the sphere of work, individual creativity and the solidarity of cooperation and common ownership must go hand in hand (Prinsloo, 1998: 277; Nzimakwe, 2014). Regine (2009: 17) and Venter (2004: 155) further propose creating environments that recognize an essential human interconnectedness between individuals and how their humanity is inextricably bound to others. Thus, if others are diminished so are they, and if others fail, so do they.

Ubuntu/Botho's stated intention as an African-centred worldview of elevating human interconnectivity and voice by fostering the critical interrogation of social relationality offers an opportunity to further refine how transformation can be implemented. The injunction to lift others as you yourself rise (which is central to the *Ubuntu/Botho* epistemology) speaks to the importance of the *Ubuntu* ethic of cooperation and collaborative work environments. Accomplishment in life may be an individual matter as a result of hard work and initiative, but mobility is sustained if and when others benefit from our achievements and movements. Thus, if rising means gaining autonomy and prestige and if lifting of others ensures that one creates opportunities and enabling environments for all and not only some to flourish, but one may also never forget where they came from as they rise or are lifted.

Ubuntu/Botho pedagogy as a transformative approach is centred on a series of principles which buttress effective implementation in diverse educational environments: understanding self and others through participation and interactions with others to share ideas, experiences, and learn from each other; building positive relationships through creating harmonious learning environment anchored on love, respect, and caring for one another; getting the class to work together through unity and solidarity; nurturing the minds of the students through active learning and engagement; teaching from a position of love and care through adhering to principles of professionalism, integrity, honest, transparency, and unbiases; and utilizing learners' linguistic resources to promote meaningful learning through accepting and embracing multilingual practices (Ukpokodu, 2016: 155; qtd. in Ngubane & Makau, 2021).

Conclusion

Dominant narratives of "transformation" have shaped the imagination of post-apartheid institutions with a clear mandate to transform the injustices, including structurally enforced and systemically embedded inequalities of apartheid and colonialism. Whilst the fiction of transformation has usefully demanded a shift towards addressing inequalities, its current priorities may undermine the potential to realize this aim. Through a process of reflection informed by an *Ubuntu/Botho* worldview, this paper has demonstrated how post-apartheid South African institutions of higher learning in their quest to transform practices are still entangled with western ways of knowing, relating, and doing. The chapter has made a call to dismantle taken-for-granted governance approaches through embracing African-centred epistemologies as a way to anchor the well-intended transformation agenda. Today's higher education context is confronted by a myriad of challenges that inhibit movement towards transformative change. Professor Adam Habib, former Vice Chancellor of Wits University, argues that the "toxic culture" of patronage politics, is becoming a strategic battleground for political warfare in a contestation for political and social capital that is threatening the functionality and credibility of academic institutions to transform. Like Habib, Jansen (2023) concurs that rent-seeking activism has become the order of the day in the higher education sector of South Africa, souring tensions and destroying the mutual trust between the academic management, staff, and the students (also see Cloete, 2020). As has been argued in this chapter, the cases of both overt and subtle violence at the top demonstrate a dysfunctionality in higher education institutions in which the concept of *Ubuntu/Botho* and its core principles are continuously compromised and undermined. As espoused by Andrews and Okpanachi (2012), indigenizing African governance through the creation of enabling environments in which African ideals of relationality can be easily accessible and transcribed into practical actions through collaboration manifest a transformed African university. Transformation in higher education presents a difficult challenge due to the evolution of its intent on the one hand, and the (in)flexibility of institutional frameworks on the other. Since most of the vigour goes into what universities do or go about doing in implementing transformational change, such an agenda requires that we expose and explicate the mistreatment on one another in academic spaces. The transformation of the structures, practices, values, culture of leadership, governance, and management are the most neglected elements in the transformation debate. As such, institutions should refocus their efforts in cultivating a culture that nurtures the intellectual, social, and cultural shifts for impactful transformation to occur. What constitutes impactful transformation ought to be left for institutions to enact, based on their histories and context.

This chapter expounds on the consortium-model and recommendations put forward by Andrews and Okpanachi (2012), Olukoshi (2006), and Moore-Sieray (1996) regarding Africa's decolonial pedagogy which is centred on three pillars: (i) indigenizing African scholarship by making it more Afro centred and detached from Western pedagogies, (ii) creating an enabling environment in which the ideals, models, and theories of African indigenous knowledge are easily accessible and translated into practical solutions; and (iii) improved partnership and sponsorship from the private sector and the African diaspora. The chapter suggest that less engagement and collaboration between universities, private sector, and community on issues of knowledge production, moreover, universities prefer to engage and collaborate more with their international fellows in the Global North and West than with other universities in the global South, African region or within their sub regions (blocks). This creates a schism in regional integration and undermines the commitment of locally produced knowledge and epistemic transformation as the international collaboration has proven to advance Western knowledge than that of Africans. African governments lack willingness and commitment to provide adequate funding for intra-Africa and South–South collaboration. This then explains why higher education institutions in the African region collaborate with the global North on knowledge production more often because they are dependent on external funding for their research activities and are required to align their research objectives to those of the donor countries. The chapter proposes that institutions as knowledge hubs need to partner and collaborate with both industry and local communities to share their expertise in the knowledge production and dissemination notably on what they value and how they interact with other key stakeholders such as policy makers in generating and transferring knowledge and technologies.

To summarize the trends in an ongoing transformation story of South African higher institutions, particularly true of the South African case, decoloniality in higher education continues to reflect on the ways in which apartheid and colonial education has shaped and continues to structure ways of knowing (knowledge production) and doing (education systems). Decolonial praxis therefore offered an opportunity and potential to realize a radical framework for examining and transforming knowledge systems and practices that shape learning in higher education. It must be said that transformation of the sector is contingent on various factors as well as implicated through the action, or, in some cases, the inaction, of institutional realities in response to these factors. Some of these factors are, arguably, more influential than others, however, it is important to concede that the state of higher education is against the backdrop of the anti-apartheid struggle and South Africa's roots in this struggle. It is evident that whatever the intentions of educational transformation are, there are obvious missteps that transformers made; missteps that ended up defeating the logic behind such reforms. Instructively, anyone doing educational reforms must identify areas that need correction or those that can do better if improved on. It is a deliberate and purposeful move which must equally be informed by context. This implies that one cannot wake up and purport to carry out transformation without a cause.

Furthermore, institutions need to be clear whether their conceptualization of transformation is realistic and/or attainable based on specific indicators. We put forward that an *Ubuntu*/Botho worldview, when embraced with the understanding and dignity it deserves, has the potential to initiate a new decolonial dialogue and reconnect institutions with values that nurture the capacity to cultivate social justice, equity, recognition, and fair participation. Thus, adapting and adopting an *Ubuntu/Botho*-based value of relating, doing, and leading would increase team effectiveness and, ultimately, organizational, and institutional effectiveness, to promote good governance. The ethic of *Ubuntu/Botho* does not necessarily ask for us to overthrow the structures that employ and feed us, but rather implores us to find consensus about what is fair and just in the way we relate to one another. In broad terms, an *Ubuntu* ethics considers the interconnected relationality we must actively work to build if we are to transform our institutions. Finding and employing indigenous approaches to enact good governance will in our view ultimately redress a recognized wrong. Leaders of institutions in this regard are responsible to ensure that the voices and pedagogies (in practice and action) of the silenced are affirmed, protected, and enhanced.

References

Andrews, N., & Okpanachi, E. (2012). Trends of Epistemic Oppression and Academic Dependency in Africa's Development: The Need for a New Intellectual Path. *Journal of Pan African Studies, 5*(8), 85–104.

Assié-Lumumba, T. (2007). *Higher Education in Africa: Crises, Reforms and Transformation*. African Books Collective.

Badat, S. (2004). Transforming South African Higher Education, 1990–2003: Goals, Policy Initiatives and Critical Challenges and Issues. In N. Cloete, P. Pillay, S. Badat, & T. Moja (Eds.), *National Policy and a Regional Response in South African Higher Education*. James Currey.

Badat, S. (2010). *The Challenges of Transformation in Higher Education and Training Institutions in South Africa*. A Paper Commissioned by the Development Bank of Southern Africa.

Badat, S. (2017, April 10). *Trepidation, Longing, and Belonging Liberating the Curriculum at Universities in South Africa* (Public Lecture). University of Pretoria.

Balintulo, M. (2004). *The Role of the State in Transformation of South African Higher Education (1994–2002): Equity Redress Revisited*. African Universities in the 21st Century. Volume II, Knowledge and Society. CODESRIA.

Bhambra, G., Gebrial, D., & Nişancıoğlu, K. (2018). *Decolonising the University*. Pluto Press.

Bhengu, C. (2023, February 23). *Vice-chancellor Dan Kgwadi Threatens Legal Action against VUT for Placing Him on Special Leave*. https://www.news24.com/news24/southafrica/news/vice-chancellor-dan-kgwadi-threatens-legal-action-against-vut-for-placing-him-on-special-leave-20230223

Bourdieu, P. (1964). *Les héritier. Les étudiants et la culture*. Minuit.

Brack, B., Hill, M. B., Edwards, D., Grootboom, N., & Lassiter, P. S. (2003). Adler and Ubuntu: Using Adlerian Principles in the New South Africa. *Journal of Individual Psychology, 59*(3), 316–326.

Brahima, A., Turner, I., & Woldegiorgis, E. T. (2021). Epilogue: A Long Way Towards a Decolonial Future in African Higher Education. In E. T. Woldegiorgis, I. Turner, & A. Brahima (Eds.), *Decolonisation of Higher Education in Africa: Perspectives from Hybrid Knowledge Production* (pp. 230–239). Routledge.

Bunting, I. (2006). The Higher Education Landscape under Apartheid. In N. Cloete, P. Maassen, R. Fehnel, T. Moja, T. Gibbon, & H. Perold (Eds.), *Transformation in Higher Education Global Pressures and Local Realities*. Springer.

Chen, M., & Taylor, J. (2011). *Quality as Transformation: Explore Understandings at Doctoral Level Education (0099) Extended Abstract for SRHE Conference 2011*. http://www.srhe.ac.uk/conference2011/abstracts/0099.pdf

Cloete, N. (2020). *Party Political Meddling Threatens Future of Universities*. https://mg.co.za/thoughtleader/opinion/2020-06-09-party-political-meddling-threatens-future-of-universities/

Cloete, N. (2023). *Comments on Jansen's Book on Corrupted: A Study of Dysfunction in Universities in SA*. https://www.universityworldnews.com/post.php?story=20230221184555640

Cloete, N., Maassen, P., & Bailey, T. G. (2015). *Knowledge Production and Contradictory Functions in African Higher Education*. African Minds.

Crossman, P. (2004). *Perceptions of 'Africanisation' or 'Endogenisation' at African Universities: Issues and Recommendations*. African Universities in the 21st Century. Volume II, Knowledge and Society. CODESRIA.

Daily Maverick. (2023). *Inside Vice-Chancellor Mamokgethi Phakeng's Messy exit from UCT*. https://www.dailymaverick.co.za/article/2023-02-22-inside-vice-chancellor-mamokgethi-phakengs-messy-exit-from-uct/

Department of Education. (2008). *Draft National Plan for Higher Education in South Africa*. Department of Education.

Department of Education (South Africa). (1996, December). *Green Paper on Higher Education Transformation* (Pretoria, Department of Education). http://www.polity.org.za/html/govdocs/green_papers/hegreenp.html?rebookmark=1#_Toc374340698, not available 04 February 2023.

Department of Higher Education and Training (DHET). (2010). Report on the Stakeholder Summit on Higher Education Transformation. In *Proceedings of the First Stakeholder Summit on the Transformation of Higher Education.*

Eckel, P., Hill, B., & Green, M. (1998). *On Change, En Route to Transformation.* American Council on Education.

Fanon, F. (1963). *The Wretched of the Earth* (C. Farrington, Trans.). Grove Weidenfeld.

Ficek, D. (2011). Reflections on Fanon and Petrification. In N. C. Gibson (Ed.), *Living Fanon: Global Perspectives* (pp. 75–84). Palgrave Macmillan.

Fox, W. (2010). *A Guide to Public Ethics.* Juta.

Gade, C. (2012). What Is Ubuntu? Different Interpretations among South Africans of African Descent. *South African Journal of Philosophy, 31*(3), 484–503.

Gildenhuys, J. S. H., & Knipe A. (2000). The Organisation of Government: An Introduction. *Van Schaik.* August 10, 2023. https://search.ebscohost.com/login.aspx?direct=true&scope=site&db=nlebk&db=nlabk&AN=1243024

Govender, P. (2018). Wit's Professors Fired for Not Disclosing Secret Affairs with Students. *Sunday Times*, August 22. https://www.timeslive.co.za/sunday-times/news/2018-08-18-wits-professors-fired-for-not-disclosing-sexual-relationships-with-students/

Government Gazette. (1997a). White Paper 3: A Programme for Higher Education Transformation. No. 18207.

Government Gazette. (1997b). Higher Education Act 101 of 1997.

Government Gazette. (1999). NSFAS Act, No. 56 of 1999.

Government Gazette. (2012). National Development Plan.

Govinder, K., Zondo, N., & Magkoba, M. (2013). A New Look at Demographic Transformation for Universities in South Africa. *South African Journal of Science, 109*(11–12), 1–11.

Harvey, L., & Green, D. (1993). Defining Quality. *Assessment and Evaluation in Higher Education, 18*(1), 9–34.

Harvey, L., & Knight, P. (1996). *Transforming Higher Education.* Open University Press and Society for Research into Higher Education.

Heleta, S. (2016). Decolonisation of Higher Education: Dismantling Epistemic Violence and Eurocentrism in South Africa. *Transformation in Higher Education, 1*(1), 1–8.

Heleta, S. (2018). Decolonizing Knowledge in South Africa: Dismantling the 'Pedagogy of Big Lies'. *Ufahamu: A Journal of African Studies, 40*(2), 47–65.

Heleta, S. (2021). *Coloniality, Knowledge Production, and Racialized Socio-economic Inequality in South Africa. The Economics of Empire*. Routledge.

Hlatshwayo, M. N. (2020). Being Black in South African Higher Education: An Intersectional Insight. *Bloemfontein Online*. https://doi.org/10.18820/24150479/aa52i2/9

Jansen, J. (2023). *Corrupted: A Study of Dysfunction in Universities in South Africa*. Wits University Press.

Kennedy, M. (2017, October 25). Cambridge academics seek to 'decolonise' English syllabus. *The Guardian*. Available at: https://www.theguardian.com/education/2017/oct/25/cambridge-academics-seek-to-decoloniseenglish-syllabus [accessed on Septermber 07 2023].

Khalema, N. E. (2018). Navigating Race in Higher Education and Beyond. In S. Swartz, A. Mahali, R. Moletsane, E. Arogundade, N. E. Khalema, C. Groenewald, & A. Cooper (Eds.), *Studying While Black: Race, Education and Emancipation in South African Universities* (pp. 50–67). HSRC Press.

Khoza, R. (1994). *African Humanism, Ekhaya Promotions, Diepkloof Extension*, South Africa.

Kumalo, S. H. (2018). Explicating Abjection: Historically White Universities Creating Natives of Nowhere? *Critical Studies in Teaching and Learning, 6*(1), 1–17.

Levy, A., & Merry, U. (1986) *Organizational Transformation: Approaches, Strategies, Theories*. Greenwood Publishing Group.

Luqman, M. O. (2022). *Curriculum Decolonization in the University of Cape Town: Research, Policy and Practice*. Faculty of Humanities.

Lutz, D. (2009). African Ubuntu Philosophy and Global Management. *Journal of Business Ethics, 84*(3), 313–328.

Makhaye, M. S., Mkhize, S. M., & Sibanyoni, E. K. (2023). Female Students as Victims of Sexual Abuse at Institutions of Higher Learning: Insights from Kwazulu-Natal, South Africa. *SN Social Sciences, 3*(2), 40.

Makhudu, N. (1993). Cultivating a Climate of Cooperation Through Ubuntu. *Enterprise*, 68, 40–41.

Mangena, F. (2016). African Ethics Through Ubuntu: A Postmodern Exposition. *Africology: The Journal of Pan African Studies*, *9*(2), 66–80.

Maphisa, S. (1994). *Man in Constant Search of Ubuntu: A Dramatist's Obsession*. Ubuntu School of Philosophy.

Mbembe, J. (2016). Decolonizing the University: New Directions. *Arts & Humanities in Higher Education, 15*, 29–45.

Metz, T. (2012). Ubuntu as a Moral Theory and Human Rights in South Africa. *African Human Rights Law Journal, 11*(2), 532–559.

Mezirow, J. (2000). *Learning as Transformation: Critical Perspectives on a Theory in Progress*. Jossey-Bass Publishers.

Mignolo, W. D. (2000). *Local Histories/Global Designs: Coloniality, Subaltern Knowledges and Border Thinking*. Princeton University Press.

Mnyaka, M., & Motlhabi, M. (2005). The African Concept of *Ubuntu/Botho* and Its Socio-moral Significance. *Black Theology: An International Journal, 3*(2), 215–237.

Moore-Sieray, D. (1996). Towards a Decolonization of Scholarship in Africa and a Vision for the 1990s and Beyond. *Journal of Third World Studies, 13*(2), 25–50.

Naidu, E. (2023, April 19). Varsity Mum over Axed Vice-Chancellor, Professor Dan Kgwadi. https://insideeducation.co.za/varsity-mum-over-axed-vice-chancellor-professor-dan-kgwadi/

Ndlovu-Gatsheni, S. J. (2020). *Decolonization, Development and Knowledge in Africa: Turning over a New Leaf*. Routledge.

Ngubane, N., & Makua, M. (2021). Ubuntu Pedagogy—Transforming Educational Practices in South Africa Through an African Philosophy: From Theory to Practice. *Journal of Humanities and Social Sciences, 13*(1), 1–12.

Nkrumah, K. (1970). *Class Struggle in Africa*. Panaf Books Limited.

Nussbaum, B. (2003). Ubuntu: Reflections of a South African on Our Common Humanity. *Reflections: The Sol Journal*, *4*, 21–26. https://doi.org/10.1162/152417303322004175

Nyamnjoh, F., & Jua, N. (2002). African Universities in Crisis and the Promotion of a Democratic Culture: The Political Economy of Violence in African Educational Systems. *African Studies Review, 45*(2), 1–26.

Nzimakwe, T. I. (2014). Practising Ubuntu and Leadership for Good Governance: The South African and Continental Dialogue. *African Journal of Public Affairs*, *7*(4), 30–41.

Olukoshi, A. (2006). African Scholars and African Studies. *Development in Practice, 16*(6), 533–544.

Pett, S. (2015, May 8). It's Time to Take the Curriculum Back from Dead White Men. *The Conversation*. Available at: https://theconversation.com/its-time-to-take-the-curriculum-back-from-dead-white-men-40268 [accessed on September 07 2023].

Prinsloo, E. D., (1998). Ubuntu Culture and Participatory Management. In P. H. Coetzee & A. P. J. Roux (Eds.), *The African Philosophy Reader* (pp. 41–51). Routledge.

Regine, B. (2009). Ubuntu: A Path to Cooperation. *Interbeing, 3*(2), 17–21.

Republic of South Africa. (1996). *The Constitution of the Republic of South Africa, 1996*. South Africa.

Santos, B. D. S. (2012). Public Sphere and Epistemologies of the South. *Africa Development, 37*(1), 43–67.

Soudien, C. (2010). Some Issues in Affirmative Action in Higher Education in South Africa. *South African Journal of Higher Education, 24*(2), 224–237.

Van Schalkwyk, F. B., van Lill, M. H., Cloete, N., & Bailey, T. G. (2022). Transformation Impossible: Policy, Evidence and Change in South African Higher Education. *Higher Education, 83*, 613–630.

Venter, E. (2004). The Notion of Ubuntu and Communalism in African Educational Discourse. *Studies in Philosophy and Education, 23*(2–3), 149–160.

Woermann, M., & Engelbrecht, S. (2019). The Ubuntu Challenge to Business: From Stakeholders to Relationholders. *Journal of Business Ethics, 157*. https://doi.org/10.1007/s10551-017-3680-6

CHAPTER 10

Agency, Africanity, and Some Propositions for Engaged Scholarship

Nene Ernest Khalema

On Discourse, Agency, and Ownership

It is the job of African scholars in Africa and the diaspora to re-imagine, expose, and decenter Eurocentric pedagogical and research practices that inform entrenched narratives about Africa and African agency. Illuminating the particularity of African scholarship, the unique contextual challenges of interrogating the entrenched modes of curricula and pedagogies, research hegemony, and practices that defines teaching about Africa should be part of our commitment. Dei (2012) agrees that African scholars in Africa and the diaspora have a significant role to play in intervening in the space of education precisely due to the benefits this intervention will achieve for Africans learners. He asserts:

N. E. Khalema (✉)
School of Built Environment and Development Studies, University of KwaZulu-Natal, Durban, South Africa
e-mail: Khalema@ukzn.ac.za

N. Andrews and N. E. Khalema (eds.), *Decolonizing African Studies Pedagogies*, Political Pedagogies,
https://doi.org/10.1007/978-3-031-37442-5_10

> Educators need to put new pedagogical approaches and classroom instructional practices in place to address schooling challenges and to ensure safe, secure, and healthy learning environments for learners. Cultural paradigms shape the construction of knowledges, as well as experiences of schooling. The work of African educators (research, writing and teachings) must affirm Indigenous/African cultures, while pointing to the creativity, resourcefulness, agency, and value systems of our cultural knowledges. We must challenge current intellectual posture, which sees how we come to know and understand our relations through the prism of the dominant. (p. 106)

For Sefa Dei (2012: 103) it is about the urgency of evoking the possibilities of "cultural engagement" versus "cultural estrangement" in promoting African education, contending that "for African learners we need to develop theoretical prisms or perspectives that are able to account for our lived experiences and our relationality with other learners". The same sentiments are expressed by Ali Abdi (2021) in his book entitled: *Theorizations of Education,* in which he states that:

> .... one can discern the slow, counter-critical, and almost osmosis-like spread of the philosophical and programmatic structures of globalizing Eurocentric education and the damages it has done to people's onto-epistemologies and overall livelihood situations. These situations were not limited to the colonized continental zones of the world, but ..., also to previously Indigenous and currently settler dominated parts of the world. (p. 3)

This volume was conceptualized in part as a response to Dei's (2012) and Abdi's (2021) calls for critical discourses that work to challenge colonial discourses and the persistent Eurocentrism that informs what we do, think, and teach. As co-editors, this collaborative journey began way over ten years ago as students and engaged scholars at the University of Alberta (Canada) where in our respective epistemic spaces we were intrigued by the way Africa and African studies were taught. Our collaboration has resulted in two volumes that unearthed the centrality of African development from a critical perspective (see Andrews et al., 2013, 2015) were produced. These two contributions were instructive in the theoretical and empirical explorations of the prescriptive notions of African development, but they had little emphasis on pedagogy. Recently and during the heart of the COVID 19 pandemic, we further collaborated on a project funded by the Carnegie African Diaspora Fellowship Program reflected on where we both are in our respective institutions as the pandemic ushered new challenges in the scholarship of teaching and learning. More specifically, in our reflections we pursued understandings of possible ways of appreciating pedagogies that enrich our knowledge of pedagogic processes, particularly during the pandemic. This discussion we felt must involve an examination of classroom discourses about Africa (what, how, and why we teach) and tease out the underlying structures of teaching and learning that influence pedagogic choice.

We also felt that as architects of knowledge and learning environments, academics play important roles in influencing ways in which curriculum and knowledge is articulated and disseminated. Thus, we shape the thought processes of students who come from different backgrounds by what we choose to share with them, while obviously being influenced by current academic, social, and political discourses in our respective fields of study. We engage with diverse students who by nature are curious about and enticed by critical approaches we might or might not adopt in our teaching and scholarship.

We work in institutions that might or might not be open to expressions of diverse academic and non-academic staff, and the theories, and worldviews expounded by different disciplines. We are further challenged by a greater social responsibility to accommodate growing numbers of students from both privileged and underserved backgrounds who are yearning for something different. The scope of the curriculum is also changing from its colonial prescriptions and challenged by a much-needed demand for an infusion of a decolonial reality that aims at expanding and including the complex diversities and intricacies experienced by those marginalized by colonial legacies to create space for new conversations about why we teach, what we teach, and how we teach (hooks, 1992; Gatune, 2010; Hua, 2013; Khalema, 2022).

Despite the sophisticated analyses and knowledge produced about Africa, the field of African studies lacks empirical analyses of the theoretical underpinning that inform it and classroom discourse on how the teaching of Africa is enacted. Although engaging about Africa as a subject matter offers a wide discussion of the knowledge about Africa; classroom knowledge without citing teacher–student exchanges particularly pedagogic discourse is limiting. The way the curriculum is organized determines or is indicative of implicit and explicit pedagogical ideas. While, on the surface, ideas appear neutral and often legitimized in terms of equality and meritocracy, the repeated message is that there is an unobserved social function which differentiates and discriminates. Thus, the way we frame and classify knowledge inherently possess claims and codes to which discourses find refuge or are nurtured. In this instance, language plays an integral role in expressing the structure, and content which favors certain ways of thinking and doing.

French sociologist Pierre Bourdieu (1991) problematized the importance of language in the academic discourse and how it operates in education. For Bourdieu (1991), academic discourse is predicated on an assumption of communication between the student and the educator, which is contradictory because it demands that pedagogical communication needs to satisfy both, which does not. For Bourdieu et al. (1994) there is an obscurity, but also implicit, present, and immanent injury relates to the power of the knowledge and how diverse students read and consume knowledge and the social interpretations derived in the classroom about the knowledge; perhaps leading to some students resisting (i.e. hostility to the hegemonic forces), others celebrating (both hegemonic knowledge to confirm what they already know or alternatively others celebrating counter-hegemonic knowledge they are privy to), and while others left with more questions in an attempt to compensate what they know and how to make sense with what they hear. These classroom scenarios pose a dilemma for African studies due to the contested terrain in which learning occurs.

On Knowledge, Teaching, and Talking Africa

The original mission for the book (which we still maintained) was to decipher what we teach, why we teach, and how we teach African studies and cognate disciplines such as international relations, sociology, development studies, and so forth. Equally important for us was to provide grounded conceptualizations about the academic project of producing African knowledge that is authentic consciousness transforming, and emancipatory to encapsulate the dynamic, ingenious ways in which African intellectuals on the continent and in the diaspora animate agency while navigating a hostile and/or toxic neo-colonial academic spaces.

The idea of producing knowledge that is critical should always be at the mind of academics teaching about Africa particularly because of the history of how knowledge about Africa is produced and circulated. As African studies scholars grapple with packaging and disseminating a balanced curriculum in classroom settings that is both emancipatory and/or factual to give a balance view of the complexities Africa and its people face; the idea of understanding the possibilities of engaging in non-essentialist decoloniality will always pose a dilemma. What is essential however is the process of critically reflecting about the knowledge in the teaching space to expand views, highlight silenced knowledge derived from lived experiences, voices, attitudes, and positionalities of African bodies to redress and contest dominant modes of thinking and practices; thus, revealing the complexities of the colonial veracities which have rationalized the continuance of the colonial project.

Fundamentally, the book set out to unpack what anchored knowledge about Africa through curriculum theorizing and praxis. The unpacking of the process of knowledge making as (and for) consciousness transformation and the possibilities of transformative curriculum change through agency was at the center of conversation with contributors. This meant seeking chapters that foregrounded pedagogical understandings and/or interpretations of multilayered meanings of stories and words about Africa and its people; thus, centering the Africanity of memory, the privileging of Black/African perspectives in teaching and learning about Africa, which is the cultural foundation that generates collective humanity and agency. These conceptual tools are fundamental in understanding and reimagining the possibilities of transforming dominant curriculum about Africa marginalized by hegemonic concepts, themes, and colonial ideas as Bhabha (1988) would argue.

The aim of examining relevant theoretical, epistemological, curriculum, and pedagogical developments in discourses about Africa was inspired by the necessary process to clarify and valorize Western-centric understanding of the world and give meaning and significance to adopting a decolonial approach that focuses on Africanity as a philosophy and method of teaching African studies for emancipation. As Boaventura de Sousa Santos (2014: 1) writes in the preface of his book entitled: "*Epistemology of the South: Justice against Epistemicide*":

> .... viewed from the perspective of the excluded, the historical record of how we teach Africa is filled with institutionalized lies at its core. It is a record of social regulation in the name of social emancipation, appropriation in the name of liberation, violence in the name of peace, the destruction of life in the name of the sanctity of life, violation of human rights in the name of human rights, societal fascism in the name of political

> democracy, illegal plundering in the name of the rule of law, assimilation in the name of diversity, individual vulnerability in the name of individual autonomy, constitution of subhumanities in the name of humanity…

For Santos (2014), the European colonial project, mired with violence, has impacted African advancement forcefully and negatively to the point of systematic epistemicide or what Jose Cossa (2020) frames as "epistemic genocide". Critical to redressing and repairing this damage is realizing producing critically engaged scholars in Africa and the Diaspora to produce conversations which can generate alternative approaches to understanding discourse about Africa given the prevailing discourses. The invitation of leading and emerging scholars who teach, research, and engage with Africa and its diaspora was meant to reflect with us on what the practical implications of decolonizing African studies curricula are likely to be and what the shifts from the current thought and content we should anticipate. Thus, offering a deep engagement with wider society, producing relevant knowledge, and pushing for epistemic freedom.

Thus, in thinking about alternatives, this volume has created space to engage with perspectives on the scholarship of teaching and learning about Africa; thus, democratizing the curriculum space as an essential part of decolonizing content, practice, and thinking. Thus, the birthing of this volume is in decolonial thinking. We question how to understand the impact of colonialism, not as an episode, but as a global process of dismemberment, subjectivation, domination, control, and exploitation. Decoloniality as posited in Chapter 1 and the rest of the volume is part of the continuing search for a new base by the excluded and subordinated subjectivities from which to launch themselves into a new world order that is humane and inclusive. In essence, a decolonial approach adopted in this volume thus searches for better ways of theorizing, explaining the meaning of liberation and freedom as well as taking the struggles forward in contemporary conjecture.

Propositions for Engaged Scholarship

The chapters in this volume have done a considerable job in shifting the discourse "on", "about", and "for" Africa to conversations "by" African and diaspora scholars for Africa's present and future by centering pedagogical approaches we utilize when we teach about Africa. Besides the visible differences in the scholarship about Africa and the interdisciplinary essence interfaced by authors there was commitment to traverse the decolonial and Afrofuturistic canon in how the chapters centered the voices, perspectives, agencies of African educators and theorists in the way African is taught and studied on the continent and the diaspora. In a very systematic manner, the book began with a detailed overview aimed at rethinking cemented storylines about Africa, focusing poignantly on the vestiges of epistemic imperialism and the place of African agency in knowledge production. The book situated its major themes alongside several debates. First, it assembled the critical perspectives of scholars engaged in African Studies and other cognate disciplines (i.e. International Studies, Sociology, and Development Studies) who are located in African academic institutions and those located in Europe and North America. This cross-geographical specification was instructive in placing the question of decolonization of knowledge in the hands of those who have been historically excluded, but whose daily lives and work intersect with such characterizations of the continent. This demonstrated the importance of reclaiming African pedagogical choices as insiders in a temporality of return and framed the idea of agency as a technique of redress.

Second, the volume contributed to a re-imagination and possible decentering of the Eurocentric pedagogical and research practices that inform entrenched narratives about Africa as a possible strategy to reclaim African/black agency. The fact that the existing scholarship on Africa has persistently marginalized African voices even on issues that are complexly connected to their daily lives calls for a reclaiming of agency neither within the context of those individuals running the field of study nor those whose perspectives are valued as legitimate knowledge. Theoretically, the volume therefore links the importance of context and voice as a prerequisite to an emancipatory discourse connected to the lived experiences of African peoples. An agency-affirming decolonial discourse approach thus provocatively expresses ways of being, knowing, and doing that are connected to ones' own positionality, drawing on the idea epistemic resistance, re-storying, and decolonizing pedagogies borne of struggle.

Third, the book positioned the reclamation of African ways of doing and knowing on debates about pedagogy, arguing that in resisting epistemic assault that still dominates the production of knowledge about Africa and its people, African scholars in Africa and the diaspora must step beyond the geopolitical critique of the western power matrix as a predominant theme and direct focus onto the dilemmas besetting contemporary post-colonial African studies. This refocus contextualizes epistemic decolonization and enables a shift in epistemology that accounts for and centers African history, culture, and context in our understanding of both the continent and the world at large.

The chapters by Zainab Olaitan and Samuel Ojo Oloruntoba (Chapter 2), Nelson Zavale (Chapter 7) and to some extent Ayandele and Oriola (Chapter 3) in this volume posit that decolonization as envisioned African scholar's positionality contributes to one's approach to teaching and researching Africa whether as an "outsider" or "insider". Africa-focused epistemology, therefore, is informed by the need for a redefinition of one's world to advance both their self-understanding and an understanding of the world around them as articulated by Dastile (2013) and Ndlovu-Gatsheni (2014). The goal was that by assembling these varying insider–outsider and home-diaspora perspectives, one can unleash diverse perspectives based on context. A point also made by Kumalo (2020: 25) insists that decolonizing the curricula should start with decolonizing knowledge through encouraging the idea of the Black Archive as a way of attaining "epistemic restitution" or epistemic justice. Thus, questions about aspects of the teaching and learning about Africa that interrogates the discourses produced and that affirms the present situation and everyday experiences of decolonization in the classroom and beyond are critical in realizing epistemic restitution. Certainly, the decolonization discourse needs to learn from its own history. And the post-colonial situation is a complex phenomenon that requires not only sufficient reflection of what the past and present means, but also how the future can be reimagined. Successively, all chapters interrogated the extent to which knowledge can be freed from traditional complicities anchored through the colonial project. The chapters distinctively underscored the prospects for a decolonial subversion itself as an enduring possibility despite the contestations presented in the case studies about the complexities enacting effective decolonial praxis in African universities well beyond intellectual intransigence.

The arguments shared in the volume have proven to be versatile in engaging the imperialist project materially and philosophically at its core to contribute pertinent decolonial critiques that give African knowledge a position in the sea of heteronormative narratives about Africa. As indicated throughout the book, the chapter authors elaborated on the notion of "re-storying" as a useful concept to imagining the possibilities of centering black agency pedagogical choices and to account for the hard work required for "true" epistemic decolonization to occur. The idea of Afrofuturism might not be a panacea of a solution, but in its essence represents a means of telling stories and giving voice to envisage a future.

Since the release of the first *Black Panther* (Coogler, 2018) and the most recent release of second *Black Panther: Wakanda Forever* (Coogler, 2022) to which I contributed as a cultural/African language expert in the film has revitalized discourses on Afrofuturism, since the black/African imaginations it raises reconfigure representations of black and African lives that have mainly been steeped in normative western categorizations. While acknowledging the criticisms of both *Black Panther* movies for what critics call the insidious ways capitalism and neo-colonial ideology has "undermined" "African values" through feelgood appropriation (here diasporic African Americans and diaspora African descendants living in the west assuming continental African roles and representing African lives) (see de B'beri, 2011; Enwezor, 2015; Yaszek, 2006; Guthrie, 2019; La Ferla, 2016); both films have managed to spark a much-needed conversation about gender representation, autonomy, the future, and agency. To imagine a greater world than the one that currently exists offers possibilities of different conversations to emerge. If stories are told differently using a variety of tools at our disposal, we might inspire others to tell different stories of their existence, perhaps in a world of tomorrow and today. While Afrofuturism presents the possibilities of being and becoming despite the othering and marginalization, (re)conceptualized and (re)imagined through multiple lenses of the future and present, it also centers experiences of black people's agency of self-articulation, social commitment, social capital, and communal empowerment. Afrofuturism further extends the possibility of the historical recovery projects that the global black experience and cultures of resistance could offer for the diaspora and beyond. Thus at the heart of Afrofuturism is creating an African space in the future through the intersection of imagination, resistance, envisaging the future, and liberation (Dean & Andrews, 2016; Eshun, 2003; Ringer, 2016; Nwagbogu, 2017; Wright, 2013).

We are acutely aware that the process invokes notions of essentialism; but alas for us and for this book it is about introspection. It is about being authentic in our experiences of teaching and learning and refining how we teach Africa and knowledge(s) of Africa from an African/diaspora source of inspiration and ownership. Ownership of a complex trauma-filled; yet survivalist-inspired legacy we have inherited and a true affirmation of the harm and achenes this heritage has indeed aided. In essence, scholarship in Africa for Africa by Africans located in the continent and the diaspora must examine how the colonization of knowledge has impacted them in particular ways. Second, scholarship in Africa for Africa by Africans located in the continent and the diaspora should elevate the discourse beyond what is wrong with Africa and emphasize what has worked for Africa. Doing so indigenizes knowledge production while remaining open to critical conversations that still occur in the discourse on Africa and its development. Thus, centers on Africa as a locus of enunciation and articulation enables a rewriting of human experience. Ndlovu-Gatsheni (2020: 10) asserts that the core of decolonization is the "re-writing of human history as opposed to a re-interpretation of the same history, thus bringing forth new facts, new voices and fundamentally opening up new possibilities for mutual learning and new beliefs and learning". Instead of relying on discourses that continue to perpetuate pedagogical injury, African academics must reclaim their role to remembering what it means to be human in the Ubuntu/Botho sense and advance what Mignolo (1995: 33) asserts that "decoloniality struggles to bring into intervening existence an other-interpretation that bring[s] forward, on [one] hand, a silenced view of the event, and on the other [hand], shows the limits of imperial ideology disguised as the true (total) interpretation of the events in the making of the modern world".

Thus, there is a need for scholars "of", "in", and "for" on the continent and the diaspora to liberate themselves from the miseducation caused by colonialism and the promises of post-colonial situations. Scholars of Africa should turn over a new page in theorizing, researching, and engaging Africa by unshackling the disciplinary boundaries that make decolonial analysis impossible. Gilroy (1993), wa Thiong'o (2009), wa Thiong'o (1986), Jéan-Paul Sartre (1964), and Mazrui (1975) cautioned about the role of imperialism in maintaining the oppressive conditions under which Africans are forced to live and struggle for survival.

The restoration and reinterpretation of what really happened and continues to happen on the continent and in the diaspora to black people is critical at this juncture and it is our collective responsibility to offer observations and interpretations. Of course, we will never agree over interpretations. However, we can agree to work according to the same epistemological principles which, by definition, will bring us together rather than drive us apart. Such an awakening is important as it allows through knowledge and understanding a new way of seeing the world. It also enables us as academics and researchers to approach the world differently both in the classroom and outside the classroom regardless of the contexts we are operating in. Thus, the exigencies of pedagogic performance through re-storying African pedagogies facilitate and embrace a return to oneself in the present, past, and future. For Jéan-Paul Sartre (1965), Africans cannot forever be incapacitated into a cycle of attributing their condition of a mental coloniality, political lethargy, and global marginalization to other. Thus, giving power and authority to those who have oppressed them.

Sartre (1964) argues in *Black Orpheus* that all humans are innately or ontologically free, which imposes a responsibility upon them to choose to either succumb to the neocolonial yoke, or to confront their reality and rise as their own liberators. What is of substantial significance in Sartre's concept of Africanity is its engagement with the possibility of Afrofuturism as a political mission for liberation and this theoretical intervention postulates a decolonial standpoint central to our arguement. For Sartre, asserting the objective subjectivity of African peoples through various literary techniques that dialectically oppose, transpose, and synthesize the dichotomies of whiteness that are subsumed within the white colonizers' language is the answer. Sartre's conceptualization of freedom as both the essence of human being and the binding pursuit of an authentic human life, as well as his aversion of the structural determinism of cultural and political institutions, coheres with the Africanist "post-modernist" appraisal of the quality of the freedom that is being delivered by both Western-liberal and post-colonial African modernity. He asserts that a sense of being places the responsibility of one's state of *being* on the subject itself. We are innately free as social beings *and* are obliged at all given instances to choose what we are becoming.

We, therefore, are responsible for what we are. The historical recovery project behind Afrofuturism engages the reclaiming of agency that is crucial to the African and diasporic past, present, and future. In the academic fields that operate according to congenital colonial practices and cultural capital, it is important to infuse knowing, doing, relating, and engaging that affirms the cultural capital (lived experiences and contexts) of those marginalized. Nene Ernest Khalema, Phumelele Zakwe, and Blessings Masuku (Chapter 9) in the volume emphasize this point as a logical extension that affirms African-centered approaches of Ubuntu/

Botho ethics to the manner transformation and governance is animated post-apartheid South Africa as an example.

It is precisely in the engagement with such theoretical and epistemological grounding that teachers and researchers grounded in context can engage and express pedagogy, curriculum, and practice inversely. What goes on in the classroom as Andrews and Patrick (Chapter 4), Mathews (Chapter 5) and Sondarjee (Chapter 8) alluded in this volume is always open to improvement, critique, and interpretation. The recognition that we are and have been producing African histories/herstories and knowledge that harm than liberate us is a case in point. The role of classroom discourse in the differential construction of pedagogic emancipation requires more than a critique of knowledge, but also a sensitivity to the way language is used in the classroom. Thus, by employing a decolonial pedagogy, with all that this employment implies in terms of theory of practice, pedagogic essence, epistemology, and methodology, we open space to reimagine our classrooms differently. We make it possible to analyze the continent and its diaspora uniquely and the process of classroom discourse changes to affirm not exclude.

This analysis is relevant beyond African contexts as it raises questions, issues, and arguments, which are relevant to colonial situations everywhere. The plight of educators and thought leaders; whose agency, embodiment, and voices have experienced maginalization and silencing will find value in the conversations and reflections in this book. As such, the volume exposes in many ways the cementation of colonial ways of doing and knowing that still haunt us today and how resistiting such narratives is possible. An aware practitioner, theorist, researcher, and educator of Africa and the world is better positioned to be a reflective teacher of Africa specifically, and knowledge(s) of the marginalized the world over.

References

Abdi, A. A. (2021). *Critical Theorizations of Education*. Brill I Sense.

Andrews, N., Khalema, N. E., & Assie-Lumumba, N. D. T. (2015). *Millennium Development Goals in Retrospect: Africa' Development Beyond 2015*. Springer (Social Indicators Series).

Andrews, N., Khalema, N. E., Oriola, T., & Odoom, I. (2013). *Africa Yesterday, Today, and Tomorrow: Exploring the Multi-dimensional Discourses on 'Development'*. Cambridge Scholars Publishing.

Bhabha, H. K. (1988). The Commitment to Theory. *New Formations, 5*, 5–23.

Bourdieu, P. (1991). *Language and Symbolic Power*. Polity.

Bourdieu, P., Passeron, J., & de Saint Martin, M. (1994). *Academic Discourse: Linguistic Misunderstanding and Professorial Power*. Stanford University Press.

Coogler, R (dir). (2018). *Black Panther*. [Film]. Marvel Studios.

Coogler, R (dir). (2022). *Black Panther: Wakanda Forever.* [Film]. Marvel Studios.

Cossa, J. (2020). Cosmo-uBuntu: Toward a New Theorizing for Justice in Education and Beyond. In A. A. Abdi (Ed.), *Critical Theorizations of Education*. Brill|Sense.

Dastile, N. P. (2013). Beyond Euro-Western dominance: An African-centred decolonial paradigm. *Africanus, 43*, 93–104.

de B'beri, E. (2011). Africanity in Black Cinema: A Conjunctural Ground for New Expressions of Identity. In K. Tomaselli & H. K. Wright (Eds.), *Africa, Cultural Studies and Difference* (pp. 15–37). Routledge.

Dean, T., & Andrews, D. P. (2016). Introduction: Afrofuturism in Black Theology—Race, Gender, Sexuality, and the State of Black Religion in the *Black Metropolis. Black Theology, 14*(1), 2–5.

Dei, G. S. (2012). Indigenous Anti-colonial Knowledge as 'Heritage Knowledge' for Promoting Black/African Education in Diasporic Contexts. *Decolonization: Indigeneity, Education & Society, 1*(1), 102–119.

Enwezor, O. (2015). A reinvented Vocabulary: Decoding the Many Dimensions of African Design, Interview with Amelie Klein. In M. Kries & A. Klein (Eds.), *Making Africa—A Continent of Contemporary Design* (20–25). Exhibition Catalogue. GmbH: Vitra Design Museum.

Eshun, K. (2003). Further Considerations on Afrofuturism. *CR: The New Centennial Review, 3*(2): 287–302.

Gatune, J. (2010, November). Africa's Development Beyond Aid: Getting Out of the Box. *The Annals of the American Academy of Political and Social Science, 632*, 103–120.

Gilroy, P. (1993). *The Black Atlantic: Modernity and Double Consciousness*. Harvard University Press.

Guthrie, R. (2019, December). Redefining the Colonial: An Afrofuturist Analysis of Wakanda and Speculative Fiction. *Journal of Futures Studies, 24*(2), 15–28.

hooks, b. (1992). *Black Looks: Race and Representation*. Boston: South End Press.

Hua, A. (2013). Black Diaspora Feminism and Writing: Memories, Storytelling, and the Narrative Word as Sites of Resistance. *African and Black Diaspora: An International Journal, 6*(3), 30–42.

Khalema, N. E. (2022). Race and Its Sociological Inquiry in Africa: Problematic Suppositions and Contemporary Predicaments. In R. Sooryamoorthy & N.

E. Khalema (Eds.), *The Oxford Handbook of the Sociology of Africa*. Oxford University Press.

Kumalo, S. H. (2020). Resurrecting the Black Archive Through the Decolonisation of Philosophy in South Africa. *Third World Thematics: A TWQ Journal*, *5*(1–2), 19–36.

La Ferla, R. (2016). Afrofuturism: The Next Generation. *The New York Times*. Retrieved April 20, 2023 from https://www.nytimes.com/2016/12/12/fashion/afrofuturism-the-next-generation.html

Mazrui, A. A. (1975). The African University as a Multinational Corporation: Problems of Penetration and Dependency. *Harvard Educational Review*, *45*, 191–210.

Mignolo, W. (1995). *The Darker Side of Renaissance: Literacy, Territory, and Colonization*. University of Michigan Press.

Ndlovu-Gatsheni, S. J. (2014, October 30). *"My Life Is One Long Debate": Ali A. Mazrui on the Invention of Africa and Postcolonial Predicaments*, Public Lecture. University of the Free State.

Ndlovu-Gatsheni, S. J. (2020). *Decolonization, Development and Knowledge in Africa: Turning over a New Yeaf*. Routledge.

Nwagbogu, A. (2017). Afrofuturism: Transhumans Imagining a New Vision for Africa. *Recontres De Bamako: Biennale Africaine De La Photographie*. Retrieved April 20, 2023, from https://www.rencontres-bamako.com/+-4_expo_Afrofuturism-+

Ringer, C. D. (2016). Afrofuturism and the DNA of Biopolitics in the Black Public Sphere. *Black Theology*, *14*(1), 53–68.

Santos, B. (2014). *Epistemology of the South: Justice against Epistemicide*. Paradigm Publishers.

Sartre, J.-P. (1964). "*Black Orpheus*," trans. John MacCombie in *The Massachusetts Review* (Vol. 6, No. 1, pp. 13–52). http://massreview.org/sites/default/files/Sartre.pdf. Accessed 12 Feb 2023.

Sartre, J.-P. (1965). *Colonialism and Neocolonialism* (S. Brewer, A. Haddour, & T. McWilliams, Trans.). Routledge.

Thiong'o, N. (1986). *Decolonising the Mind: The Politics of Language in African Literature*. J. Currey.

wa Thiong'o, N. (2009). *Something Torn and New: An African Renaissance*. Basic Civitas Books.

Wright, M. M. (2013). Can I Call You Black? The Limits of Authentic Heteronormativity in African Diasporic Discourse. *African and Black Diaspora: An International Journal*, *6*(1), 3–16.

Yaszek, L. (2006). Afrofuturism, Science Fiction, and the History of the Future. *Socialism and Democracy*, *20*(3), 41–60.

INDEX

N. Andrews and N. E. Khalema (eds.), *Decolonizing African Studies Pedagogies*, Political Pedagogies,
https://doi.org/10.1007/978-3-031-37442-5